T0333429

Pamela R. Cummings
Francis A. Kwansa
Marvin B. Sussman
Editors

The Role
of the Hospitality Industry
in the Lives
of Individuals and Families

The Role of the Hospitality Industry in the Lives of Individuals and Families has also been co-published simultaneously as *Marriage & Family Review,* Volume 28, Numbers 1/2 1998.

Pre-publication
REVIEWS,
COMMENTARIES,
EVALUATIONS . . .

"**T**here are many relevant and extensive studies cited! The information is comprehensive and interesting. The information will be beneficial for a class on history, trends in the hospitality industry. The information can be used as the core of hospitality management."

Cynthia Mayo, MBP, PhD, RD
Professor and Department Chair
Virginia State University

The Role
of the Hospitality Industry
in the Lives of Individuals
and Families

The Role of the Hospitality Industry in the Lives of Individuals and Families has been co-published simultaneously as *Marriage & Family Review*, Volume 28, Numbers 1/2 1998.

The *Marriage & Family Review* Monographs/"Separates"

These books were published simultaneously as special thematic issues of the *Marriage & Family Review* and are available bound separately. Visit Haworth's website at http://www. haworthpressinc.com to search our online catalog for complete tables of contents and ordering information for these and other publications. Or call 1-800-HAWORTH (outside US/Canada: 607-722-5857), Fax: 1-800-895-0582 (outside US/Canada: 607-771-0012), or e-mail: getinfo@haworthpressinc.com

Cults and the Family, edited by Florence Kaslow and Marvin B. Sussman

Alternatives to Traditional Family Living, edited by Harriet Gross and Marvin B. Sussman

Intermarriage in the United States, edited by Gary A. Crester and Joseph J. Leon

Family Systems and Inheritance Patterns, edited by Judith N. Cates and Marvin B. Sussman

The Ties that Bind: Men's and Women's Social Networks, edited by Laura Lein and Marvin B. Sussman

Social Stress and the Family: Advances and Developments in Family Stress Theory and Research, edited by Hamilton I. McCubbin, Marvin B. Sussman, and Joan M. Patterson

Human Sexuality and the Family, edited by James W. Maddock, Gerhard Neubeck, and Marvin B. Sussman

Obesity and the Family, edited by David J. Kallen and Marvin B. Sussman

Women and the Family, edited by Beth B. Hess and Marvin B. Sussman

Personal Computers and the Family, edited by Marvin B. Sussman

Pets and the Family, edited by Marvin B. Sussman

Families and the Energy Transition, edited by John Byrne, David A. Schulz, and Marvin B. Sussman

Men's Changing Roles in the Family, edited by Robert A. Lewis and Marvin B. Sussman

The Charybdis Complex: Redemption of Rejected Marriage and Family Journal Articles, edited by Marvin B. Sussman

Families and the Prospect of Nuclear Attack/Holocaust, edited by Teresa D. Marciano and Marvin B. Sussman

Family Medicine: The Maturing of a Discipline, edited by William J. Doherty, Charles E. Christianson, and Marvin B. Sussman

The Role
of the Hospitality Industry
in the Lives of Individuals
and Families

Pamela R. Cummings
Francis A. Kwansa
Marvin B. Sussman
Editors

The Role of the Hospitality Industry in the Lives of Individuals and Families has been co-published simultaneously as *Marriage & Family Review*™, Volume 28, Numbers 1/2 1998.

The Haworth Press, Inc.
New York • London

The Role of the Hospitality Industry in the Lives of Individuals and Families has been co-published simultaneously as *Marriage & Family Review*™, Volume 28, Numbers 1/2 1998.

The development, preparation, and publication of this work has been undertaken with great care. However, the publisher, employees, editors, and agents of The Haworth Press and all imprints of The Haworth Press, Inc., including The Haworth Medical Press® and Pharmaceutical Products Press®, are not responsible for any errors contained herein or for consequences that may ensue from use of materials or information contained in this work. Opinions expressed by the author(s) are not necessarily those of The Haworth Press, Inc.

Cover design by Thomas J. Mayshock Jr.

Library of Congress Cataloging-in-Publication Data

The Role of the hospitality industry in the lives of individuals and families / Pamela R. Cummings, Francis A. Kwansa, Marvin B. Sussman, editors.

      p. cm.

      "Co-published simultaneously as Marriage & Family Review, Volume 28, Numbers 1/2, 1998."

      Includes bibliographical references and index.

      ISBN 0-7890-0524-7 (alk. paper). – ISBN 0-7890-0526-3 (pbk. : alk. paper)

      1. Hospitality industry–United States–Social aspects. 2. Family–United States. I. Cummings, Pamela R., 1944- . II. Kwansa, Francis A. III. Sussman, Marvin B. IV. Marriage & family review.
TX911.2.R65 1998
647.9473–dc21

                                     98-8597
                                          CIP

INDEXING & ABSTRACTING

Contributions to this publication are selectively indexed or abstracted in print, electronic, online, or CD-ROM version(s) of the reference tools and information services listed below. This list is current as of the copyright date of this publication. See the end of this section for additional notes.

- *Abstracts in Social Gerontology: Current Literature on Aging*
- *Abstracts of Research in Pastoral Care & Counseling*
- *Academic Abstracts/CD-ROM*
- *Academic Search: database of 2,000 selected academic serials, updated monthly*
- *AGRICOLA Database*
- *Applied Social Sciences Index & Abstracts (ASSIA) (Online: ASSI via Data-Star) (CDRom: ASSIA Plus)*
- *CNPIEC Reference Guide: Chinese National Directory of Foreign Periodicals*
- *Contemporary Women's Issues*
- *Current Contents: Clinical Medicine/Life Sciences (CC:CM/LS) (weekly Table of Contents Service), and Social Science Citation Index. Articles also searchable through Social SciSearch, ISI's online database and in ISI's Research Alert current awareness service*
- *Expanded Academic Index*
- *Family Studies Database (online and CD/ROM)*
- *Family Violence & Sexual Assault Institute*
- *IBZ International Bibliography of Periodical Literature*
- *Index to Periodical Articles Related to Law*
- *INTERNET ACCESS (& additional networks) Bulletin Board for Libraries ("BUBL") coverage of information resources on INTERNET, JANET, and other networks*
- *MasterFILE: updated database from EBSCO Publishing*
- *National Periodical Library*
- *PASCAL, c/o Institute de L'Information Scientifique et Technique*

(continued)

- *Periodical Abstracts, Research I (general & basic reference indexing & abstracting data-base from University Microfilms International (UMI)*
- *Periodical Abstracts, Research II (broad coverage indexing & abstracting data-base from University Microfilms International (UMI)*
- *Population Index*
- *Psychological Abstracts (PsycINFO)*
- *Sage Family Studies Abstracts (SFSA)*
- *Social Planning/Policy & Development Abstracts (SOPODA)*
- *Social Science Source: coverage of 400 journals in the social sciences area, updated monthly, EBSCO Publishing*
- *Social Sciences Index (from Volume 1 & continuing)*
- *Social Work Abstracts*
- *Sociological Abstracts (SA)*
- *Special Educational Needs Abstracts*
- *Studies on Women Abstracts*
- *Violence and Abuse Abstracts: A Review of Current Literature on Interpersonal Violence (VAA)*
- *Women "R" CD/ROM*

Special Bibliographic Notes related to special journal issues (separates) and indexing/abstracting:

- indexing/abstracting services in this list will also cover material in any "separate" that is co-published simultaneously with Haworth's special thematic journal issue or DocuSerial. Indexing/abstracting usually covers material at the article/chapter level.
- monographic co-editions are intended for either non-subscribers or libraries which intend to purchase a second copy for their circulating collections.
- monographic co-editions are reported to all jobbers/wholesalers/approval plans. The source journal is listed as the "series" to assist the prevention of duplicate purchasing in the same manner utilized for books-in-series.
- to facilitate user/access services all indexing/abstracting services are encouraged to utilize the co-indexing entry note indicated at the bottom of the first page of each article/chapter/contribution.
- this is intended to assist a library user of any reference tool (whether print, electronic, online, or CD-ROM) to locate the monographic version if the library has purchased this version but not a subscription to the source journal.
- individual articles/chapters in any Haworth publication are also available through the Haworth Document Delivery Service (HDDS).

ABOUT THE EDITORS

Pamela R. Cummings, PhD, is Associate Professor in the Department of Hotel, Restaurant, and Institutional Management at the University of Delaware. She teaches courses in hotel management and in the distance education program and coordinates a hotel practicum. Dr. Cummings is a member of the International Council on Hotel, Restaurant, and Institutional Education for Hospitality and Tourism Educators, The National Restaurant Association, and the American Hotel and Motel Association. Her research interests include issues related to international hosting, human resource development, and hospitality management education. Presently, Dr. Cummings is researching hotel turnover and self-managed teams, a project funded by the Research Alliance of the Educational Institute of the American Hotel and Motel Association.

Francis A. Kwansa, PhD, is Associate Professor in the Hotel, Restaurant, and Institutional Management Department at the University of Delaware, where he teaches courses in financial management and managerial accounting. He is the past president of the Association of Hospitality Financial Management Educators, a member of the Financial Management Committee of the American Hotel and Motel Association, and serves on the Publications Council of the Council on Hotel, Restaurant, and Institutional Management Education (CHRIE). He is currently the Associate Editor of *Journal of Hospitality Financial Management.*

Marvin B. Sussman, PhD, is UNIDEL Professor of Human Behavior Emeritus at the College of Human Resources at the University of Delaware. He is also a member of the CORE Faculty of the Union Graduate School of Union Institute in Cincinnati, Ohio. A member of many professional organizations, he received the 1980 Ernest W. Burgess Award of the National Council on Family Relations. In 1983, Dr. Sussman was elected to the prestigious Academy of Groves for scholarly contributions to the field, as well as awarded a lifelong membership for services to the Groves Conference on Marriage and the Family in 1984. In 1985, Dr. Sussman received the Distinguished Family Award of the Society for the Study of Social Problems (SSSP) and was honored with the Lee Founders Award, the SSSP's highest professional award, in 1992. In the same year, he was the recipient of the State of Delaware Gerontological Society Award. Dr. Sussman is the author or editor of 30 books and more than 220 articles on family, community, rehabilitation, health and aging, and organizational transformation.

The Role of the Hospitality Industry in the Lives of Individuals and Families

CONTENTS

Preface

Research directed at analyzing the development and practices in the hospitality industry is often initiated and implemented around economic issues. The "bottom line" is certainly important, but the editors of this book had additional interests in mind when we requested manuscripts of inquiry into the hospitality industry as related to individuals and families. The evolution of the hospitality industry, using a longer and wider lens, was the overall objective of this endeavor. Topics of interest included an examination of the philosophical, social and spiritual underpinnings of hospitality. Also of interest was the history of hospitality from preliterate times to the development and commercialization of the industry up to its present practices. We sought topics with marketing implications for families and individuals across family life cycles, as consumers of hospitality products. We also sought manuscripts aimed at a better understanding of the human resources issues surrounding employment in this industry and the consequences on family and individual development. Cross-cultural differences in hospitality industry practices were sought for the purposes of determining successful employment and training practices across diverse human resource pools, and for identifying characteristics of successful international hosting practices. Additionally we were interested in the psychological and sociological implications of employment in this industry on family structures and roles for individuals and families from varied cultures, including those in developing nations. "Inclusive" was the term used to describe the topics of interest to the editors who developed this book.

The actual contributions to this volume are representative of the diverse range of topics we had hoped to receive. There are three broad themes in this volume: (1) chapters related to the spiritual, philosophical and historical

[Haworth co-indexing entry note]: "Preface." Cummings, Pamela R., Francis A. Kwansa, and Marvin B. Sussman. Co-published simultaneously in *Marriage & Family Review* (The Haworth Press, Inc.) Vol. 28, No. 1/2, 1998, pp. xv-xvii; and: *The Role of the Hospitality Industry in the Lives of Individuals and Families* (ed: Pamela R. Cummings, Francis A. Kwansa, and Marvin B. Sussman) The Haworth Press, Inc., 1998, pp. xv-xvii. Single or multiple copies of this article are available for a fee from The Haworth Document Delivery Service [1-800-342-9678, 9:00 a.m. - 5:00 p.m. (EST). E-mail address: getinfo@haworthpressinc.com].

provision of hospitality; (2) chapters related to the human resources and work issues for employees in the hospitality industry; and (3) chapters examining individual consumer and family demand issues and subsequent marketing strategies for hospitality organizations.

What we have in this volume is an important initial effort in the exploration of the relationships of the hospitality industry and families and individuals, but many important topics from the original list remain and other new ones have surfaced. Further examination of the historical evolution of providing food, shelter, protection, friendship and entertainment for the traveler would help us understand cultural variations and how they have developed from early laws, religious traditions and customs.

- What are the most significant "universal needs" to be met for strangers who are called guests?
- How has the profit motive influenced the hospitality industry's response to the need of travelers for a "home away from home"?
- How have we dealt with the social and health issues of the public across time and what is the role of the industry in educating and protecting guests?

The hospitality industry is replete with ethical dilemmas that affect hospitality employees and need the further attention of researchers.

- What is the extent of sexual harassment in an industry that hires many women, who may be selected and rewarded for their pulchritude and friendliness?
- What behavior and apparel constitute going too far in an effort to please the hospitality guest?
- How are employees protected from demanding guests who are under the influence of alcohol?
- What are the issues of gender equity, at all levels of employment?
- How are the values of the individual manager, which may include compassion, generosity and idealism, balanced with the corporate profit maximization mandate?
- How are the values of equity and justice internalized by the hospitality employee when the corporate philosophy states that "the customer is always right"?
- What are the sources of industry "burn-out" for employees, and what are the successful therapeutic interventions taken to reduce unwanted turnover?
- Do any hospitality companies have a reward system for longevity?
- Is there a long-term commitment in the industry to its employees?

Other topics of research and analysis that focus on human resource issues include an examination of the role of the hospitality industry in the maturing process and socialization of American youth. Additionally, what are the personality attributes as well as the socialization and developmental experiences that predict success in the hospitality field?

- Have part-time jobs in the fast food industry become rites of passage, like scout camp, church camp or military training?
- What are the components of leadership development for hospitality executives?
- What are the life experiences of industry leaders such as Ray Kroc, Dave Thomas or Norman Brinker, that predict success in the industry?
- What are the personality attributes of successful hospitality employees?
- What has been the role of racial, ethnic and cultural groups in creating family businesses in the hospitality industry?
- How has immigration to the United States altered and developed employment pools for hospitality industries?

Finally, in the broader sense, what have been the contributions of companies in the hospitality industry to serving and helping their communities through voluntary involvement in nonprofit projects? What happens to cultural understanding, attitudes and values when international travelers make new friendships across geographic boundaries? How might hospitality practices designed to serve guests graciously, meet their most basic needs and extend understanding and friendship contribute to brotherhood and world peace?

Would it be possible to create a hospitality industry think tank designed to look at some of the issues mentioned above? Systematic examination and research into these varied issues could significantly contribute to the hospitality industry, hospitality employees and the individuals and families it serves. There is more to be done in further understanding the relationships between the hospitality industry and individuals, families, communities, and the world.

Pamela R. Cummings
Francis A. Kwansa
Marvin B. Sussman

Acknowledgments

The co-editors would like to acknowledge the people who have contributed to this volume. First, we would like to thank Dene Klinzing for initiating and encouraging this effort. Additionally, we thank all of the authors of the manuscripts in this volume for their scholarly endeavors and their perseverance. We are also truly grateful to the people who served as reviewers by critiquing manuscripts. The following colleagues provided this necessary assistance:

Kathleen Pearl Brewer
University of Nevada, Las Vegas

Anne E. Camasso
University of Delaware

Kaye S. Chon
University of Houston

Ronald P. Cole
University of Delaware

Virginia Felstehausen
Texas Tech University

Angela Farrar
Pennsylvania State University

Michelle Grottola
Cornell University

Kimberley J. Harris
Florida State University

Linda C. Hoover
Texas Tech University

Sandra Kapoor
California State Polytechnic University

William E. Kent
Auburn University

Bonnie J. Knutson
Michigan State University

Elizabeth M. Lieux
University of Delaware

Robert R. Nelson
University of Delaware

Robin J. Palkovitz
University of Delaware

David V. Pavesic
Georgia State University

Ania Zajicek
University of Arkansas

PART I:
SPIRITUAL, PHILOSOPHICAL AND HISTORICAL PROVISION OF HOSPITALITY

The Spiritual Essence of Hospitality Practice: Seeing the Proverbial Stranger as a Pretext to Reading Ourselves

Michele Grottola

SUMMARY. This paper is consciously interdisciplinary. The literature of theology, myth, and folklore is juxtaposed with the literature of family systems, organizational studies, and service management to explore the multifaceted meaning of the term *hospitality practice.* The related origins of such words as *guest, host,* and *stranger* are presented to create a model of possibility capable of imagining how

Michele Grottola is a doctoral candidate at Cornell University. Her interests focus upon ethno-cultural studies in the areas of human resource management and organizational behavior.

[Haworth co-indexing entry note]: "The Spiritual Essence of Hospitality Practice: Seeing the Proverbial Stranger as a Pretext to Reading Ourselves." Grottola, Michele. Co-published simultaneously in *Marriage & Family Review* (The Haworth Press, Inc.) Vol. 28, No. 1/2, 1998, pp. 1-22; and: *The Role of the Hospitality Industry in the Lives of Individuals and Families* (ed: Pamela R. Cummings, Francis A. Kwansa, and Marvin B. Sussman) The Haworth Press, Inc., 1998, pp. 1-22. Single or multiple copies of this article are available for a fee from The Haworth Document Delivery Service [1-800-342-9678, 9:00 a.m. - 5:00 p.m. (EST). E-mail address: getinfo@haworthpressinc.com].

1

the ancient image of the proverbial *stranger at the door* remains an apt metaphorical model for hospitality practice to be enacted on both private as well as public levels of social interaction. The interconnectedness derived from such meanings, drawn between older forms of hospitality practice and its contemporary reincarnation in a formalized industry niche, called *Hospitality,* are intended to articulate how service quality is an attribute that the industry owes as much to its employees as to its customers. *[Article copies available for a fee from The Haworth Document Delivery Service: 1-800-342-9678. E-mail address: getinfo@haworthpressinc.com]*

KEYWORDS. Hospitality, Hospitality management, Hospitality industry, Service management

. . . for I was hungry and you gave me food,
I was thirsty and you gave me drink,
I was a stranger and you welcomed me.

Matthew 25:35

Hospitality practice is the humanistic art of being able to give as well as to receive and, in the spirit of that exchange, requires us to understand how both acts comprise a unified experience. It may be said that such practice comprises the essence of what it can mean to live successfully in a global world on both individual and collective levels.

The term *hospitality* derives from the word "hospice," a house of rest for pilgrims during medieval times (Metelka, 1990, p. 73), but as Russell Lockhart has written in his book, *Words as Eggs,*

behind every word we use–for the most part so casually–there lies a story to be found, if we are willing to attend to its inner meaning. There is a level on which the essential story will be the same for all seekers, but also a level where it will be unique for everyone of us . . . so also are the stories that nourish every single human life. (Luke, 1990, p. 17)

In her paper *The Stranger Within,* Helen Luke uses Lockhart's words about meaning to further explore such words as *hospitality, guest,* and *stranger.* We learn that these words are more intricately bound to one another than common vernacular would automatically tell us. Luke writes:

The American Heritage Dictionary tells us that the Indo-European root of the words "host," "hospice," "hospitality," and "hospital" is *ghosti*; it is, surprisingly, also the root of the word "guest.". . . Moreover, in the Indo-European Appendix the meaning of this root includes another word: *ghosti* meant "stranger" as well as "guest" and "host," properly, "someone with whom one has reciprocal duties of hospitality." (1990, p. 17)

What are these reciprocal duties that exist? One excellent source of readings that lends insight to this question is found in the special issue about the multiple meanings of hospitality that was published by *Parabola: The Magazine of Myth and Tradition* in 1990. In the opening editorial, a section called *Focus,* D. M. Dooling writes:

Do we ever take an idea seriously enough? That is a question that arises after some years of pondering themes for Parabola. By pondering, I don't mean only cerebrating, whether alone or in company, nor reading what others who ponder with us have written. Spending weeks with the predominating thought of a certain theme opens other avenues than those of the ordinary mind.

One begins to experience the idea in action and to feel it in a certain way. It makes its own surprising connections; one idea links itself with another, or perhaps with several. There seems to be an endless network of relationships in which every concept expands into a bewildering infinity; and what becomes clear is that we cannot take any word for granted and say we understand it.

So we cannot take for granted the familiar word *hospitality* when we begin to see it in its rich context. All our contributors agreed that hospitality is a form of exchange, not a one-sided beneficence. The soup kitchen, though necessary, isn't in itself hospitality; maybe the lack of real hospitality in our day is the reason why people are homeless and soup kitchens exist. The exchange we speak of requires another level, and seems to correspond with a human need even deeper, and far harder to satisfy, than physical hunger. Its nature is a profound question. (1990, p. 2)

In this paper, I wish to explore the *possibility* of expanding the term, hospitality practice, in richly interdisciplinary layers so that an often forgotten soulful essence can not only be remembered, but also be savored. Then, I want to associate *hospitality practice* with both how an individual acts in the role of guest and/or host, as well as, later on in this paper, how an industry may do the same for its employees as well as its customers.

Such interconnectedness as the above quote by Dooling suggests, helps us to "experience the idea in action" (1990, p. 2) and build a bridge between the theory and the need for a renewed practice.

THE INTERCONNECTEDNESS BETWEEN STRANGERS AND OURSELVES

From the special issue of *Parabola,* one learns that the reciprocal duties of hospitality practice as they exist among and between hosts, guests, and strangers are well documented in the most ancient biblical texts of our civilization, the mythic literary traditions such as those to be found, for example, in Chaucer's *Canterbury Tales* or the plays of the *Oresteia* from Greece's golden age of drama, as well as in plebian folklore customs.

In *Philoxenia and Hospitality,* Lambros Kamperidis (1990) uses the vehicle of his own childhood memory to recount one such custom. He describes how, at Christmas, his parents insisted upon setting a place at the table for the stranger or the wayfarer who might happen by their rural farmhouse door. This same ritual would be repeated again on New Year's Eve when his mother would save and permanently reserve a slice of homemade St. Basil's bread for the same purpose.

Kamperidis stresses that it did not matter whether a stranger ever physically appeared on the holiday scene because "even if not physically present, a stranger occupied a certain place in the household. In case he or she materialized, usually brought by a friend, the stranger would be treated as a member of the family and entertained in a most cordial way. An inviolable rule of the hospitality offered to strangers is to accept them unconditionally. No questions concerning their origins or their station in life are permitted, and nothing is expected in return" (1990, p. 5).

Such ritualistic holiday traditions originated in the religious belief systems of agrarian peasant cultures. Symbolically, their ritualistic forms speak to preserving the *sacred character* of the stranger so often written about in parables discovered throughout the world as written literature or as oral tales handed down from generation to generation. In such stories, a major character theme emerges whereby the stranger turns out to be either "God-sent" or the incarnation of the Lord, himself, who initially poses as a humble street beggar specifically to test the degree of charity for others held in the hearts of the leading characters in the parable.

Kamperidis reminds us that the first biblical reference to just such a charity-laden parable can be found in Genesis (18:1-8, 19:1-3) where the story is told about how three strangers appeared to Abraham as he sat at the door of his tent in Marme. The bible reports that Abraham knew immediately to welcome the three strangers as being *God-sent* by running to greet them and then, later, inviting them to accept his hospitality of food and beverages. This same sense of hospitality can be found in Bedouin culture, today, which is why "throughout history Abraham has been recognized as the exemplar of hospitality. The Talmud asserts, 'Whoever on showing compassion is bent, from the Patriarch Abraham may claim his descent'" (Wolk, 1990, p. 80).

The story goes on to tell us that after greeting the new guests, Abraham invited the three strangers to sit beneath the shade of his oak trees where he washed their feet with water and served them a meal of cake baked from fine grain, curds, and milk. Later, Abraham accompanied the strangers to Sodom where they encountered Lot who was seated by the gate of the city. Lot repeats the same rites of hospitality for the strangers as did Abraham.

This parable recounts a culture of hospitality practice that clearly extends the meaning of one of the Ten Commandments, namely: Love thy neighbor as thy self. One pretext, or subtext, to this commandment may well be: one's neighbor is yourself, in the form of another human being. The metaphorical use of the term, "God-sent," with reference to strangers conveys the *possibility* of God existing in each one of us, and how all strangers and wayfarers are interconnected to us in a very direct way.

Later in the parable about Abraham and Lot, the bible tells us that the wicked men of the city gathered around Lot's house demanding that the strangers be turned over to them, but Lot refuses and tells the intruders that he would rather submit his own daughters to their lust than give them the strangers "for they have come under the shelter of his roof" (Kamperidis, 1990, p. 6). Lot and Abraham are enacting the rule of hospitality: once a stranger comes under the roof of the host, it is the host's sacred obligation to protect him or her.

This sacred character of the stranger is intricately associated with the belief that each of us shares with the stranger the same journey or predicament in this life through the vital bond of sheer humanity. In fact, one can say that this is the essence of how hospitality practice came to evolve beside the many cultural tales of the proverbial stranger at the door.

In re-telling this story, Kamperidis is illustrating how "the host feels responsible for what may happen to his guests; if he cannot avoid disaster, he is willing to meet it himself, rather than involve the strangers who are under his protection" (1990, p. 6). Kamperidis writes:

> The practice of hospitality, the sharing of the goods of the earth with another fellow creature, the unconditional acceptance of the stranger and his or her integration into our life, constitute the very essentials of a eucharistic relationship with the Creator of all.

By giving generously of what has been bestowed on us to the stranger, by sharing the fruits of the earth, we render to God our thanksgiving for what has been offered to us. The stranger becomes the *pretext,* the means through which we enter into eucharistic communion with the Creator. Thus the stranger acquires a sacred character. (1990, p. 5)

An unmistakable ecology of themes in this summation evokes the consciousness of knowing that when we give to another human being, we are also nourishing ourselves; and, when we allow ourselves to receive from another, we are allowing him or her to do the same. The Buddhists call this karma. Other equally non-dogmatic terms could be *humanism* or *voluntarism.* Such an essence has many faces and belief systems and is not the territory of any one formalized religious dogma. However, the culturally, comparative, shared meaning is strikingly similar.

The inviolable bond of reciprocity is also illustrated in Homer's *Odyssey,* when, for example, the guest departs from the host, he or she is given an *astragalos,* a die, or a *symbolon,* a ring, which is broken between the two. This symbolizes that the host and guest are one in the union of the hospitality that they have shared with each other.

Each person possesses part of the ring, symbolic of the union. The broken die, or the ring, becomes whole again upon reunion. However, reunion may or may not occur between these two people, but they in turn may host and be guest to others. The ring, or circle, may be said to stand for the metaphorical power of the intangible *shared experience* between those who share hospitality with one another.

Most cultures have spoken of hospitality practice among strangers from the most ancient to the contemporary day. Much of our contemporary terminology comes from ancient Greek and Latin. Kamperidis' paper *Philoxenia and Hospitality,* in fact, takes its title from such meanings and readings to be found about Zeus who was known for his love of the sojourner. He writes:

Just as Yahweh loves the sojourner, so does Zeus, who takes on special attributes as the protector of the strangers. Xenos, in Greek, is the stranger, and an appeal to *xenios* Zeus–Zeus of the strangers–entitles the stranger to the rites of hospitality. *Philoxenia,* love towards strangers, especially in the Homeric age, is a sacred virtue to be cultivated, in the same way as *philosophia,* love of wisdom, in the classical age.

In the ecumenical age of Hellenism and Christianity, *philadelphia*

(love of one's brother and sister) and *philoxenia* are coupled to form
one indivisible virtue of charity and philanthropy (Hebrews 13:2).
Only monsters unfit for human fellowship are deprived of the virtue
of *philoxenia*. (1990, p. 7)

Within the context of parables, most modern families probably can
relate to some form of ceremony that they practice which honors the
stranger in some way. Surely, as the gap between the secular versus the
older religious celebration of holidays widens in modern times, such per-
sonalized ritual as preserving a place at the table for a wayfarer probably
becomes far less common.

Agrarian cultures, where such customs were easier to preserve, have
evolved into a far more urbanized and crowded service economy. Due to
the changing values and customs that result from such social change, the
once-honored ritual of preserving a place setting at one's table may only
be a memory in our grandparents' minds if it exists there at all, now.

"Charity," in fact, may not be immediately recognized as a word once
used in ancient scripture as a synonym for "love." For example, in the
New Testament, when Paul writes to the Corinthians (13:13), he says,
"Though I speak with the tongues of men [and women) and of angels, and
have not charity, I am become as sounding brass, or a tinkling cymbal."
Charity, today, may mean a financial donation that one gives via the more
acceptable distance of a mailed check, or a periodic donation of clothing
left outside the front door that is carted away by and given to others who
we never actually meet in person.

Hospitality, today, may in fact more easily translate into very private
acts of generosity that are viewed as the natural terrain of the nuclear
family circle. When we think of the types of social exchanges that take
place along these lines between strangers in larger public places, many of
us may be more apt to think in terms of the service economy where one's
host, more often than not, is the local restaurateur, and one's role of guest
is viewed as that of any paying customer whose primary concern is with
receiving a certain quality of service that will be judged by the modern
language of efficiency in a competitive market arena.

IN AN INDUSTRY CALLED "HOSPITALITY"

The relationship between a provider and client
is a special kind of "stranger" relationship.

–Czepiel, Solomon, and Surprenant, 1985, p. 5

Moving away, now, from the individual and into the collective, private service sector, specifically into an industry called *Hospitality,* we can further appreciate how words and concepts change and adapt their meanings as the contexts in which they are embedded expand and shift.

The global hospitality industry is, at best, an elusive collection of businesses and purposes that are difficult to grasp for the outsider and insider, alike. The term "hospitality industry" as it will be used in this paper is sometimes "used interchangeably with the words 'tourism' and 'tourism industry' but focuses attention on the responsibility of industry personnel to be hospitable hosts. Sometimes the term 'hospitality' is also used to refer as a category to the hotels, motels and other accommodations which comprise a significant part of tourism" (Metelka, 1990, p. 73).

The term "tourism" is also "variously defined contingent upon context. Usually, it is an umbrella term for the variety of products and services offered and desired by people while away from home. Included are restaurants, accommodations, activities, natural and manmade attractions, travel agencies, government bureaus, and transportation. The meaning of the word also includes an awareness that this myriad of products and services are interrelated and interdependent" (Metelka, 1990, p. 154).

The hospitality industry is the largest employer in the world. By 2005, as reported in The World Travel and Tourism Council Research Report (1994), the number of people employed in this industry is estimated to be 300 million, a figure that represents approximately 12 percent of the global workforce.

Strangers, in this industry context are thought of as "paying customers," or "clients." Industry employees are "service agents" or "service providers" and they do not so much befriend clients in a purely humanistic spirit as they sell services to them in an exchange commonly known as "the service encounter" (Czepiel, Solomon, Surprenant, & Gutman, 1985, p. 5).

In a book entitled *The Service Encounter: Managing Employee/Customer Interaction* (Czepiel, Solomon, & Surprenant, 1985), the concept of the stranger is specifically noted as changed or altered due to the economic context of all commercial and public market places.

> Face to face service encounters are the focus of this book, although other forms are also discussed. As one aspect of marketplace behavior, the service encounter is particularly interesting. By one perspective its shape is determined by thousands of years of history in defining the roles of buyer and seller.
>
> Differently perceived, it encompasses the totality of feelings and activities that define what happens when two strangers meet, interact, and take leave of one another. It can also be interpreted and

understood as an example of social organization using such themes as class, power, control, and authority. (Czepiel et al., p. 1)

To aid the industry and its customer-service workers to understand what this means in terms of operational realities, certain tenets of the *service encounter relationship* are defined and accepted by most professional hospitality practitioners as SOPs (standard operating procedures), both theoretically and practically speaking. These conceptualizations have modernized the hospitality industry's ability to forge a relationship with "strangers and wayfarers" in ways that make tangible the rather abstract nature of hospitality practice in public places.

I will, at this time, present an example of one highly relevant blueprint, if you will, to illustrate how hospitality practice takes place in an industrial service setting. Service encounters (Czepiel, Solomon, Surprenant, & Gutman, 1985, pp. 4-7) are defined as human interactions with the following characteristics:

1. *Service encounters are purposeful.* The interaction between two individuals can occur for a wide variety of reasons. It may be accidental. They may be friends. It may be educational, emotional, familial, or political. In contrast, service encounters belong to a special class of human interaction which is goal-oriented.

2. *Service providers are not altruistic.* While there are individuals and classes of people who provide services for altruistic reasons (such as physicians or lawyers with Pro Bono clients, or volunteers with charitable organizations), the primary raison d'etre of a service provider is to provide a specified service as part of a job for which he or she is paid.

3. *Prior acquaintance is not required.* The relationship between a provider and client is a special kind of "stranger" relationship. While one does not normally have extended interactions with strangers, service providers are strangers who may be approached with societal approval as long as the approach occurs within the limits of the service setting. . . .

4. *Service encounters are limited in scope.* While service encounters have both latent and manifest functions, it is the latter that dominate and define the area of legitimate intercourse. The scope of the interchange is restricted by the nature and content of the service to be delivered. A bank teller is not expected to give medical advice.

5. *Task-related information exchange dominates.* In many service settings, especially the less formal, there is a difficult-to-separate mixture of task and nontask information exchange. In an informal set-

ting such as a local barber or beautician shop, for example, an observer might code the content of conversation as 10 percent task and 90 percent nontask. More formal service settings, such as airline ticket counters or fast-food restaurants might be coded 90 percent task and 10 percent nontask in terms of content.

6. *Client and provider roles are well defined.* Purposeful interactions between strangers require rules if the task is to be completed. The basic set of rules which give structure to the interchange are contained in the roles that each actor assumes in the interchange. (Solomon, Surprenant, Czepiel, & Gutman, 1984)

While some role expectations may be specific to a particular type of service, other role expectations may be generalized across many different settings. The expectations clients hold about the behavior of the person behind the counter–whether fast-food restaurant, bank, or airline–may be very similar.

The "counter person" is expected to acknowledge the client's presence, smile, and be pleasant, but also accomplish the task with minimal nontask commentary. For services with closer personal contact such as dentist or hairdressing services, the provider's role includes making the client feel at ease, which may require more nontask conversation.

7. *A temporary status differential occurs.* The concept of role definition and expectations highlights a final characteristic of service interactions. It is that the roles of provider and client provide for a temporary suspension of the "normal" social status enjoyed by each party.

A lawyer, for example, normally a high-status person in our society, may work for clients of lower social status. Such an inversion of the accepted social order in which those of lower social status generally work for those of a higher social status adds a degree of role ambiguity or piquancy to the interaction.

What we've come to call "service quality," as you can see from the above blueprint of the service encounter relationship is, at best, an extremely complex array of human interactions that are symbolic, intangible, physical, behavioral, psychological, and artistic in their very essence (Klaus, 1985). And, a blueprint of words does not do proper justice to such dynamic, real time encounters, for sure. Nonetheless, one insight that emerges is how the role of the service employee is more complex than the average customer may think at first glance.

Hence, "any attempts to manage service quality *directly*–by prescribing specific attributes–cannot work" (Klaus, 1985, p. 17) because the sum total of elements in human interactions are as elusive as a work of artistic design. Klaus writes:

> The charm of an impressionistic painting has to do with the colors and the painting technique used by the artist, the choice of the motif, but also with appropriate framing, lighting, and other contextual factor.
>
> Yet "charm" is not equivalent to nor determined by a specific arrangement of colors, or any other analytical category by which a painting is usually described. To suggest the use of specific colors or a certain painting technique to the artist as the means of enhancing the charm of a piece would seem naive advice.
>
> But what then is charm, and how does it come about? The answer is: It is a consequence of a delicate configuration of elements–an epiphenomenon. (Klaus, 1985, p. 17)

In fact, such "a delicate configuration of elements" (p. 17) is not devoid of a certain spiritual quality that transpires between the art form and the observer. A truly excellent service encounter is both an art form and a science of operational reality in the hospitality industry. And, despite all efforts to try to efficiently pre-script how business and management cultures may most profitably operate, today, the simple truth remains that the core and the heart of excellent service provision is still very much all about certain special stranger relationships that take place on a face-to-face basis between strangers at the doors and a hospitality labor force of employees who interact with them.

Without exception, so much of this simply depends on employees who are well treated, well trained, and enabled, if not empowered, to move in their varied operational spaces. Whether they are cooks in a restaurant kitchen, or clerks behind a hotel-front desk, providers need to work in a free and fluid dance that allows them access to the varied tools necessary to do their jobs.

Due to the stressful, "emotional labor" (Hochschild, 1983) laden nature of being a service provider who constantly mediates between satisfying customer needs and a myriad of inconsistent operational realities, service employees require working conditions that rest securely upon their rights to progressive and rich human resource management environments that enable them to feel respected for the jobs they perform.

Such a humane environment is just as crucial for the service provider as it is for the customer, a fact that is widely touted in the "talk" of industries, but not so widely demonstrated in the "walk" or day-to-day operational realities in which service employees must function. Such a humane environment, however, is not as carefully blueprinted for the employee as it is for the customer.

Employees are the charm and the true spirit of the hospitality industry. In some ways, they are *family*.

IN THIS INDUSTRIAL EMPLOYEE FAMILY THERE ARE COMPLEX CHALLENGES

Family is a word or term that has gained both depth and breadth from redefinition during the last decade (Scanzoni & Marsiglio, 1991; see also Marciano & Sussman, 1991). In a paper entitled "Wider Families As Primary Relationships," the authors' presented a sampling of various definitions of family to illustrate that family is "a group of people who love and care for each other" (Seligman, 1989) and that this conceptualization may equally apply to any group of people involved in a "strong symbol system" (Gittens, 1986, p. 117) of myriad societal variety.

Ultimately, the authors conclude that a wider definition of the word, family, encompasses "non-kin exchanges" and "primary networks" (Scanzoni & Marsiglio, 1991, p. 125) of both an intrinsic and extrinsic nature that are constructed, ideally speaking, to support and enhance an individual's total well-being. Hypothetically, the notion of the wider family could be thought to include an organization of workers and managers in which an individual is employed.

To those of us who have labored in the front- and the back-of-house jobs in the hospitality industry, "family" is a familiar term that, in fact, has been used to describe "the help" for many, many years. While it is true that, traditionally, the term, family, was more applicable to smaller hospitality businesses such as the Mom-and-Pop type of restaurant operations, the vernacular has stuck and it is not uncommon to hear a manager in an employee meeting of one kind or another employ this term while trying to rally a collective sense of commitment among his or her troops.

Of course, within the market place of the industry nicknamed *Hospitality,* just as in our popular culture, the concept of the God-sent or sacred stranger has strayed a considerable distance away from the original meanings of ancient religious and folklore literature. However, it has not strayed as far as one might think.

When one begins to study *The Law of the Innkeeper–For Hotels, Motels, Restaurants, and Club* (Sherry, 1981), one learns that it is still the legal if not the sacred duty of hosts to protect guests in many different ways when they take shelter in a wide variety of hospitality businesses for a myriad of reasons. John Sherry writes of how the contemporary laws regulating hospitality industry businesses evolved from those followed by early innkeepers in England:

> Such being the business and such the customs of innkeepers, their responsibility, which through modern eyes seems anomalous, is easily explained. They undertake as a business to furnish food, protection, and shelter to the wayfaring guest.
>
> Having undertaken such a public business, and the public need being concerned, the innkeeper must supply his service to all; and in order to perform his undertaking he must furnish not merely sufficient food and a tight roof, but sufficient protection against the dangers of country traveling. (1981, pp. 7-8)

Tremendous advances have been made in the hospitality industry concerning how service employees can successfully greet and welcome the proverbial stranger at the door who is our customer. Nevertheless, a troubling irony continues to exist as the industry less seldom evaluates how well it is doing with greeting, welcoming, and successfully building long-term relationships with its employees. These employees, more often than not, may actually be the real strangers in its midst: those soon to be 300 million global workers who, these days, go by the name of "family" less and less within organizational boundaries.

TROUBLED EMPLOYEE RELATIONS

As late as 1996, some of these labor relations problems were articulated in a virtual Internet conference entitled "Hospitality Management: The State of the Art," sponsored by the Hospitality and Tourism Forum, an initiative by MCB University Press in the United Kingdom to provide an on-going global Internet forum for those providing professional and academic services to the hospitality industry (http://www.mcb.co.uk/services/hospitality_forum/home.htm).

Within the context of this conference, a human resource management discussion group took place and a selection of papers were presented by hospitality researchers and writers from Australia, Canada, and the United Kingdom that rather bravely addressed the serious challenges facing the hospitality industry in the pervasive area of global labor relations. Not only was the caliber of the discussion admirable in terms of its professional integrity, but the forum's relevance to global industry concerns touched upon similar problems seen in the US with respect to employee relations.

Rosemary Lucas (1996) identified a serious paradox, namely, that despite the fact that the hospitality industry, at large, is very well populated with human resource specialists in its ranks, oftentimes, the industry is characterized by "a poor state of personnel management and associated practice" (1996, p. 2) with respect to progressive quality of work life outcomes for employees.

Lucas cited the following problems with which human resource management must more progressively grapple: "high quit rates, sickness absence, injury rates and dismissals, pervasive low pay, and above average use of disciplinary sanctions and grievance procedures" (1996, p. 2). She also explains that "trade union density in hotels and catering, the British equivalent of what Americans refer to as the Food Service Industry, is "a mere 3% compared to 48% in the economy as a whole" (Lucas, 1996, p. 2).

It deserves to be mentioned that Lucas is specifically talking about the hospitality industry in Great Britain, but this author began working in the food service industry in the US in the early '70s, and these problems speak to ones I and others have personally observed for many years.

Julia Chistensen-Hughes (1996, see also 1992), from the University of Guelph, explored the organizational and institutional "barriers that prevent organizations from making more progress towards a longer term view of human resource management" (1996, p. 1). She discussed concerns that most North American hospitality organizations are faced with today such as "government sanctions in labor relations, work force diversity, the need to raise the level of professionalism, the need to increase efficiency and productivity through automation and down sizing, and the need to increase the quality of entry level employees," citing the work of Allen (1994), in part, to complement her own ethnographic fieldwork research (p. 1).

Chistensen-Hughes writes that "one of the most critical issues organizations are facing today is the ability to address their short-term financial challenges while demonstrating a "commitment to, and investment in, the development of effective, long-term human resource practices" (1996, p. 2).

Citing the work of Shames (1989) as well as her own fieldwork observations, Christensen-Hughes notes how hospitality industry organizational cultures, in general, are traditionally known to deploy "rigid and highly stratified hierarchical structures, autocratic leadership styles, centralized decision making, predominant emphasis on cost controls and short-term profits, the rigorous enforcement of standardized procedures and controls, and limited downward information sharing" (1996, p. 2).

Such antiquated, Tayloristic, managerial practices derived from the school of scientific management studies initiated during the Industrial Revolution have been well noted by other researchers who have collected qualitative, field research data about employee working conditions in the hospitality industry (Christensen-Hughes, 1992; Fine, 1996; Leidner, 1993; Mars and Nicod, 1984; Prus & Irini, 1988; Whyte, 1949, 1948, 1947; Whyte & Hamilton, 1973).

Christensen-Hughes reminds us that such an approach has been previously noted with such descriptors as "manufacturing in the field" (Levitt, 1992) and the "service factory environment" (Lovelock, 1990). She quoted the work of Schlesinger and Heskett (1991) who wrote that such terms were highly appropriate and based on a number of key assumptions inherent in the managerial strata of the hospitality industry including such beliefs, values and norms as "it is better to rely on technology than people; front-line jobs should be designed to be as simple and narrow as possible; employees should be paid as close to minimum wage as possible; sales promotions and marketing drive the top line; and cost control is the unit-level manager's primary responsibility" (p. 81).

In a candid quote based on her own 1992 ethnographic study of a large American based, food-service multi-national, Christensen-Hughes observed many of the problems listed above while she worked in the field, saying "while managers privately expressed their concern about the impact of these practices on their employees and customers, they felt controlled by an autocratic management style and the organization's short-term, results-oriented culture. The National Director of Operations proudly described his management style as encompassing 'the 5 F's.' He explained, 'be friendly, fair and firm, if that doesn't work use fear, if that doesn't work, they're fucked'"(1996, p. 3).

In terms of offering what may be a strategy for longer termed effects towards building a more genuinely progressive human resource environment leading to improved quality of work life experiences for industry employees, Christensen-Hughes suggests remembering the advice of Schlesinger and Heskett (1991) to put front-line workers first and design the business system around them.

This, it deserves to be mentioned, is different from merely "talking" or "writing" about *TQM* or an infinite variety of so-called *leadership* styles–as well as the all too commonly used *academic journalese* terms of *employee commitment* and *employee empowerment*. Putting employees first involves cultivating a deeper and more humane industrial gaze into just why corporations and organizations actually owe nurturing quality of work life experiences to their employees.

One might say this genuinely means that it is the responsibility of management to know how to enable employees to move with agency, grace, and ease in the physical as well as the psychological service space in which they operate to do their various jobs. In operational practice, as opposed to some forms of popularized *worker-motivation* jargon, there is a definite difference between such an enabling managerial capability and a latent industry managerial value that primarily focuses solely upon customer satisfaction.

Such a difference manifests in results that are at the emotional expense of employees who, in many ways, end up being treated like "service machines" in a factory-like setting instead of being treated as valued employees and professional service agents. Lundberg (1995) reminds us that "the milieu of a factory illustrates this . . . although this scenario applies equally well to service, education, health care, and most other institutions" in our postindustrial age (p. 36).

In such a factory-like work world, "efforts to retrieve and rediscover preindustrial values of self-expression and self-actualization in the service of personal growth are nullified because behaviorally they embody autonomy" (Lundberg, 1995, p. 36).

Christensen-Hughes cited industry leader Isadore Sharp, past chairman, president and chief executive officer of Four Seasons Hotels and Resorts (Sharp, 1991, p. 18), who said "command and control is out; people cannot be ordered to think . . . The manager as disciplinarian will have to give way to the manager as mentor, communicator and coach . . . someone who creates unity, not divisiveness, who generates energy rather than directing it" (Sharp, 1991, p. 4).

Christensen-Hughes concluded her Internet conference paper on a note of honesty. She writes:

> Over the past several years, corporate America has taken off its paternalistic gloves, revealing some hard truths about the Darwinian world of business.
>
> Within this climate, significant barriers exist with respect to the implementation of sound human resource management practices. Many hospitality organizations will continue to expect more from their employees while forcing wage rates and human resource management budgets down.
>
> In these organizations many negative outcomes may result: financial security and employee loyalty will be scarce; productivity, product quality and customer service may suffer; turnover rates will remain high; employee/employer relationships will become further strained; and control systems will become increasingly necessary as a culture of maximizing one's own self-interest prevails. (1996, p. 5)

Troubled employee relations speak to "family" in a shadow-like dysfunctional way. The research cited above illustrates this by imaging what are persistent, serious industrial labor problems. This question begs to be asked: Can any genuine sense of *industrial family* exist in a setting where employees are made to feel like machines while, at the same time, they are also expected to perform the most delicate service of hospitality work? We know the answer to such a question.

PRESERVING ORGANIZATIONAL HOSPITALITY IN A TIME OF POSTINDUSTRIAL MALAISE

Craig C. Lundberg (1995, see also 1989, 1985) insightfully and sensitively captures a cultural description of a postindustrial malaise of which the hospitality industry is but a part. He states that much of the malaise in organizations derives from the extreme power that corporations play in all of our lives as well as in certain "philosophical errors" that have become too institutionalized and rooted in our corporate cultures (Lundberg, 1995, p. 32). Within this corporatized Myst Game, individuals and groups have become so conditioned, so erased, so eviscerated of whatever they might once have become, or have been, that all they can think to do is what they are conditioned to do.

Lundberg reminds us that "all modern societies are 'organizational,' (Presthus, 1962) in that organizations, especially business organizations, are the dominant institutions and both mirror and shape society and its citizens" (1995, p. 31). He describes the values of the now-past industrial age and suggests that some corporations are still enacting them almost without realizing it "including unquestioned beliefs about competitive relationships, private property, the subjugation of nature, delayed gratification, working hard, and the separation of management and labor" (1995, p. 32).

Certainly, not all of these beliefs were harmful, but the last one, the separation of management and labor, is perhaps the main reason why the hospitality industry, across the board on a global level, faces tremendous challenges in terms of employee relations.

Lundberg poses two crucial questions which it would do well for all industries to ask now, especially *Hospitality* precisely because it will employ 300 million people throughout the world by 2005 and is the world's largest employer: "What is the organizational archetype likely to engender the work-related behaviors desired in the future? And, what are the values that will enhance our capabilities, as individuals and as organizational members, to cope with increased levels of complexity which more and more characterize the turbulent postindustrial environment?" (1995, p. 32).

To those of us who now labor in postindustrial organizations of various types, Lundberg reminds us how, when we are very honest about it, we know the answer:

> As we move into the postindustrial era with its contextual turbulence and uncertainties, organizations will no doubt continue to be the backbone of society. Clearly, the dominant organization designs of the past no longer suffice. Contemporary organizational innovations are all mostly flawed because they are designed utilizing no longer appropriate conceptions of humans, human relationships, and human values.
>
> Optimum organizational designs are still sought even when contextual circumstances increasingly become ambiguous due to rapid and proliferating change. Needed, it now seems clear, is a greater variety of organizations each of which promotes a multifaceted excellence.
>
> High-performing systems, sharing certain characteristics but varying widely in formal organizational terms, may well be the exemplar of the organizations and human systems required in a postindustrial society. While unique in superficial ways, what these systems fundamentally share is a culture in which their members can experience deep, existential values of intensity, dignity and freedom while pursuing purposive, collective action. (1995, p. 44)

High performing systems (HPS) vary enormously but share some common features such as shared values among members; a healthy respect for how employees are genuinely motivated; a sense of integrated, germane team spirit; reliable and predictable leadership; a feeling for what workforce creativity actually means; a certain bounded insulation or degree of socialized comfort from the larger environment; internalized control structures that are more democratically determined; and possess a sense of community spirit that defies pat corporatized metaphors (Lundberg, 1995; also see Vail, 1982, pp. 26-27).

Most importantly, such systems, however they manifest themselves, "appear to be human systems that encourage degrees of proaction, passion, collaboration, shared meaning, flexibility, and learning which conventional organization thinking would deem extraordinary if not inappropriate" (Lundberg, 1995, p. 41). What surfaces here is that such a democratically determined organizational structure may be capable of *hospitality practice* towards those who work within its bounds as well as towards those who visit as customers, suppliers, and other types of boundary spanners.

Given the tremendous breadth and latitude of what a high performing organizational system might look like in each specific manifestation, Lundberg asks "What is the core of the characteristics?" and posits "the quality and the form of process is what is paramount" (1995, p. 41). If successful, "HPS members discover, over time, their systems' uniqueness, specialness, organic unity and contextual resiliency–in a word, their culture. Beyond the facts of any particular HPS then, it is here hypothesized that it is some set of deep and latent values that both enables their excellence and peak performances as well as distinguishes HPS from other organizations" (Lundberg, 1995, p. 41).

It might be said that in a time of postindustrial malaise, what organizations as well as whole industries need to do is to re-examine their own sense of hospitality practice towards those who are *employee relations,* or part of their *wider families* (Marciano & Sussman, 1991).

TOO MANY TIMES, WE ARE THE STRANGERS INSIDE OUR OWN DOORS

Learning is the very essence of humility,
learning from everything and from everybody.
There is no hierarchy in learning. Authority
denies learning and a follower will never learn.

–Krishnamurti's Notebook

Culture, whether it be "organizational" or not, has been written about by more than one author in more than one country or language. Culture can be likened to a map with multivariate human variations, a social but invisible map that depicts the essence of our human consciousness traveling through the moments of history, if only we know how to deeply read such a highly sentient form of soulful cartography.

Hospitality, both as an ancient humanistic act of grace and as a global industrial niche holds the promise of modeling its own archetype to the world. Here, it is wise to ponder how the word "model" means to be a smaller imitation of the real thing.

The act of honoring the stranger at the door as well as those who are already standing beside us, and thus genuinely honoring ourselves in the process, personifies the spiritual essence of all that is exemplary about how human beings can and, at times, do acknowledge one another.

Remembering and, if necessary, re-learning the ancient archetype of hospitality practice and how it can exist in our wider family life, both in our homes and in our corporations and industries may be a good place to begin anew.

> So we cannot take for granted the familiar word *hospitality* when we begin to see it in its rich context. . . . The soup kitchen, though necessary, isn't in itself hospitality; maybe the lack of real hospitality in our day is the reason why people are homeless and soup kitchens exist. The exchange we speak of requires another level, and seems to correspond with a human need even deeper, and far harder to satisfy, than physical hunger. Its nature is a profound question. (Dooling, 1990, p. 2)

Shared meaning is a rare cultural resource in a time of postindustrial malaise. The interconnectedness between our civilization's earliest cultural images, or archetypes of the hospitality exchange, and who we are today at home as well as in the market place is a matter of re-organizing an awareness of what we model and why, both internally to ourselves and then to others who are only strangers until we reshape our own structural social need for them to remain so. The uneasiness and discomfort of any social malaise holds the promise of *possibility* for new as well as renewed bridge building between theory and practice on both individual and collective levels.

AUTHOR NOTE

In 1991, Michele Grottola received the MS degree from Cornell University in the department of Management: Operations and Human Resources, located in the School of Hotel Administration. In 1988, Michele graduated from the Culinary Institute of America in Hyde Park, New York. In 1980, she received a Bachelor of Arts degree, awarded *magna cum laude* in English Literature and Educational Studies from Wesleyan University in Middletown, Connecticut.

The author is indebted to many others. Several of the major ideas are freely borrowed from and inspired by the special issue about hospitality published by *Parabola: The Magazine of Myth and Tradition,* particularly the work of Lambros Kamperidis and Helen M. Luke. The author is equally indebted to the organizational scholarship of Craig C. Lundberg (Cornell University) and Julia Christensen-Hughes (University of Guelph), as well as to my many discussions with Frances Calloway-Parks (Chicago State University) about the need for industrial compassion in the private service sector. A very special debt is extended to Francis Kwansa and Pamela Cummings at the University of Delaware for their sincere interest in promoting a different voice in hospitality and tourism management scholarship.

REFERENCES

Allen's article (as cited in Christensen-Hughes, 1996).

Christensen-Hughes, J. (1996). Human resource management: Barriers to a longer term view. [On-line], Available: [http://www.mcb.co.uk/services/conference/apr96/hospitality/themes. htm#subtheme2]. Internet Conference. Hospitality Management: The State of the Art.

Christensen-Hughes, J. (1992). Cultural diversity: The lessons of Toronto's hotels. *The Cornell Quarterly.* April, 78-87.

Czepiel, J. A., Solomon, M. R., & Surprenant, C. F. (Eds.). (1985). *The Service encounter: Managing employee/customer interaction in service businesses.* Massachusetts: Lexington.

Czepiel, J. A., Solomon, M. R., Surprenant, C. F., & Gutman, E. G. (1985). Service encounters: An overview. In J. A. Czepiel, M. R. Solomon, & C. F. Surprenant (Eds.), *The Service encounter: Managing employee/customer interaction in service businesses (pp. 3-16).* Massachusetts: Lexington.

Dooling, D. M. (Ed.). (1990). Hospitality [Special Issue]. *Parabola, XV* (4).

Fine, G. A. (1996). *Kitchens: the culture of restaurant work.* Berkeley, CA: University of California Press.

Gittens's study (as cited in Scanzoni & Marsiglio, 1991).

Hochschild, A. E. (1983). *The managed heart.* Berkeley, CA: University of California Press.

Kamperidis, L. (1990). Philoxenia and hospitality. *Parabola, XV* (4), 4-13.

Klaus, P. G. (1985). Quality epiphenomenon: The conceptual understanding of quality in face-to-face service encounters. In J. A. Czepiel, M. R. Solomon, & C. F. Surprenant (Eds.), *The Service encounter: Managing employee/customer interaction in service businesses* (pp. 17-34). Massachusetts: Lexington.

Leidner, R. (1993). *Fast food, fast talk: Service work and the routinizartion of everyday life.* Berkeley, CA: University of California Press.

Levitt's study (as cited in Christensen-Hughes, 1996).

Lockhart's study (as cited in Luke, 1990).

Lovelock's study (as cited in Christensen-Hughes, 1996).

Lucas, R. (1996). Of paradox and paradigm. [On-line], Available: [http://www.mcb.co.uk/services/conference/apr96/hospitality/themes.htm#subtheme2]. Internet Conference. Hospitality Management: The State of the Art.

Lundberg, C. C. (1995). Are high performance systems an existential organizational exemplar for post industrial society? *Quarterly Journal of Ideology, 18,* (3,4), 31-48.

Lundberg, C. C. (1989). On organizational learning: Implications and opportunities for expanding organizational development. In R. W. Woodman & W. A. Pasmore (Eds.), *Research in Organizational Chance and Development,* Vol. 3 (pp. 61-82). Greenwich, CT: JAI Press.

Lundberg, C. C. (1985). On the feasibility of cultural intervention in organization. In P. Frost, L. Moore, M. Louis, C. Lundberg, & J. Martin (Eds.), *Organizational culture and the meaning of life in the workplace* (pp. 169-186). Newbury Park, CA: Sage.

Luke, H. M. (1990). The stranger within. *Parabola, XV* (4), 17-23.

Marciano, T. D., & Sussman, M. B. (Eds.). (1991). *Wider families: New traditional family forms*. Binghamton, NY: The Haworth Press, Inc. [Also published in *Marriage & Family Review 17*(1/2).]

Mars, G., & Nicod, M. (1984). *The world of waiters*. London: George Allen & Unwin.

Presthus, 1962 (as cited in Lundberg, 1995).

Price's study (as cited in Christensen-Hughes, 1996).

Prus, R., & Irini, S. (1988). *Hookers, rounders, and desk clerks: The social organization of the hotel community*. Salem, WI: Sheffield. (Original work published in 1980.)

Seligman' s study (as cited in Scanzoni & Marsiglio, 1991).

Scanzoni, J., & Marsiglio, W. (1991). Wider families as primary relationships. In T. D. Marciano & M. B. Sussman (Eds.), *Wider families: New traditional family forms* (pp. 117-133). Binghamton, NY: The Haworth Press, Inc. [Also published in *Marriage & Family Review 17*(1/2).]

Schesinger, L. A., & Heskett, J. L. (1991). The service driven company. *Harvard Business Review*, September-October, 71-81.

Shames' study (as cited in Christensen-Hughes, 1996).

Sharp's comments (as cited in Christensen-Hughes, 1996).

Sherry, J. E. H. (1981). *The laws of innkeepers*. (Rev. ed.). Ithaca, NY: Cornell University Press.

Solomon et al. study (as cited in Czepiel, J. A., Solomon, M. R., Surprenant, C. F., & Gutman, E. G., 1985).

Travel & Tourism–A New Economic Perspective. (1994). *The World Travel and Tourism Council Research Report*.

Vail's study (as cited in Lundberg, 1996).

Whyte, W. F. (1949). The social structure of a restaurant. *The American Journal of Sociology, 54*, 302-310.

Whyte, W. F. (1948). *Human relations in the restaurant industry*. New York: McGraw-Hill.

Whyte, W. F. (1947). Solving the hotel's human problems. *The Hotel Monthly* (June).

Whyte, W. F., & Hamilton, E. L. (1973). *Action research for management*. Columbus, Ohio: Grid, Inc. (Originally published by Richard D. Irwin Inc. January, 1965.)

Wolk, D. S. (1985). And he ran to greet him. *Parabola, XV* (4), 81-85.

Cultural Heritage
of American Food Habits
and Implications for the Hospitality Industry

H. G. Parsa

SUMMARY. This study has profiled the cultural heritage of American food habits. American food habits remained predominantly European until the middle of the 20th century, and became distinctly American by late 20th century. This study indicates that the relationship between the culture and the food habits is bi-directional. Analysis of changes in the family structure, and their impact on food habits in the Western civilization from the period of the Roman and Greek empires through the 20th century are included. Contrary to the earlier beliefs, food habits of individuals were found to be more permanent and stable than their socio-economic, cultural, religious, educational, and ethnic preferences. American food habits of the 20th century are influenced by its cultural sub-groups.

Food habits include not only food consumption habits but also the food procurement, production, preparation, and preservation practices. The food habits are often passed on from one generation to

H. G. Parsa is Associate Professor, Hospitality Administration program, State University of New York College–Buffalo, and a member of several professional organizations.

The author acknowledges Kathleen O'Brien and William Scheider of SUNYC-Buffalo, and Francis Kwansa of University of Delaware for their valuable comments and suggestions in the early stages of the manuscript development.

The author is very grateful for the invaluable suggestions and comments provided by the three anonymous reviewers in revising the manuscript.

[Haworth co-indexing entry note]: "Cultural Heritage of American Food Habits and Implications for the Hospitality Industry." Parsa, H. G. Co-published simultaneously in *Marriage & Family Review* (The Haworth Press, Inc.) Vol. 28, No. 1/2, 1998, pp. 23-48; and: *The Role of the Hospitality Industry in the Lives of Individuals and Families* (ed: Pamela R. Cummings, Francis A. Kwansa, and Marvin B. Sussman) The Haworth Press, Inc., 1998, pp. 23-48. Single or multiple copies of this article are available for a fee from The Haworth Document Delivery Service [1-800-342-9678, 9:00 a.m. - 5:00 p.m. (EST). E-mail address: getinfo@haworthpressinc.com].

23

another like sacred texts and family traditions. Changing food habits and their impact on the hospitality industry are discussed. *[Article copies available for a fee from The Haworth Document Delivery Service: 1-800-342-9678. E-mail address: getinfo@haworthpressinc.com]*

KEYWORDS. Food habits, Culture, Family structure, Hospitality, Western civilization, Ancient

INTRODUCTION

International tourism is one of the few trade surplus industries in the United States netting $17 billion annually with revenues at hundreds of regional destinations throughout the country. It is one of the largest industries in the USA. How the U.S. hospitality industry relates to families of today's world may include a broad number of issues. Many of these issues are about how the needs and expectations of international and domestic travelers are met by the hospitality industry. The travelers are not a homogeneous group. The travelers as a group are distinctly diverse in cultural, ethnic, linguistic, political, and religious backgrounds. With this multiple diversity they offer unique challenges to the hospitality industry. Hospitality firms that provide food, lodging and entertainment to the travelers will need to pursue philosophies and practices that effectively satisfy the needs and wants of these complex market segments.

Needs and wants of various cultural groups are uniquely different from each other especially in the case of food. What impact does cultural diversity have on the products (food) offered by the hospitality industry? To answer this question, it is important to understand the dynamics of cultural diversity, and the impact of cultural changes on the food habits over several generations. Cultural roots extend beyond language, clothing, customs, traditions, life styles, gender and preferred art forms; they also include food habits, their selection, preparation, preservation and consumption, and family traditions. Food habits of families are often more entrenched than art, language, clothing, and art expressions of their members. They are often religiously preserved and passed on to the future generations.

Food habits that include procurement, production, preparation, preservation and consumption are often passed on from one generation to another like sacred texts and family traditions. Many ethnic groups take more pride in the preservation of their food habits than any other factor that holds them together. For an example let us consider some of the ethnic groups of USA. Even after centuries of isolation and lack of communication with the native lands, ethnic communities such as Jews around the world, and Africans in Caribbean Islands and the U.S. take pride in their distinct food habits that are well preserved through the centuries, and are meant to hold them together through the difficult times. Similar preservation and passage of food habits can be noticed in other ethnic groups such as Irish-Americans, Asian-Americans, Italian-Americans, Native Americans, and Hispanics. High consumption of rice by the Asian-Americans, beans by the Hispanics, pasta products by the Italian-Americans, beef by the Euro-Americans, and corn-based products by the Native Americans, as well as avoidance of pork by Arab-Americans, are some of the examples of preservation of food habits. Religious beliefs, ethnic identity and health further add to the phenomenon. In addition, food habits are often intertwined with religious meanings, and used as vehicles of transportation of religious messages. Therefore, preservation and passage of food habits become paramount in maintaining and passing on the religio-cultural identity of social groups.

As the U.S. hospitality industry prepares to welcome the "world-customer," it needs to understand the value of food habits and their ability to withstand generational passage. Management of hospitality establishments need to show greater appreciation for different cultures and ethnic groups, honor human values, and realize the value of diversity over homogeneity in their work force as well as their guests. It is a paradigm shift requiring a holistic approach. Hospitality companies that are willing and able to make that change will be successful in meeting the needs of international and domestic travelers and their families. Earlier studies have shown that food habits of American society have strong European roots. But through the 20th century the food habits of the American consumers became distinctly American. Therefore it is necessary to further investigate the changing nature of American food habits.

LITERATURE REVIEW

Multicultural strategies in tourism outlined by Jaffari and Way (1992) discovered at least three cultures at work in the interaction between hotel employees and international guests. One of these is identified as "home culture." This typically is associated with the behavioral aspects of families that are retained in spite of the fact that they are away from home (Haviland 1993). West and Olsen (1990) discussed strategies pertinent to successful restaurants. They suggested that innovation and development in menu choices and focus on the specialized market as "grand strategies" will offer restaurants a better chance of meeting the needs of their guests.

Kittler and Sucher (1989) see culturally-based food habits as a "daily reaffirmation of cultural identity" and note that these habits are not easily dropped. The correlation between home culture, grand strategies and food habits may reveal the significance of culture on food procurement, selection, preparation, preservation and consumption for families. Further, we may see broad-based implications for the hospitality industry. Hertzler, Wenkam and Standal (1982) noted that food habits of individuals are significantly influenced by their culture, and food habits can be further classified depending on their content or context. While analyzing the menu trends of the U.S. from 1919 to 1988, Parsa and Khan (1992) recognized the impact of socio-economic and cultural factors on food habits. They also noted that changing food habits in the U.S. have dramatically modified the hospitality industry.

Every cultural (ethnic) group that came to the U.S. brought its own distinct food habits with it. This fact is exemplified by the food habits of Southern European, Irish, Mediterranean, Oriental, and Asian groups that are clearly noticeable in the contemporary American food habits. In the process of assimilation into the mainstream culture, the newly arrived groups have stretched the cultural tent of the U.S. a little wider and longer. As this process continued, new values and new cultures have evolved that are reflected in the changing food habits of America.

Over the past 400 years, the American food culture has evolved into its own. It is distinctly different and reflects the contributions of each of its participating groups. For example, during the 1920s, the primary food item in the U.S. hospitality industry was beef (steaks). In 1949, hamburger replaced steak as the most favored food. The hamburger was replaced by pizza as the choice of young American adults in the 1980s. These noted changes in food preference reflect the choices that each generation made during that period as a part of the dominant culture of that period. The question of how this choice is made deserves further investigation. To understand how different generations select their food choices it is necessary to have a clear understanding of the term "food habits." To accomplish this, a review of literature on "food habits" follows.

FOOD HABITS DEFINED

The term food habits is commonly perceived as a reflection of food consumption patterns. That is not necessarily true. According to Wenkam (1969) food habits are an adaptation of nutritional behavior patterns. As humans seek food to meet their physiological need they tend to select foods, intentionally or unintentionally, that meet their nutritional balance. According to Kittler and Sucher (1989), food habits are more than simple nutrient selection, they are symbols of an individual's choice of culture, religion, ethnicity, and regional affiliation. According to McIntosh (1995), food habits are culturally acquired, environmentally constrained, and affected by socio-economic, cultural, and religious factors. The food habits are a group phenomena as much as an individual's traits. In summary, the food consumption patterns of people are the result of various factors such as the cultural practices; religious affiliations; socio-economic status; occasion of food consumed (meal time); availability of foods; resources available to prepare the meal; tools available to consume the food; status of the food technology (food preservation, transportation, packaging, and storage); method of food preparation; and finally and most importantly, immediate and extended family.

In America, food habits can also be used to reflect an individual's political views. For example, environmental groups selecting only organic foods; liberal groups choosing vegetarian, "vegan" (devoid of animal of derivatives) and politically-correct food products; conservatives displaying preference for traditional "beef and potato" meals; and ethnic groups such as Cuban-Americans, African-Americans, Native Americans and Asian-Americans preferring foods that reflect their political views as well as cultural identity. To make a statement of political solidarity and cultural identity ethnic groups prefer to serve foods that represent their cultural heritage. For example, Polish-Americans try to display Polish sausage as a symbol of political and cultural identity. Informal political gatherings of Italian-Americans are often held at restaurants that serve foods of Italian heritage. It is not uncommon, during an election campaign, for political candidates and groups to use food as a symbol of their support to the cause of targeted groups. During the U.S. presidential campaigns political candidates carefully chose to display their preference for ethnic/regional foods to appease the ethnic/regional groups. For example, while campaigning in Texas, Democratic as well as Republican candidates prefer to participate in backyard Bar-B-Q parties to identify with the dominant culture of that region.

Similarly, during the 1992 presidential campaign, candidate Bill Clinton's visits to McDonald's restaurants were well publicized. With Quick Service Restaurants as the backdrop, candidate Bill Clinton tried to identify with the younger groups and the "common man," and differentiate himself from President Bush. But in 1996, while campaigning, President Clinton purposely avoided McDonald's restaurants to appear more presidential and formal than Senator Bob Dole, the Republican candidate. In America, most of the political fund raising activities include feasting as the focal point of the evening. The practice of using food as a symbol of political statements is well established in American society. Dining with different ethnic, religious and geographic groups and tasting foods of various ethnic/regional groups to solicit their political favors is a well-known practice in American politics.

Food habits are also affected by the choice of mealtimes. Typically, Americans consume breakfast and lunch in a different manner than they do dinner. Dinners are often taken seriously and consumed in a formal manner. They are often in the company of family members or friends. In contrast, lunch is often consumed either in the company of colleagues at work or alone at home/work. Presence of others during lunch time is not a necessary condition, while eating dinner alone is considered something less than desirable by many American families.

Food habits are also affected by the advances in food technology (food preservation, packaging, transportation, and storage) and production (preparation, cooking, serving, and saving). A good example is the increasing preference for convenience foods as the primary food choice and increasing use of pre-packaged, nutritionally balanced foods to replace traditional home-made meals by Americans. Discovery of frozen food technology during the early part of the twentieth century has given impetus to the birth of fast food restaurant industry in America (Parsa and Khan 1992). Introduction of microwave ovens has dramatically changed the way Americans prepare meals, especially the breakfast and lunch meals. Similarly, advances in food technologies such as freeze drying, cook-chill system have dramatically changed the way foods are prepared in institutional and industrial food services. Progress made in food delivery systems has significant impact on American food habits as noted in the popularity of ubiquitous Quick Service Restaurants with drive-thru, double drive-thru, and home delivery services.

Impact of religion on food habits is well documented in the literature. Every major religion has a set of guidelines, implicit or explicit, prescribing a specific manner to collect, select, prepare, consume, preserve, and store food (Tannahill 1988; Kittler and Sucher 1989; Kilara and Iya 1992; Chaudhry 1992; McIntosh 1995). Likewise every religion has restrictions and guidelines regarding the food habits of its believers. Similar to religious groups, every cultural group has its own distinct food habits. Food habits of cultural groups are passed on from one generation to another more as a part of tradition rather than as a rational process of understanding.

Finally and most importantly food habits are influenced by the changing nature of families. The concept of family had a different meaning at different times in human evolution. Earliest man was a 'food gatherer.' During this period no effort was made to increase the amount of food available. At that time, the concept of family was a group of nomads traveling together in search of food. The nomadic groups probably best lived as 'one big family.' It is done more for the convenience, safety, and security of the group members than any cultural, religious, or social norms. As Beals and Hoijer (1971) explained, 'food gatherers' slowly learned the techniques of 'food foraging' where animal and plant foods were collected and assembled, probably even stored, for later consumption. This tradition continued for an extended period through the Paleolithic period (McIntosh 1995). Food habits of the 'food foraging' period probably required a family structure that separated single-unit nomadic families into 'food collectors' and 'food preparers.' This was the first indication that food habits impacted the family structure.

Later, specialized food procurement practices such hunting, fishing, and scavenging developed requiring specialized use of tools and techniques (Gordon 1987). These newly acquired food habits further refined the concept of family. Now there was a head of a family that controlled the source of food for the family and another that controlled the food storage and distribution. By now the nomadic groups had learned the concept of settlement, although very temporarily. As the sources of food became scarce the humans learned to domesticate small animals and developed the practices of gardening. This eventually led to the development of agriculture. With the advent of agriculture, the concept of the family changed, giving men, women, and children more defined roles. The new defined roles for men and women in relation to foods have resulted in new innovations in food habits. The families of agri-based societies invented food preparation/preservation techniques such as drying, smoking, salting, pickling, cooking, and heating. While developing food preservation methods they also invented appropriate food consumption practices for new foods, and ensured their passage from one generation to another.

Food habits of human beings are continually evolving. As human beings make adaptations to the societal changes they modify their food habits as well. To better understand the process of continual adaptation to the societal changes and consequential changes in food habits, it is prudent to trace the changes in food habits through the early civilizations. The following section will present a review of food habits of the early civilizations.

FOOD HABITS OF THE ANCIENT CIVILIZATIONS

Human history began with the pursuit of food. When food supply dwindled, the ape-like man, in pursuit of food, descended onto the lower plains seeking small animals, herbs, roots, edible leaves, and fruits which resulted in the evolution of *Homo erectus* somewhere between 10 and 4 million years ago. According to some archaeological reports about 70 percent of Peking Man's (*Homo erectus*) diet is made up of venison. This is the first indication of change in human's food habit from fruits and nuts to meat. As the land resources became scarce, around 25,000 BC, invention of hooks using natural thorns to catch fish was introduced. It was followed by the invention of the bow and arrow in Central Asia around 13,000 BC (Tannahill 1988, 10). These two new innovations in food procurement have contributed the most to the evolution of human species, *Homo sapiens.*

Methods of controlling fire were developed about 500,000 BC in Africa or Central Asia. But it is not clear when these methods were used for the preparation of foods. Probably there was a delay as the earlier civilizations were waiting for the invention of cooking utensils. In Asia, the first cooking utensil used with fire was a bamboo stick and in Africa, many archaeologists believe, it was an earthen pit. Food preparation methods changed with the discovery of metals such as bronze, iron and steel. Using the newly discovered metals early civilizations prepared large quantities of foods. Evidence for such activities may be noted in the discovery of earthen ovens [Dumas 1969 (as quoted by Tannahill 1988)]. These metals may have contributed to the development of various food preparation techniques such as roasting and baking, and much later smoking. Thus, food habits indirectly influenced the development of earlier civilizations.

These evolutionary changes are not without consequences on the family structure. Women of the stone age primarily held the responsibility of bearing and raising the children while men spent their time collecting food either by hunting, fishing, gathering, or scavenging. As metals were invented, animals were domesticated, crops were harvested and the role of women changed dramatically. Now the woman had to spend more time caring for the crops, husking and grinding the grains, looking after the house, and bearing and rearing the children. In contrast, man's work had changed from mentally and physically demanding hunting to peaceful tending of flocks. Men had more time to attend to the needs of society beyond their immediate families (Tannahill 1988, p. 32). The man's work was changed from hunting to farming, and developing systems to maintain the new social order and communal unity. Since men took a more active role in establishing societal rules and norms, a male-dominant family structure was established. This is the first indication of the family structure that most of the world knows today. Therefore, it is clearly evident that from the beginning of human civilizations food habits have played a key role in the development of the human family structure.

As men were involved in developing societal norms and traditions for the common good of the society the women at home took active part in adapting individual family living practices to the societal norms and expectations. In other words, as men were involved in developing norms and traditions for the communities (macro-level) women became active in adapting the community policies to the individual families (micro-level). Over time, in some communities, women that were responsible for developing family level (micro-level) norms and customs have achieved greater power than men that were entrusted with the community level (macro-level) policies, resulting in matriarchal societies.

Until this period, food was collected and consumed as a community affair. A family was a tribal unit comprised of several individuals of both genders and some offspring that secured and consumed food collectively. People lived as hunting groups similar to present day animal groups such as monkeys and elephants. With the advent of animal domestication and flocking, the concept of family changed. A limited number of individuals functioning as one economic unit (family) replaced the old tribal commune systems. In other words, the concept of family changed from that of a social entity to an economic one.

The evolution of civilizations was connected to their food habits. The four great civilizations: Sumerian civilization (about 3500 BC) near Mesopotamia between the Tigris and Euphrates rivers; Egyptian civilization (about 3000 BC) near the Nile river in Africa; Indus Valley civilization (between 4500 and 2500 BC) near the Indus (Sindhu) river in the Northwestern part of India; and Hung He civilization (2000 BC) near the banks of Hung He river in China all evolved near a major river, a rich source of food and water. Some of the staple foods of these civilizations included sheep, milk, rice and flour. Bronze was used in preparing meals indicating advances in food preparation techniques. Therefore, emergence and growth of human civilizations was intricately linked with the foods collected and consumed.

Since the arrival of Pilgrims and colonists, the American culture has remained predominantly European in nature. Even though numerous African, Asian and Native American groups have contributed to the American cultural heritage it still remains primarily the culture of the Western Hemisphere. Therefore, to better understand the effects of food habits on the American culture it is necessary to review the historic role of food habits in the evolution of Western civilizations such as the Greek and Roman civilizations.

FOOD HABITS OF EARLY WESTERN CIVILIZATIONS

The food habits of Greek civilization were influenced both by the Central Asian tribes and the nomads from the upper north. From the Central Asian tribes, the Greeks learned animal husbandry, use of dairy products, winery, and bread making. The Northern nomads slowly settled in Central Europe depending on agriculture as a food source. From them, the Greeks learned the techniques of agriculture (McIntosh 1995, p. 46). Some of the primary foods of the Greeks were breads from wheat and barley, porridge, olives, fish, figs, honey, cheese, and wine.

During the Golden Age of Greek civilization, food habits took a new turn. Until that period, the primary purpose of food habits of the earlier civilizations was to meet the basic physiological needs of the people. The family was considered a social unit. Irrespective of the economic status of families, people consumed similar foods. But the Greek empire gave a new meaning to the term food habits. During the period of Greek rule separate foods were developed to indicate the social status of the families. The foods of the higher classes were significantly different from that of peasantry (Tannahill 1973, p. 31). The upper class dined on more wine and several types of meats and imported foods while the lower classes consumed black pudding made from animal blood, eggs, and hens.

During the early periods of the Roman empire, food remained simple with emphasis on vegetables and breads. Salt was used extensively. Due to the lack of utensils for food consumption, the bread was used as a 'mop' or a spoon (McIntosh 1995, p. 49). As the Roman empire expanded into Northern Africa, the Mediterranean, and Central Europe new foods were introduced. Grapes were introduced to Central Europe. As a result, an abundance of wine was available to meet the increasing demands of the fast-growing upper classes. The lower classes meanwhile remained true to their simple meals. To further distinguish themselves from the peasantry, the upper classes devised new food habits such as catered meals for larger gatherings. A typical catered group consisted of nine members. This is the first indication of food being catered for an event. In the process to accommodate the emerging demand for food service, new techniques evolved to prepare food in large quantities and of high quality. This tradition of inventing food preparation practices to meet the needs of the upper classes (royalty) continued to the later periods by the Central European empires of

France, Germany, Spain and Italy. This was the beginning of culinary practices as an art form.

To accommodate the large quantity of cooking needed for the upper class banquets, men were recruited for the kitchens and held as bonded laborers. This is the first indication of men entering the culinary profession. Men were specially recruited to make breads from scratch and they were called "magieros" (Anderson 1976, p. 10). These men were treated with respect as artists. The head magiero was often publicly acclaimed at the end of the dinner by the guests. Thus began the tradition of honoring chefs at the end of formal dinners. After attaining a certain status, magieros were released from bondage. Therefore, the culinary profession began as a way out of bondage. This was the beginning of the culinary profession and one may state that magieros were the forefathers of the current chefs.

During Greek rule the practice of three meals per day also slowly evolved. The first meal was called "ariston" (bread dipped in wine). It was eaten shortly after sunrise. The second meal was known as "diepnon" (simple meal). It was eaten sharply at noon or little after. The third meal was called "cena" or "derpon" (two courses with meat followed by a dessert). It was eaten at sunset (Anderson 1976, p. 10-11).

Food habits related to food consumption of the Greeks remained very close to the Central Asian cultures, consuming food while sitting on floor mats and reclining on cushions. Food was consumed with the right hand and baskets (or bowls) were held in the left hand. A spoon-like utensil was also used where appropriate. These customs remained an integral part of Western cultures until the times of the Roman empires.

Several new food processing technologies were also introduced during this period. One was a commercial donkey-mill to make wheat flour and the other was a large commercial oven to make breads. According to Tannahill (1988, p. 78), Romans consumed various types of gourmet breads. The food habits of Romans evolved along class lines. Rome's contribution to the food habits of Western cultures included grandiose dining events that were catered. Large banquets of Romans became a characteristic feature of later Western royalties. The word banquet was derived from an ancient word "banc" meaning "wooden bench" (Anderson 1976, p. 18). As mentioned earlier, during the Greek rule food was consumed while leaning on cushions laid on floor. But to accommodate the banquets, dining tables were added to the earlier dining formalities of cushions on the floor. This tradition of grandiose banquets still continues in Western countries in all public and private celebrations.

Romans also used food preparation methods to reflect their feelings towards their guests. If the guest was more important food was prepared differently than if the guest was less important (Toklas 1967, p. 201, referred by Tannahill 1988, p. 80). In addition, Romans also introduced the concept of cook book to the world. The Roman empire was particularly interested in learning about and promoting agriculture. They showed keen interest in taking ideas in agriculture from all corners of their empires and propagating them to other parts. During this period, numerous inventions in foods and food preparations were developed.

The newly acquired food habits of the Romans included a taste for Eastern spices such as peppers, cloves, and cinnamon. As the Romans' preference for these spices increased it impacted the levels of trade between the Roman empire and the Arabs. Arabs brought spices from the East to distribute in the Roman empire. The need to satisfy the Roman food habits increased the contact between the West and East (through Arabs). This resulted in a greater cultural exchange and fusion between the Roman empire and the East. This is the earliest indication of food habits being the source of the cultural exchange process. Arab traders not only traded food but other items such as art, cotton, and information also. Arab traders also played a very important role in exchanging knowledge between the East and West. This is another indication of the effect of food habits on cultural heritage that resulted in cultural exchanges leading to knowledge exchanges.

By the time of the Greek and Roman empires, the family structure in Europe was well established. Men played the dominant role while women attended to the housekeeping. In addition to the duties of earlier women, the women of the Greek and Roman empires were also expected to hire and manage the servants (McKay, Hill and Buckler 1987, pp. 90-91). This new role of home management for women was the contribution of this era. The family structure became more complex with specific norms and traditions for the upper classes and different rules for the lower classes. With the addition of a new class, the servant class, food habits were further refined. There were now different foods for the upper classes, lower class families, and the servants.

Another major contribution of the Roman empire to the food habits of the Western cultures was the introduction of commercial food service places. To meet the food needs of traders and travelers, commercial food-service establishments were introduced. These establishments were primarily three kinds: "Taberna Meritoria," taverns of merit, for the upper classes; "Caupona," simple inns for lower classes; and "Cabarets," usually located in the basements or caves for gambling and entertainment (Anderson 1976, p. 19).

Romans also introduced several new utensils for serving food. Until this period, food had been consumed with the hands, using a piece of bread as a spoon or "mop." With the addition of banquets and catered group dinners in upperclass abodes, the food serving technology slowly evolved. New serving utensils using metals such as iron, bronze and silver became commonplace. Silver salt containers were a common attraction at the banquet tables and the "seat of the salt" indicated the position of the most important person at the table.

FOOD HABITS OF MEDIEVAL EUROPE

The Medieval period played an important role in shaping the food habits of contemporary Western societies. After the fall of the Greek and Roman empires, Western civilization became leaderless. Past empires were broken into smaller kingdoms, thus allowing development of new ideas and practices in family structures and food habits. With the absence of a dominant political force and unifying authority, new and unique customs and traditions developed all over Western Europe. Until this period the food habits and family structure were molded around the example of a dominant rule. With newly acquired freedom, the Germans, French, Spaniards, and Italians developed food habits and family structures independent of each other. This was the beginning of regionalization of Western cuisine as we know it today.

The culture and lifestyles of Medieval Europe was largely influenced by Central European kingdoms. This period can be divided into three segments: Early Medieval Times; The Era of Crusaders; late Medieval Times. In spite of their chronological differences, they all have one thing in common, the famines (Tannahill 1988, p. 50). Part of the reason for famines was the lack of innovations in food production (agricultural) methods. The soils were depleted of nutrients and existing irrigation techniques did not meet the changing needs of the society. Thus, demand for food outpaced production and importation of food became almost impossible due to lack of royal support. This resulted in a long plateau in the development of Western food habits. During these bleak years people relied on the food habits of earlier times, making breads from grass and seeds (Germans) and from bark and straw (Swiss). Obviously changes in the levels of food supplies impacted the food habits. This phenomenon of continuous adjustment of human food habits to meet the levels of available food sources is noted in other cultures too. The family structure had to be redefined to adapt to the new food habits.

Common foods of this time were bread, ale and salt pork. "Except for cabbage, leeks and onions, vegetables were scarce or absent from the diet during this period" (McIntosh 1995, p. 51). The supply of meats was limited at best. Therefore, spices were used more to camouflage the tainted meat. Similar practices were already in existence in the Eastern cultures, the home of spices. This was the beginning of new uses of spices in the Western cultures. In other words, Western cultures, in the earlier times, used spices more as food preservatives and extenders than as food flavorings or seasonings. This tradition has continued until modern times. Some of the food habits that were prevalent during this period were salting, drying, smoking, cooking in large iron kettles, and using tables for food consumption even by the lower classes.

During this period, culinarians developed the idea of preserving food preparation techniques in a written form. The cooking techniques and recipes were passed on from one generation to another in written form thus giving birth to the cookbooks of recent times.

At the same time, Northern Europeans developed the practice of preserving fish by smoking. This was helpful in ensuring a continuous supply of food through the long winters of Northern Europe. The use of fresh fish however became problematic for its salty taste. To overcome this limitation, cooks started placing bland foods such as carbohydrates (rice and potatoes), boiled vegetables, bread crumbs, whole grains, and various pastes of peas and beans, along with meats on the same plate. This practice of a multi-item plate at dinner was an innovation in Western food habits. Prior to that food was served one item at a time. This period also gave birth to desserts and snacks.

Prior to the Medieval period, Western societies consisted of primarily two classes of citizens: the higher classes, and the lower classes. During Medieval times a new class emerged which was slightly higher than the common peasantry but much lower than the royalty. Emergence of this class had its own influence on the food habits of the times. As mentioned earlier, higher classes enjoyed multi-course catered dinners during the Greek and Roman periods while the lower classes often consumed basic foods with a single course. The new class that emerged during Medieval times preferred to distinguish themselves from the lower classes but could not duplicate the grandiose banquets of the higher classes. To meet the need of the new class to differentiate itself from the others, new menus consisting of three courses were developed.

A typical menu in Paris in 1393 consisted of three primary courses. The first course was a meat item (beef, lamb, saltwater fish, eels) in some kind of sauce. The second course was a meat-based item or another meat (roast, freshwater fish, capon pastries, Blank mang). The third item was a light item with or without meat (frumenty, venison, lampreys) (Power 1928, quoted by Tannahill 1988, p. 185). Even though menus of the "new class" consisted of more than one course, the primary product remained either a meat or a meat-based product. A possible explanation for this practice could be lack of choice in vegetables, lack of skills in preparing the available vegetables, or the symbolism that meat was the choice of the wealthy. This tradition of serving multi-course dinners was later accepted as standard practice in commercial foodservice operations of later years. This tradition became the precursor of the modern day multi-course dinner.

Until this period, desserts were not served as a part of the meal. Sweets and desserts were considered as a post-meal snack to foster communication or aid in digestion. Sometimes nuts, cheese, wine, and dry whole spices to 'aid in digestion' were also served as post-meal snacks. The practice of wrapping dry spices in a dry leaf to 'aid in digestion' probably came from India where it was practiced for thousands of years, and even today (Parsa, 1994).

According to Tannahill (1988, p. 187), one of the major contributions of this period to the food habits of Western civilization was the use of knives and forks while consuming foods. But Anderson (1976) reports that knives and forks were also used by the Romans during their later periods. The art of using tools to carry food from the plate to the mouth was not accepted easily. To break the habit of thousands of years was probably not easy. It took almost three centuries before it became more acceptable to use a fork throughout the rest of the West. The use of knives to break food into pieces was well established by the time of the Roman Empire, and it was often done by the cooks for the guests. The use of spoons was later added to scoop up the gravies and soups. But the need to use forks to move food from the plate to the mouth was never perceived necessary. The use of forks became more acceptable, probably, with the introduction of salads and soft desserts during the post-Medieval and early modern periods.

To meet the changing needs of the upper classes and the middle classes, food preparation techniques had to be modified. A major innovation of that time was the addition of indoor chimneys so that food could be prepared indoors. The culinarians were able to make several animal shaped breads and desserts. In some instances live animals such as frogs and birds were used as a part of the display of culinary skills.

During Medieval times the family structure also experienced numerous evolutionary changes. With the emergence of the new middle class, the role of men and women changed. The role of a woman in the middle class was, probably, more complex than that of her contemporaries in the higher and lower classes. The management of household duties became more complex with the development of new food preparation methods, new food habits, and ever changing socio-political systems, the wars of Crusaders, decline in food importation, and changes in agricultural practices. The woman's role changed to include numerous additional responsibilities.

In sum, Medieval times contributed the most to the food habits of the contemporary Western societies. Some of the highlights of this period include the emergence of the middle class, introduction of new food preparation methods, introduction of cookbooks, the concept of recipe writing, catered banquets, the use of spices, the introduction of desserts, popularization of the use of cutlery at the dining tables, the separation of foods into three classes (higher, middle, lower), the development of banquet menus, the development and enhancement of bread making, popularization of salt, new food preservation techniques, and the introduction of multi-item food plates.

As the Pilgrims and new colonists settled in the American continent, they brought with them the family structure and food habits of Medieval Europe. The cold, cruel, and bitter winters of the American colonies forced the early colonists to adapt to the new conditions. Such an adaptation required blending of native crops and methods with the European technologies. This was the beginning of American food habits. The following section describes the changes that emerged in the American food habits.

AMERICAN FOOD HABITS

The early colonists defined roles for men, women and children in their family structure. The colonial men retained the role as food procurers. The colonial women and children prepared, served, stored, and disposed of the food and assisted in other food production related activities. In such an arrangement, large size families had an advantage in food production since more people could get involved in the production process. The larger the size of the family the greater the production of food. Abundance of food that was produced demanded new techniques of food preservation. The new preserved foods required changes and adaptations in food preparation methods as well as changes in the food consumption patterns. This practice of maintenance of larger family size to secure greater food resources is also observed in other civilizations. Preference for larger families still remains true in all agri-based societies. Therefore, the interdependent relationship between the family structure and food habits has its roots in the early development of human civilizations.

The above-mentioned interdependent relationship between the food habits and American families is also obvious in contemporary American society. As America became more industrialized, the role of men in the family continued to be limited to food procurement while the role of women included preparation, preservation, and distribution (serve) of the food, and the children had limited assisting roles. This arrangement was further reinforced, to an extent, by greater industrialization. After the World War II, Americans experienced a dramatic increase in personal disposable incomes. The new prosperity impacted American food habits. It placed more emphasis on food with cultural, socio-economic, and political symbolism. Thus, the beginning of the American hospitality industry as we now know it (Parsa and Khan 1992). Changes in the cultural values of American lifestyles and family structure have often been reflected in American food habits. So the old adage remains true, "tell me what you eat, I will tell you who you are." It is fairly evident that the American food habits are a product of the dynamic changes that occur in the socio-economic system, technology, cultural values, and the changes in family structure. The food habits are always changing and evolving reflecting the impact of underlying forces.

The food habits of America can be divided into two major periods: the colonial period (until late 19th century), and the modern period (from late 19th century to present). To maintain the chronological order, the Colonial period will be discussed first followed by the contemporary period.

The meals of colonial times were very simple for obvious reasons such as lack of resources, technology, and lack of familiarity with native foods, and due to the abundance of natural food sources. The early settlers were primarily ex-tradesmen, craftsmen, and sailors from the lower classes of Europe. They did not have adequate skills to cultivate crops or domesticate animals. Consequently, they had to learn the agricultural techniques and hunting tricks from the Native Americans.

The basic foods of the colonists consisted of pork, maize, fish, and beans. Women made breads in small ovens and stew in a large pot hung over the fire similar to the European methods. Wheat and rye were introduced later. Prior to cooking food inside the homes, colonists successfully attempted an outdoor fire to roast and smoke meats as done commonly by the natives. The cold winter and lack of food resources made it difficult for the early colonists. Meals of the wealthy (high socio-political status) consisted of fresh meat, bread and butter while lower classes used baked beans, salted meats, and corn breads (McIntosh 1995, p. 75). The trade and greed for gold fostered a faster transfer of technology from Europe to the new colonies allowing numerous advances in the food habits of colonists. The colonists were able to rely on European traders to bring tea, coffee, grains, and others in exchange for corn, tomatoes, sugar cane, etc., to take back to Europe.

The family structure in the colonies was primitive, but it quickly changed with the arrival of new craftsmen, skilled workers, farmers and the expansion of agriculture. Culturally speaking, the colonists remained true to their native cultures (English, Dutch, Ireland, Swiss, French, and German) and their religious beliefs through most of the first 200 years.

The food habits of the early colonists were influenced by the availability and affordability of foods. Pork and poultry were more popular than beef because it was less expensive to raise chicken and pigs. Southerners ate sweet potatoes while the northern colonists preferred white Irish potatoes (Tannahill 1988, p. 3). An inadequate supply of dairy cattle prevented the colonists from consuming sufficient quantities of milk and milk products.

By the end of the nineteenth century, American foods developed into four major types: the urban foods; rural foods; southern foods; and soul foods. Urban foods were high in baked goods, breads, meats, and low in dairy products and fresh vegetables. Rural foods were primarily composed of seasonal choices. Southern foods were made up of local crops, fruits and vegetables. During later colonial times, slaves on the farms concocted their own recipes using most of the leftovers and molasses. These experiments led to the development of 'soul foods.'

By the second half of the colonial period, several urban centers were developed with the addition of commercial foodservice establishments. To accommodate the boarding needs of the travelers and the traders, as in Europe and other parts of the world, taverns (lodging, entertainment, and food) and inns (lodging and food only) were permitted to operate in the colonies. One of these inns was owned by Samuel Cole in Boston in 1734. But he did not allow guests to stay overnight, thus, the beginning of the commercial foodservice industry in America. Delmonico's restaurant in New York City, owned by John Delmonico, a Swiss captain, opened in 1827 and was considered as the first fine dining restaurant in the USA.

The influence of French culture on American formal dining food habits is evident since the first four American Presidents hired their chefs from France to serve in the White House. But this passion for French cuisine could not be shared by the average American, consequently mainstream American cuisine remained American. Of all the practices, one European practice that remained firmly with the American food culture was the dislike for vegetables, vegetarian dishes, and fresh milk.

American food habits changed dramatically with the rapid industrialization during the nineteenth and early twentieth centuries. Three innovations that impacted American food habits the most were the invention of pressure cooker in 1874, the invention of frozen foods later by Dr. Birdseye in 1928, and the introduction of canned meats. In contrast to their counterparts in Europe, Americans enjoyed the abundance of beef though pork (ham and bacon) was still popular.

The food habits of Americans were also influenced by government regulations such as the US Department of Agriculture policies on meat inspections, the Food and Drug Administration's campaign for nutrition education, and government subsidies for selected food production systems.

As new immigrants from Italy, Poland, Russia, Eastern Europe and Asia came to the shores of America, they quickly flocked to urban centers in search of employment. This infusion of new cultures impacted American food habits. Italian foods were easily accepted as healthful alternatives. A major innovation in American food habits was the introduction of breakfast cereals by William R. Kellogg and Charles W. Post. This phenomenon is truly American and was developed out of concern for better health.

In European cultures, the trend in food habits had always been towards sophistication in food preparation and consumption. In contrast to the European cultures, developments in early American food habits have been more towards simplification of meal preparation methods rather than sophistication and expansion. The European food habits of the 18th and 19th centuries were driven by the sophistication in culinary arts advanced by the chefs. In contrast, American food habits of the 18th and 19th century were driven by simplicity in preparation and efficiency in mass production. This was the reflection of the political system of the land. In early Europe, the political systems were feudalistic and ruled by the royal families. Here conspicuous consumption was a norm and expected. The democratic political system of America did not encourage indulgence in excessive food consumption by their national leaders since it symbolized concentration of power.

The Great Depression of the 1920s and World War II had the same effect on American food habits as did the famines in Europe. During this period Americans learned to accept chicken as a viable alternative to beef. In addition, Americans also learned to use pre-portioned food products such jams, sugar, ketchup, etc., in place of bulk products. Later postwar prosperity and the emergence of a middle-class population led the way in several innovations in American food habits (Parsa and Khan 1992).

By the middle of the twentieth century single entree (meat) meals, accompanied by a starch and some vegetables, followed by a dessert, became the standard American meal. For all formal occasions, beef was the preferred choice of entree, and poultry was considered not good enough for special occasions. This trend changed by the mid-1980s when the demand for beef declined while the demand for poultry rose. Similarly, the demand for seafood increased dramatically. The emerging trend in American food habits was the demand for vegetarian meals.

As American food preferences changed during the 20th century, the meal patterns also changed. By the mid-1980s, many Americans were eating only two meals a day, often skipping either breakfast or lunch. These changes were mostly due to lack of nutrition education of American families. The American family structure also changed dramatically during the second half of the 20th century. Post war prosperity resulted in more disposable income for American families. Consequently, more American families went out to eat more often than before because now they could afford to. This food habit was aided by the popularity of motor vehicles and the interstate highway system.

Prior to the 1950s, dining in America outside of home required a special occasion. By the mid-1950s, many commoners in America were able and willing to dine out more as a part of their daily activities than to celebrate a special occasion. By the late 1980s, dining out had become a part of normal daily activities and was almost a requirement. This was primarily due to the increasing number of families becoming dual income families. The dual income families had less time for food preparation and had more disposable incomes resulting in more eating out. To meet the increasing demand for convenience by the American consumers hospitality firms introduced drive-thru restaurants. Food purchased at drive-thru restaurants was often wrapped with wax paper without requiring any knives or forks to consume food. Consumption of food purchased at these drive-thru restaurants required adaptation in food habits.

Through most of the first half of the 20th century, the American diet remained predominantly European. After World War II, many Americans were willing and able to try new foods from other parts of the world such as Eastern Europe, Asia, and Latin America. By the mid-1980s, numerous ethnic restaurants (ethnic restaurant chains) mushroomed. This influenced Americans' daily food habits. The daily food consumption pattern of average Americans evolved into a truly American tradition. It consisted of foods from various parts of the world. They reflected cultural (ethnic) diversity of the American society. During the golden age of the Roman empire, a similar phenomenon of feasting on world foods was observed but it was limited to the upper classes and for formal dinners. In contrast, by the 1990s, the American daily food consumption patterns of commoners included foods from various parts of the world, but the formal meals remained predominantly Euro-American. That means, in America, food offerings at formal dining places remained Eurocentric while the menus of informal dining places, that were meant for the commoners, became international offerings of various ethnic foods from different parts of the world. Over a period of time, certain ethnic foods may earn respectability to be included in the formal menus.

As the American cultural umbrella expands and experiences infusion of new ideas and cultural values from other parts of the world, food habits continue to emerge and become distinctly American. The hospitality industry must adapt its strategies to meet the emerging needs of American society. As America prepares for the 21st century it must understand the nature of emerging cultural changes and their impact on the American food habits.

DISCUSSION

Analysis of the trends in the cultural heritage of American food habits reveal that the dynamics of food habits of an individual are very complex. Food habits are not simple food consumption habits but they are symbols of an individual's perception of oneself. Food habits also may symbolize the political, socio-economic, religious, or cultural views of an individual. They are very personal and people are emotionally attached to their food habits. Therefore, any desired permanent changes in one's food habits often require monumental effort. To make a permanent change in food habits, the change has to come from "within." To achieve this goal, an individual may have to sacrifice some personal identity. This may lead to some changes in personal food habits that symbolize cultural, emotional, socio-economic, political, and sentimental opinions. This fear of loss of personal identity is the crux of the reluctance to change food habits by many.

It is commonly believed that food habits are easily acquired and people learn to adapt to new ways with little effort. It can be illustrated by the fact that meals served at most non-commercial institutions such as schools, hospitals, and industrial sites tends to be standardized without any regard for cultural, ethnic, religious, or regional differences of the consumers. Many governments (rulers) of the past and present have tried to change the food habits of their citizens to meet the adopted official policies and achieve political objectives. Even though the adopted policies of many may be rational, the practice of food habits of individuals are not. For many people, adherence to the established and accepted food habits is more an emotional, sentimental, and cultural choice than a rational one. This explains why numerous nutritional education programs, patient care programs related to diets, and community educational programs often fail to achieve the desired objectives.

The author supports the fact that food habits are more permanent than was thought earlier. The simple task of using a fork for food consumption during dinner was resisted for three hundred years. It took Romans about four hundred years to adapt and standardize the use of table and benches for formal dinners instead of cushions. Similarly, European cultures have resisted the consumption of vegetables for over two thousand years. Still many Americans are reluctant to accept poultry as a menu choice for formal dinners. Similarly, after hundreds of years of exposure to European cultures, Asian cultures still insist on using fingers to transfer food from a plate/bowl to the mouth. This reluctance to change is not limited to food consuming habits. It is also noted in food production, preparation, preservation, and selection processes.

Therefore, a study of food habits provides researchers an opportunity to study factors that are preserved and passed on from one generation to another in a cultural group. Food habits are better indicators of human ancestry than many other cultural variables such as language, arts, music, clothing, and shelter. As noted by many sociologists, when immigrants come to America they often adapt quickly to American values and way of life in terms of shelter, education, clothing, music, art, and lifestyle. They may even adopt one of the religions of America. Adoption of a religious faith is often considered to be the most difficult choice. In spite of all these adaptations, they still retain food habits of their native lands. To survive in the new land, they may make some adaptations to the original food habits but the core values remain intact. Because of this resiliency in food habits, many European subcultures were able to preserve and adapt their regional specialties and cultural differences to America and blend with the culture of the new lands.

In sum, many American food habits are a collage of various cultural subgroups with distinct flavors representing each group. As the cultural fabric of America expands, modifies, and evolves, at least in food habits, contributions of each ethnic group and their distinct identity will be well preserved and passed on to the next generations. This can be supported by the fact that over hundreds of years after the Roman and Greek empires, we still retain their way of consuming foods and conduct formal banquets. Even after hundreds of years of colonization, many former colonies of Britain and France in Asia and Africa retained their native food habits intact. These former colonies adapted European cultures, education, political and economic systems, social norms and even religious faiths. But they kept their food habits as distinctly Asian and African as possible.

Developing countries were quick to adopt practices and technology of the Western nations as long they did not interfere with their basic food habits. This can be substantiated by the fact that McDonald's was not allowed to operate in India, unless they agreed to sell only non-beef menu items, yet India was exposed to Western food habits over 200 years during the British rule. This exemplifies the fact that many societies consider food habits as sacred rituals that are passed on from one generation to another.

Changes in American food habits are of significant importance to the hospitality industry. As the hospitality industry prepares for the 21st century, it must consider the changing nature of American food habits. As American food habits become distinctly American, the current practices in food preparation, preservation, and service in the hospitality industry need to be reviewed for possible adaptations and modifications. For example, catering operations of many hospitality firms need to be reassessed in light of changing American food habits. The menu selections of fine dining restaurants and formal dining places need to be expanded to accommodate the increasing demand for vegetarian foods. Similarly, the menu offerings of institutional foodservices in America have to be modified to reflect the ethnic, regional, cultural, and religious diversity of the American society. The hotel industry may also have to evaluate its food and beverage operations to accommodate the needs and demands of international travelers as well as the domestic travelers.

Finally, this study has described the nature of food habits and traced the lineage of American food habits. The literature cited and the examples presented provide some insights into the nature and roots of American food habits. This study further described the intricate relationships that were observed between food habits and socio-political, economic and technological systems, and cultural and religious changes. The actual direction and magnitude of the relationship between food habits and other factors could not be established in this study. Further studies involving empirical data are necessary to establish such a relationship.

CONCLUSION

In this study the author has profiled the cultural heritage of American food habits. In spite of apparent differences, American culture remains predominantly European in its content and basic practices. It remained predominantly European until the first half of the 20th century. During the second half of the 20th century, the cultural practices, norms, and traditions of America have slowly become uniquely American and distinctly different from its mother culture, Europe. This process of Americanization of the old colonial cultural practices had a significant impact on the food habits of society. This study indicated that the relationship between cultural practices and food habits is bidirectional. In some instances food habits affected the culture as in case of the Roman and Greek empires. Other times, changes in cultures impacted the food habits as in the case of contemporary American food habits.

The food habits, as mentioned earlier, are not limited to just the food consumption habits of the society but the food procurement, production, preparation, preservation and consumption of food products. Nature of the food habits in a society is the byproduct of numerous factors such as its culture, sub-cultural groups, economy, religion, political system, traditions, customs, and the environment (ecology). This study has demonstrated that in addition to the above-mentioned factors the "family structure" of the society plays a very important role in the evolution of food habits. As the nature of family structure changes, the food habits also change accordingly. In other words, families continue to adapt new food habits to meet their changing structure. For example, large size families have different food habits compared to the smaller ones. This is clearly demonstrated in the changing nature of American food habits from the colonial times with larger families to the 20th century with the relatively smaller families. This phenomenon could be observed also in the changing food habits of developing nations with a trend towards smaller families is prevailing. Finally the food habits are often passed on from one generation to another as a part of family traditions and/or rituals, and food habits are one of the intangible things that bind family units together.

The present paper also includes analysis of changes in the family structure, and their impact on food habits in the Western civilization during the various times. Evolution of food habits and their effect on family are also included. This study has showed that, contrary to the earlier beliefs, food habits of individuals could be more permanent and stable than their cultural, religious, educational, and ethnic preferences. According to this study, sub-cultural groups are equally capable of influencing the food habits of the mainstream culture as it happened in the 20th century America.

The hospitality industry thrives by providing the foods that people need and demand away from home. As American food habits change the hospitality industry has to change to provide the products its customers need and demand. For example, during the 19th and early 20th centuries the American hospitality industry depended heavily on beef as the primary food source, and dinner as the main meal away from home. But during the late 20th century, the American families became more mobile and nutrition-conscious, and the American restaurants started serving foods at all three traditional meal times, breakfast, lunch and dinner, and offered foods that are more nutritionally balanced and considered healthful. To survive in the 21st century, the hospitality industry must continue to analyze the emerging trends in family structure and the consequential changes in the American food habits, and must adapt its product offerings appropriately. Understanding of the relationship between the American family structure and the changing food habits is essential for long-term survival of the hospitality industry.

AUTHOR NOTE

H. G. Parsa holds a PhD in Hospitality Management from Virginia Polytechnic Institute and State University, MS in Food Science from University of Arkansas, Fayetteville; MS in Biology and BS in Chemistry from India.

He is a member of several professional organizations in the area of marketing, franchising, and hospitality management. His research interests include menu trends in American restaurants, franchising, foodservice marketing, and strategic management. He has published in academic journals such as Cornell Quarterly; Hospitality Research Journal; Journal of Nutrition in Recipe and Menu Development, and the Journal of College & University Foodservice. He has presented papers at conferences such as American Marketing Association; Society of Franchising; Council on Hotel, Restaurant; Institutional Education; Franchising Association of Australia-New Zealand. He has over 13 years of professional experiences in food service industry managing institutional as well as commercial operations.

REFERENCES

Anderson, W. H. (1976), The Modern Foodservice Industry: An Introductory Guide, Dubuque, Iowa: Wm. C. Brown Company.

Beals, R. L. and H. Hoijer (1971), An Introduction to Anthropology (4th ed.) New York, NY: Macmillan Company.

Chaudhry, K. N. (1978), The Trading World of Asia and the English East-India Company 1660-1760.

Dumas, M. (1969), (ed) *Histoire Generale des Techniques* 3 t, Paris. 1962-1969.

Gordon, K. E. (1987), Evolutionary Perspectives in Human Diet. in F. E. Johnston (ed), *Nutritional Anthropology, (3-39,)* New York, NY: Alan R. Liss.

Haviland, Wm. A. (1993), Cultural Anthropology, New York, NY: Harcourt Brace College Publishers.

Hertzler, A. A., N. Wenkam, and B. Standal (1982), Classifying Cultural Food Habits and Meanings, *Journal of American Dietetics Association,* V 80, p. 421-425.

Jaffari, S. and Way A. (1992), Cultural Tourism and Regional Development, *Annals of Tourism Research* (3).

Kilara, K. and K. K. Iya (1992), Food and Dietary Habits of Hindus, *Food Technology*, 46(10), 94-104.

Kittler, P. G. and K. Sucher (1989), Food and Culture in America: A Nutrition Handbook, New York, NY: Van Nostrand Reinhold.

McIntosh E. N. (1995), American Food Habits in Historical Perspective, Westport, CT: Praeger.

McKay, J. P., B. D. Hill and J. Buckler (1986), A History of Western Society, Dallas, TX: Houghton Miffin Company.

Parsa, H. G. and M. A. Khan (1992), Menu Trends In Quick Service Restaurant Industry During the Various Stages of Industry Life Cycle (1919-1988), *Hospitality Research Journal*, V15(1) p. 93-107.

Parsa, H. G. (1994) personal communication while travelling in India.

Power, E. (1928), (ed. & trs) *Managier De Paris*, (c. 1939) translated as "The Goodman of Paris."

Tannahill, R. (1988), Food in History, New York, NY: Crown Trade Paperbacks.

Toklas, A. B. (1954), The Alice B. Toklas Cook Book, p. 207.

West, J. J. and M. D. Olsen (1990), Grand Strategies: Making Your Restaurant A Winner, *The Cornell Hotel and Restaurant Administrative Quarterly*, V31(2).

Wenkman, N. S. (1969), Cultural Determinants of Nutritional Behavior, Nutrition Program News, July/August.

Black-American Entrepreneurship: The Case of the Foodservice Industry

Francis A. Kwansa

SUMMARY. This paper discusses Black-American entrepreneurship in the U.S.: its beginnings, the context for Black enterprise, and the philosophy of Black-American business. Then it focuses on the food-service industry and the participation that Black-American entrepreneurs have had in it. The paper highlights the role that Black food-service entrepreneurs have played in employment and wealth creation in the Black community. It concludes with a series of issues that are suggested to form the basis for a research agenda in Black entrepreneurship in the foodservice industry. *[Article copies available for a fee from The Haworth Document Delivery Service: 1-800-342-9678. E-mail address: getinfo@haworthpressinc.com]*

KEYWORDS. Entrepreneurship, Black-American, Foodservice industry

INTRODUCTION

Business enterprise has been considered the fundamental source of economic stability for many ethnic groups in the U.S. Particularly for

Francis A. Kwansa is Associate Professor in the Hotel, Restaurant and Institutional Management Department at the University of Delaware. He teaches courses in Financial Management and Managerial Accounting.

[Haworth co-indexing entry note]: "Black-American Entrepreneurship: The Case of the Foodservice Industry." Kwansa, Francis A. Co-published simultaneously in *Marriage & Family Review* (The Haworth Press, Inc.) Vol. 28, No. 1/2, 1998, pp. 49-68; and: *The Role of the Hospitality Industry in the Lives of Individuals and Families* (ed: Pamela R. Cummings, Francis A. Kwansa, and Marvin B. Sussman) The Haworth Press, Inc., 1998, pp. 49-68. Single or multiple copies of this article are available for a fee from The Haworth Document Delivery Service [1-800-342-9678, 9:00 a.m. - 5:00 p.m. (EST). E-mail address: getinfo@haworthpressinc.com].

Black-Americans, Henderson (1993) believes that business ownership is an important source of financial wealth, community capital formation, self-esteem for the owners and employees, skills and capacity-building, and even political power. Thus some believe that success and growth in entrepreneurial activity within the Black-American community will lead to economic and political empowerment. Yet data from the Census Bureau's Survey of Minority-Owned Business Enterprises cited by Henderson showed that, although by 1987 the number of Black-owned businesses had increased by 37.3% compared to 26.2% by all U.S. firms, only 3.1% of all U.S. businesses were owned by Blacks. Such representation is at variance with Black-American demographic representation in the U.S. Based on census data Henderson suggested that albeit growing in number, Black-owned businesses essentially remained small and had little influence in the overall American business community.

A closer look at the industry distribution of Black-owned businesses from the census data showed that by 1987 almost 50% of these businesses were in the services sector (compared to less than 20% of all small businesses) followed by 10% in the retail sector. This suggests that the services and retail sectors, which include the hospitality industry, have been a haven of success for Black-American enterprise. The purpose of this paper is to describe Black entrepreneurship in the foodservice industry. It will include a historical overview of entrepreneurship in the Black-American community, the evolution of Black business in the foodservice industry, and suggest questions for a research agenda in Black entrepreneurship in the hospitality industry. The paper will further highlight the role that the foodservice industry has played in the past and will continue to play in the future in the Black-American community with respect to employment development, capital formation and growth.

Beginnings of Black-American Entrepreneurship

Africans, brought to America via the slave trade, possessed some business experience from trading among themselves and through prior contacts in commercial activity with Europeans. Such trading involved agricultural products, jewelry/ornaments, fabrics, liquor and others. This experience and know-how served as the basis for their engagement in commercial activity during the years of slavery in the 19th century.

According to Joseph Pierce (1947) there were 2 types of Black entrepreneurs prior to 1865: one group was the Free Negroes who established businesses through their own accumulated capital and the other type was those slaves who became business people through their own industry and initiative and with their slave masters' blessings and support. For both of these types of entrepreneurs, however, acquiring initial business knowledge and techniques was difficult because they were denied opportunities to apprenticeship with the more successful White businessmen. Additionally, they had little opportunity for formal business training. In spite of such difficulties and the rigid enforcement of racial separation, especially in the south, some of the Black-owned businesses managed to survive. Their businesses had greater chances of survival in cities that had large concentrations of Blacks, such as Charleston, Savannah, New Orleans and Richmond.

They were mostly successful in the service-oriented businesses such as mechanics, restaurateurs, hoteliers, barbers and artisans. By contrast, in the north, Black entrepreneurs found success in lumber, pickle making, sail manufacturing, coal, jewelry, bed manufacturing and catering. During this period, most of these businesses remained very small due to lack of capital, credit, and a consumer market that was characterized by poverty and little purchasing power (Pierce, 1947). Yet, the foodservice catering business was the one business in which Black entrepreneurs, men and women, found considerable success and made fortunes.

After 1865 a few significant changes began in the Black business community, according to Pierce, although the number of Black entrepreneurs did not increase significantly. One such change was the creation of fraternal orders which sold insurance policies to Blacks whose policies had been canceled by White insurance agents. This marked the beginning of capital formation in the Black business community. As the need for more capital arose as a result of businesses seeking expansion, Blacks entered the banking industry. The first banks organized and operated by Blacks were the Savings Bank of the Grand Fountain United Order of True Reformers in Richmond, Virginia and the Capital Savings Bank in Washington, DC in 1888. Following the establishment of banks was the establishment of credit unions, industrial loan associations, and building and loan societies.

Although only a few of these new endeavors in the financial arena between 1864 and 1900 flourished and were profitable, a very critical purpose had been achieved. That is, through the failures of the banks and credit institutions, Blacks had gained an incredible level of confidence, courage, experience and training that would prepare them for their entry into other businesses.

Context for Black Business Enterprise

Black-owned businesses were typically confined to the black neighborhoods of urban cities due to segregation. As a result they were constrained by some realities. One was that they had to depend solely on Blacks in the community for business and could not count on White patronage. The other was that they faced competition from White-owned businesses that would locate and often did locate in the Black neighborhoods since Whites were not prohibited from locating there.

With respect to the size of the market available to Black business owners, it was as large as the population of Blacks that lived in the large cities. The market of the rural areas, in the south especially, was virtually non-existent because Blacks shopped from the stores or commissaries owned by White landlords. In addition to this, the rural Black population was declining as Blacks began moving to the urban areas for jobs in the industrial sector. Jobs in the industrial sector for which Blacks were qualified tended to be mostly unskilled or semi-skilled and paid relatively low wages. Therefore, the overall market that was available to Black business owners was severely limited. Furthermore, there were also political factors that helped shape the context in which Black enterprises operated in the early 20th century. For example, municipal authorities in the south prohibited Blacks from owning and operating saloons and beer bars in the Black communities. Other businesses in which Blacks would directly compete against White businessmen in the Black communities were similarly off limits to Blacks.

Some of the consequences of these unique features of the Black businesses' operating environment included reliance on race solidarity as a basis for attracting customers. The downside to this practice was the expectation by Black owners that their commercial interaction with businessmen of their color would be based on friendship and race solidarity rather than on strict business principles and practices. Needless to say, the profitability and efficiency of the Black-owned businesses suffered as a result. Also the nature of employment and wage rates of the majority of working class Blacks meant a customer market with largely low purchasing power. This continually posed a serious threat to the expansion, even survival, of Black enterprises. Myrdal (1944) estimated that Blacks' share of the GNP was no more than 4%. To compound the problems of the Black-owned businesses, the relatively small Black consumer market had to be shared with White-owned businesses. Indeed Myrdal estimated further that only about 10% of the total expenditures of Blacks went to Black-owned businesses and the rest was captured by their White counterparts during the 1940s.

Philosophy of Black-American Business

Within the Black community entrepreneurship was always looked upon as prestigious. Thus one way for Blacks to escape the societal confines of the poor working class and to achieve social status was to be in business. Pierce (1947) found from a survey of Black entrepreneurs that 65.2% entered business for economic reasons, 15.5% for their special interest and ability, 10.1% due to family influence, and 9.2% to meet a racial need. By contrast, an earlier study of White graduates from the Wharton School showed that only 4% entered business for economic reasons while 24% were motivated by family traditions. Thus, for the majority of Blacks, the desire to elevate the family's socioeconomic status was of paramount importance in the post-emancipation years, and entrepreneurship was perceived as the means to achieve that goal. Another reason for the interest in business enterprise was that Black leaders and business owners considered success in business as one critical way of solving the race problem in America and insuring that Blacks would enjoy the full rights and privileges of citizenship. Blayton (1941) stated that for Blacks to gain the respect of other Americans, they would have to become efficient conductors of commercial and industrial enterprises.

The lack of wealth and access to capital in Black families also contributed to an attitude in the early entrepreneurs that later would become detrimental to their businesses. Most of the early businesses were driven to accumulate capital in order to pursue larger and better enterprises, while neglecting such fundamental aspects of enterprise as planning, cost controls, overhead management, and business location. The result of this pre-occupation with growth and neglect of business fundamentals was a significant number of business failures.

Another philosophical dilemma that had an impact on Black entrepreneurs in this era was whether to integrate their businesses into the general American economy or remain separate and self-sufficient within a Black economy. Although the practice of segregation placed limitations on Black enterprises, it also ensured a captive and predictable market for the Black entrepreneur. Thus many Black businesses capitalized and built their businesses on race pride and loyalty. Yet the dilemma remained, should they reject segregation because it limited their access to the larger market, or embrace segregation because it guaranteed a Black consumer market? Later, there emerged a trend toward bi-racial partnerships which helped many Black businesses survive and gain better access to credit and capital and to the larger market.

In summary, entrepreneurship has had a long history in the Black community and it has served both economic and social purposes. The social circumstances before and after emancipation, to a large extent, defined the context within which Black enterprises operated. Limited markets, very low purchasing power of Black consumers, political encumbrances, little or no access to capital, and reliance on racial solidarity were all character-istics of the business environment in which Black entrepreneurs operated.

THE FOODSERVICE INDUSTRY

Historical Evidence of Black Entrepreneurship in the Foodservice Industry

Historical accounts show that large cities in the eastern and southern U.S. had a larger concentration of Black businesses. The city of Philadel-phia provided one such example of how Black families entered and became successful in the foodservice industry. In an address to the Ameri-can Historical Society in 1913, Henry Minton, MD, chronicled the early history of Blacks in business in Philadelphia. He was motivated by the fact that whereas numerous books had been written about slavery and the suffering of Blacks, there was a lack of writing in those days about Black contributions in the commercial world. He cited a publication called, "A Register of Trades of Colored People in the City of Philadelphia Districts" which represented the first Black-American directory of businesses. In it were listed 57 occupations including bakers, blacksmiths, boot and shoe-makers, carpenters, chairbottomers, dressmakers, tailors, sailmakers, and caterers.

The catering business brought the most prestige and fame to Black entrepreneurs in Philadelphia because no other city in the U.S. was more famous for its efficient and successful caterers. Pioneer Peter Augustine, who came from the West Indies and began his catering business in 1816, was famous in Paris and other world cities where he exported terrapin. Other famous families in this line of business included the Dorsey and Jones families. Robert Bogle, however, is credited with being the origina-tor of the catering business in Philadelphia. While working as a waiter in the early 1800s he conceived of the idea that instead of those who desired to entertain being inconvenienced by having to temporarily enlarge the retinue of their kitchens to prepare a formal dinner, he would contract to prepare and serve the entire meal with his own help. Minton (1913) writes,

> He was a versatile man, and a natural executive as is shown by the fact that he was also a conductor of funerals, often within one twenty-four hours serving a dinner and directing a prominent funeral, at one using all the suavity and pleasantness of manner desirable, and at the other evincing a solemness and dignity that was most impressive. (Minton, 1913, p. 12)

According to Minton, Nicholas Briddle, who was then President of the Bank of the United States and a leader in the financial community of Philadelphia, wrote an "Ode to Bogle" in 1829 to immortalize Robert Bogle.

Similarly, Drake and Cayton (1945) wrote about the early years of Black entrepreneurship in the city of Chicago. In the early part of the 1800s, according to Drake and Cayton, Blacks were engaged in service businesses such as catering, wigmaking, hairdressing, barbering and livery. By 1885 the number of Blacks engaged in businesses had multiplied such that 200 businesses in 27 different fields were listed in the first "Colored Men's Professional and Business Directory of Chicago" published in that year. The most popular of these 27 fields of business was barbering, and restaurants competed with "sample rooms" (combination of liquor stores and saloons) as the second most popular. The reason for their popularity was that these businesses required little capital and little experience. Another reason provided by Kinzer and Sagarin (1971) was that there were certain skills and crafts that were taught to slaves so that slavemasters would not have to perform these tasks or pay White labor for them. These include blacksmithing, tailoring, barbering, shoemaking, carpentry, and cooking. The philosophy in those times was that it was in the interest of slaveowners, before emancipation, to use slave labor wherever it was possible in handicraft and manufacture (Rose, 1948). Consequently, the knowledge of these skills was concentrated almost exclusively in the hands of Blacks, free and slave (Kuzer and Sagarin, p. 52).

The foodservice industry continued to be popular in the post-emancipation era through the 1940s. Data presented by Pierce (1947) covering 12 cities in the U.S. with large Black populations, show that of 1,642 retail businesses owned and operated by Blacks, 43.5% were in the foodservice industry (Pierce, p. 35). Further analysis of the data showed that indeed of the 3,866 Black businesses located in the 12 cities he studied, the restaurant industry had the most representation of Black entrepreneurs in 1944 (see Table 1).

Characteristics of the Businesses

Although specific information about characteristics of Black restaurant businesses is unavailable, Pierce (1947) provides general characteristics of all the Black businesses during the early 1900s including those in the foodservice industry. In his study he found that the median amount of start-up capital was $549.50 (Table 2 shows more detail). The source of the initial capital is typically money saved from earnings and family savings. Other sources used, albeit to a relatively smaller extent, were rela-

TABLE 1. Classification by Line of Business for Twelve Cities, 1944

Line of Business	Number	Line of Business	Number
Accounting offices	1	Building and loan associations	2
Apartment houses and office buildings	10	Business schools	3
Auto accessories	1	Carnivals	1
Bakeries	9	Cemeteries	7
Barber colleges	2	Cleaning and pressing shops	288
Barber and beauty shops	10	Coal, ice, and wood dealers	61
Barber shops	404	Coin operated machines, rentals, repairs	5
Beauty schools	17	Concessions	1
Beauty shops and schools	6	Confectionaries	114
Bicycle shops	3	Contractors, builders	14
Blacksmith shops	5	Clinics	3
Booking agencies	2	Dairies	1
Book stores	7	Decorators	6
Bottling works	2	Delicatessens	8
Bowling alleys	2	Dress shops	5
Line of business	2	Junk dealers	3
Drug stores	67	Laundries	15
Dry good stores	5	Liquor stores	13
Egg and poultry dealers	3	Loan and investment companies	7
Electrical Appliance stores	5	Locksmiths	4
Employment agencies	4	Men's clubs and recreation places, pool rooms	52
Fish and poultry markets	31	Meat markets	2
Five-and-Ten cent stores, variety, sundries	28	Millinery shops	8
Florists	33	Moving and hauling	47

Line of Business	Number	Line of Business	Number
Fruit and vegetable stores	30	Manufacturing, cabinet	1
Furniture stores	10	Manufacturing, casket	5
Garages	6	Manufacturing, chemical	2
Gift shops	3	Manufacturing, cosmetic	8
Grocery stores	293	Manufacturing, flower	1
Hardware stores	2	Manufacturing, food	1
Hospitals	4	Manufacturing, hair	1
Hotels, Inns	30	News stands	19
House cleaning	1	Newspapers	8
Insurance life, branch offices of	21	Nurseries	2
Insurance, other	5	Optical stores	2
Insurance brokers	3	Orchestras	5
Jewelry stores	8	Photographers	29
Plumbers	9	Sign-painting Shops	7
Printing and publishing	39	Stocking shops	3
Public stenographers	1	Tailor Shops	42
Radio repair shops	39	Taverns, cabarets, etc.	88
Real Estate Agencies	51	Taxicabs and taxicab companies	36
Record Shops	14	Theaters	1
Restaurants	627	Toilet preparation stores	3
Secondhand stores	12	Undertakers	126
Shoe-repair shops	130	Upholstery, furniture repairs	8
Shoe-shine shops	53	Uniform shops	1
Shoe stores	2	Watch and jewelry stores	3
Total			3,866

TABLE 2. Percentage of Respondents and the Amount of Initial Capital

% of Respondents	Initial Capital
15.8	< $100
41.0	< $ 400
35.6	> $1,000
8.0	> $5,000
3.6	> $10,000
1.1	> $20,000

Source: Joseph Pierce (1947). *Negro Business and Business Education*. New York: Harper & Row.

tives, banks, and the sale of stock. This further explains why the majority of Black businesses were concentrated in the foodservice and other service industries during the 1800s and early 1900s since businesses in these industries required little start-up capital.

Another characteristic relates to the number of years the business has been in existence–length of establishment. Pierce's data show that on the average the length of establishment for Black businesses is 6.7 years. Businesses that fall in the foodservice group had been in existence for 5.8 years on average, and the length of establishment did not vary whether the business was owner-operated or manager-operated. With respect to owner-ship type, 85% of all the businesses in this study were sole proprietorships, 9% were partnerships and 3% were corporations. The sole proprietorships and partnerships had a higher mortality rate than the corporations.

Pierce also provided data on some selected financial and operating ratios. Black enterprises in the restaurant industry along with dairy stores and bakeries had the highest inventory turnover rate: 365 times per year (see Table 3), that is, they were able to sell all the inventory purchased for each day. The average mark-up (profit margin over cost) for all retail businesses was less than 50% with the exception of bakeries, dairy stores, cosmetic stores, and florists. However, across all retail businesses for example, mark-up ranged from 25% to 100% (see Table 4). These profit margins were relative to a median sales volume for all 3.866 business in 1944 of $3,260.01. A little over 30% of the businesses had annual sales less than $2,500 while only 4.8% had annual sales of $25,000 or more. Service businesses reported the smallest median sales of $2,496.66, fol-

TABLE 3. Average Inventory Turnover Rate-Per Year by Line of Business, 1944

Line of Business	Turnover Rate	Line of Business	Turnover Rate
Apparel stores	4	Furniture	3
Bakeries	365	Giftshops	4
Book stores	3	Grocery stores	12
Coal, ice, and wood	12	Jewelry stores	0.5
Confectionaries	12	Liquor stores	52
Cosmetic stores	12	Newstands	156
Dairy stores	365	Optical stores	12
Drug stores	12	Record shops	12
Electrical appliances	4	Restaurants	365
Filling stations	156	Second-hand stores	27
Fish and poultry	156	Taverns	52
Florists	52	Uniform shops	1
Fruit and vegetable	24	Variety shops	4

Adapted from: Pierce, Joseph (1947). *Negro Business and Business Education*. New York: Harper & Row, p. 67.

lowed by retail stores with $3,579.05, and miscellaneous businesses with $7,245.26. Restaurants, as a group of businesses in the retail sector reported median annual sales of $3,274.50. One explanation for restaurant businesses' relatively low median sales is that they generally have a high mortality rate, and in the Black business community, the longer a business had been established, the greater its annual sales volume was. Also, on the average, sole proprietorship, which was the predominant form of business organization for Black restaurant enterprises, reported the lowest median annual sales of $3,049.07. This was followed by partnerships with $3,961.36, cooperatives with $12,499.50, and corporations with $22,499.50.

Table 5 provides an illustration of how a dollar is spent after it is received in a Black business enterprise. Again, foodservice businesses are found in the retail stores category, and food and beverage cost (merchandise, supplies, etc.) represent the largest expense item followed by labor cost (salaries and wages).

TABLE 4. Profit Margin in the Retail Sector by Line of Business

Line of Business	Average Margin	Line of Business	Average Margin
Apparel stores	33.3%	Furniture	100.0
Bakeries	75.0	Gift shops	33.3
Book stores	26.0	Grocery stores	39.0
Coal, ice, and wood	25.0	Jewelry stores	33.3
Confectionaries	35.0	Liquor stores	41.5
Cosmetic stores	50.0	Record shops	37.5
Dairy stores	60.0	Restaurants	28.8
Drug stores	48.0	Second-hand stores	30.0
Electrical appliances	35.5	Stocking shops	25.0
Fish and poultry	35.0	Variety shops	33.3
Florist shops	50.0		

Adapted from: Pierce, Joseph (1947). *Negro Business and Business Education.* New York: Harper & Row, p. 68.

In summary, the foodservice industry has been a line of business with a disproportionate representation of Black entrepreneurs relative to other business sectors. It was also the kind of business in which the culinary and service skills of Blacks were very well known. The predominant form of business organization was the sole proprietorship, and these businesses tended to have relatively low sales and high mortality rates.

CURRENT STATE OF BLACK ENTREPRENEURSHIP IN FOODSERVICE

Current Statistics of Black Entrepreneurship in the Foodservice Industry

In the 1980s and '90s the foodservice industry has not been as popular as a line of business for Black-American entrepreneurs as it was in the middle and latter parts of the 1800s. Whereas in 1944 restaurants represented 16.2% of all Black-owned businesses (Pierce, 1944) there were 11,834 Black-owned foodservice establishments in 1987 and they represented only 3% of all Black-owned businesses (Census Bureau, 1987).

TABLE 5. Sample Profit and Loss Statements for Selected Business Groups

	Retail Stores	Service Establishments	Miscellaneous Business
Median Annual Sales	$3,579.05	$2,496.66	$7,245.26
Expenses:			
Salaries & Wages	15.5%	32.4%	41.3%
Rent Heat, Power, Repairs	3.4	5.4	5.3
Property Taxes, Licenses	1.3	1.9	1.7
Advertising	0.7	1.1	1.1
Bad debts	0.2	0.2	
Merchandise, supplies, etc.	56.3	22.4	23.8
Other Expenses	3.4	5.3	4.4
Total Expenses	80.8	68.7	77.6
Net Profit including owner's salary	19.2	31.3	22.4

Source: Pierce, Joseph (1947). *Negro Business and Business Education.* New   York: Harper & Row.

These foodservice establishments contributed a little more than 5% of the total sales of all Black-owned businesses, making them the sixth largest line of business. From another point of view, these establishments represented 4% of all restaurants in the U.S.

Table 6 shows changes in Black-owned foodservice businesses between 1982 and 1987. Although there was little change in the number of foodservice businesses over this five year period, total sales for Black-owned foodservice firms almost doubled from $619.1 million to $1.1 billion. This was due in part to a 41% increase in the number of businesses with paid employees since such businesses tended to be larger. These businesses with paid employees accounted for 71% of the total sales of all Black-owned foodservice firms in 1982 and 85% in 1987. Although the bulk of Black-owned foodservice businesses tended to be owned and operated solely by the family, the trend was toward an increase in those with paid employees. The percentage of all Black-owned foodservice firms with

TABLE 6. Black-Owned Foodservice Firms: 1982-1987

Indicator	1982	1987
Total sales for all firms	$619.1 mill.	$1.1 bill.
Total number of firms	11,406	11,834
Number with paid employees	3,365	4,747
Percentage with paid employees	29.5%	40.1%
Firms with paid employees		
Total sales (in 000)	$437,183	$918,321
Ave. sales per firm	$129,921	$193,453
Ave. sales per paid employees	$26,397	$28,393
Number of paid employees	16,562	$32,343
Ave. number of employees per firm	4.9	6.8

Source: U.S. Census Bureau, Survey of Minority-Owned Business Enterprise: Black 1987.

paid employees rose significantly from 29.5% in 1982 to 40% in 1987, and their sales almost doubled from $437 million to $918 million during the same period.

In terms of the number of firms with paid employees, the Black-owned foodservice firms represented the fifth largest line of Black-owned businesses with employees in 1987. Yet these foodservice firms ranked second to business service firms in the aggregate number of paid employees in any kind of Black-owned business. They employed 15% of all the paid employees of Black-owned businesses in 1987, and an over-whelming majority of these employees were Black (Michalski, 1991).

Table 7 shows the growth that occurred in Black-owned foodservice businesses between 1987 and 1992. Black-owned foodservice businesses, as a percentage of all Black-owned businesses, declined from 3% in 1987 to 2.2% in 1992. With respect to total sales of all Black-owned businesses, foodservice businesses contributed about 5.5%, similar to 1987 (see Table 8).

TABLE 7. Black-Owned Foodservice Firms: 1987-1992

Indicator	1987	1992
Total sales for all firms	$1.1 billion	$1.8 billion
Total number of firms	11,834	13,832
Sales per firm	$91,640	$129,090
Total number of paid employees	32,343	54,393
Number of paid employees per firm	6.8	11.9

Source: U.S. Census Bureau, Survey of Minority-Owned Business Enterprise: Black 1992.

However, there was a 16.9% increase in the number of Black-owned foodservice firms from 1987 to 1992 compared to the over-all restaurant industry growth rate of 7.4%. Whereas the entire restaurant industry sales grew by 41.8%, the Black-owned foodservice firms sales grew by 64.7% (Michalski, 1991). Although the foodservice business is no longer as popular with Black entrepreneurs as it was six or more decades ago, it continues to be a major contributor to the Black-American economy in terms of sales and employment. Black-owned foodservice businesses were the fourth largest employer of all Black-owned businesses in 1992. Those businesses with paid employees accounted for 89% of the sales of all Black-owned foodservice businesses (see Table 8).

In summary, the Black foodservice entrepreneur has made very significant contributions to the over-all foodservice industry during the eighties and nineties. Census data show that 4% of all foodservice businesses are owned by Blacks yet they have a higher sales growth rate relative to the industry as a whole. These businesses represented the fourth-largest employer of all Black-owned businesses, and in 1992 this group doubled their total payroll from 1987 to more than $400 million (Michalski, 1991). Given that in 1995, 47.9% of racial and ethnic minorities in the U.S. were Black and, furthermore, 47% of Black adults patronized a foodservice establishment on any given day, the prospects for more prosperity for the Black foodservice entrepreneur is promising.

TABLE 8. Ranking by Sales of Black-Owned Businesses

Industry	All Black-Owned Businesses		Black-Owned Businesses with Paid Employees	
	1992 Sales (000)	Rank	1992 Sales (000)	Rank
All Industries	$32,197,361		$22,589,676	
Health Services	2,858,582	1	2,010,937	2
Automotive dealers and service stations	2,384,443	2	2,250,442	1
Business services	2,371,433	3	1,576,771	5
Wholesale trade–non-durable goods	1,836,949	4	1,728,854	3
Eating and drinking places	1,785,569	5	1,590,634	4
Real estate	1,552,796	6	792,740	9
Personal services	1,468,760	7	583,994	13
Special trade contractors	1,465,642	8	987,598	7
Engineering & management services	1,352,798	9	916,084	8
Trucking warehouse	1,346,941	10	538,453	14
Miscellaneous retail	1,246,999	11	721,475	10
Wholesale trade durable goods	1,107,372	12	1,016,558	6

Source: *Restaurants USA* (1996), *16*(5), 43.

Threats and Opportunities

There is ample evidence to assert that during the last three decades the number of Black-owned foodservice businesses has increased dramatically, and their impact on the industry as a whole continues to be significant. However, obstacles continue to persist. Ahiarah (1993) identified several factors that threaten the survival and growth of Black entrepreneurship in all industries. These include (1) inadequate managerial capability and operational neglect, (2) choice of unfavorable business location, (3) fraudulent practices, (4) lack of relevant training and experience, (5) random disturbances–acts of God, (6) lack of access to capital, (7) lack of supportive network, (8) lack of role models, (9) inadequate Black patronage, and (10) racial discrimination and Black powerlessness.

The first four factors he described as individual-specific and are within the control of the Black entrepreneur. These factors can sometimes be addressed through education and training. The remaining six he referred to as environment-consequent factors and these are typically beyond the entrepreneur's control. Removing these obstacles, except for random disturbances, requires institutional and legal changes, and sometimes an awareness that the future growth and success of non-minority owned business enterprises is linked with the spread of capitalism and spurring of economic empowerment within the Black community. The recent creation (1997) of the Multicultural Foodservice and Hospitality Alliance (MFHA) as a consortium of influential foodservice corporations in the U.S. dedicated to supporting and encouraging diversity in the hiring process, career advancement, and vendor selection in the hospitality industry is one example of promoting economic empowerment (Prewitt, 1997).

Black-owned foodservice businesses face less of a threat in the operational aspects of the business, such as food purchasing and preparation. It is in the areas of business management skills and service management skills where there is greater threat. This threat is significant because the average consumer today is more sophisticated with regard to his or her expectations and how they are to be met. In addition, consumers have a better understanding of pricing, promotions, service delivery, and value.

Against the backdrop of fierce competition in the foodservice industry, Black foodservice entrepreneurs cannot afford to be lax in the areas of business and service management. More and more hospitality management programs have appeared on University campuses over the last twenty years and Black foodservice entrepreneurs must seek access to faculty and small business institutes available on some of these campuses.

Furthermore, more college-bound Black students must be told the history of Black-Americans in the foodservice industry, and the success they have had over the years. To ensure that a new generation of better-trained and educated Black foodservice entrepreneurs will be available for the next century, bright college students must be pursued, recruited and nurtured into the hospitality major. The Asian-American Hotel Owners Association (AAHOA), for example, has recognized the need to encourage Asian-American youth, especially children of AAHOA members who are enrolled in non-hospitality majors, to give serious consideration to careers in this industry. At their 8th annual convention a program was unveiled to target a minimum of 100 Asian-American students throughout the U.S. to be mentored and educated about the history and business of hospitality (Shaw, 1996).

The growth of restaurant franchising is one of the opportunities that have evolved over the last three to four decades. Franchised restaurants, because of their brand affiliation, are easily recognized and accepted by diverse customers. This type of business form offers greater opportunities for the business to have instant access to a larger market than other forms. Black-owned foodservice businesses that are franchised have been more successful at attracting and serving a racially diverse clientele, and this has contributed to their significant sales growth.

Minority business opportunity has become a priority in the 1990s to franchisors. From a company like Denny's, which launched its first-ever minority franchise recruitment program in 1993, to Burger King which has re-vamped its existing minority franchise program, franchise companies have recognized that effective minority business development is good business. The appeal of franchising to the potential Black-American entrepreneur is the idea of running a small business with the financial, marketing and managerial support of a nationally recognized corporation. If the brand is a strong one, then the franchisee can count on a broad patronage that crosses racial lines, although minorities provide the most patronage, especially in the foodservice sector of the franchise industry. The franchisee can also be confident that the consumer is assured that the product and service are standardized. Therefore, the best opportunity for entry into today's foodservice industry by a prospective Black entrepreneur is through franchising.

CONCLUSION

Although the percentage of Black-owned businesses in the United States is very small relative to the representation of Blacks in the population, the services industry in general and foodservice in particular show a disproportionate representation of Black entrepreneurs. Their relatively large representation in foodservice may be due to the long history that Blacks have had in the culinary field during the days of slavery and the post-emancipation era. Over the years Black-Americans have found success and wealth as entrepreneurs in the foodservice industry, and today Black-owned foodservice businesses as a group represent one of the largest in terms of sales and employment of all Black-owned businesses in the U.S. Franchising has also emerged as emerged as a vehicle for Black foodservice entrepreneurs to conteract racism as well as inadequate Black patronage.

Considering the history that Blacks have had in the foodservice industry, relatively little published research exists in the hospitality literature about their participation in the industry. Given that the foodservice industry will continue to be important in attracting potential Black entrepreneurs, as well as provide opportunities for wealth creation and employment in the Black community, more studies must be conducted to shed light on Black entrepreneurship in this industry. Some of the research issues may include:

1. Black foodservice owners' access to non-minority markets,
2. capital formation and access to capital for Blacks in the foodservice industry,
3. characteristics of successful Black entrepreneurs in the foodservice industry,
4. comparative analysis of Black entrepreneurs and entrepreneurs of other ethnic minorities in the foodservice industry,
5. comparative analysis of Black entrepreneurship in foodservice versus other selected industries.

AUTHOR NOTE

Prior to the University of Delaware, Francis A. Kwansa was on the faculty of the Hospitality and Tourism Management Department at Virginia Tech where he taught graduate and undergraduate courses in hospitality financial management and managerial accounting. While there he chaired and served on several doctoral and masters committees. He is currently the Associate Editor of the *Journal of Hospitality Financial Management,* and has published widely in both academic and trade journals. He is the past President of the Association of *Hospitality Financial Management Educators,* member of the Financial Management Committee of the American Hotel and Motel Association, past Editor of the Hospitality Financial Management Review, past Chair of the Financial Management Special Interest Section of the Council on Hotel, Restaurant and Institutional Management Education (CHRIE), and also serves on the Publications Council of CHRIE. Dr. Kwansa's graduate training is in Financial Management and Statistics in Hospitality and Tourism Management from Virginia Tech and Economics from Virginia State University.

REFERENCES

Ahiarah, Sol. (1993). Black American' business ownership factors: A theoretical perspective. *The Review of Black Political Economy, 22*(2), 15-40.

Blayton, J.B. (1941). Education and Negro business. *Proceedings of the National Negro Business League,* August.

Drake, St. Clair & Horace Cayton. (1945). *Black Metropolis.* New York: Harper and Row, Torchbook Edition.

Gardner, Karen. (1996). Black-owned foodservice firms are booming. *Restaurant USA, 16*(5), 42-44.

Henderson, Lenneal. (1993). Empowerment through enterprise: African-American business development. In B.J. Tidwell (Ed.), *The state of Black America.* New York: NUL.

Kinzer, Robert & Edward Sagarin. (1971). Roots of the integrationist-separatist dilemma. In Ronald Bailey (Ed.), *Black business enterprise.* New York: Basic Books Inc.

Michalski, Nancy. (1991). Black-owned eating and drinking place firms: 1987. *Restaurants USA, 11*(3), 38.

Myrdal, Gunnar. (1944). *An American dilemma.* New York: Harper and Brothers.

Pierce, Joseph. (1947). *Negro business and business education.* New York: Harper and Row.

Rose, Arnold. (1948). *The Negro in America.* New York: Harper and Row.

Quantity Feeding
During the American Civil War

Danielle M. Torisky
Reginald F. Foucar-Szocki
Jacqueline B. Walker

SUMMARY. Quantity feeding has always been an integral part of hospitality. This chapter provides a historic description of the food production, quality, and safety challenges facing those individuals who fed Union and/or Confederate soldiers during 1861-1865. *[Article copies available for a fee from The Haworth Document Delivery Service: 1-800-342-9678. E-mail address: getinfo@haworthpressinc.com]*

Danielle M. Torisky is Assistant Professor in the Dietetics Program of the Health Sciences Department at James Madison University. Reginald F. Foucar-Szocki is currently the J.W. Marriott Professor of Hospitality Management at James Madison University and serves as the director of both the Hospitality Program and the Center for Experiential Learning for the College of Business. Jacqueline B. Walker is the Associate Professor of History and Co-Director of African and African American Studies Program at James Madison University in Harrisburg, Virginia, where she teaches courses in American, African-American, and Civil War and Reconstruction history.

Many have provided valuable assistance in the research for this paper. The authors wish to acknowledge Kenneth Boichuk, Dr. Patricia Brevard, Patricia Garrison, Dr. F. Terry Hambrecht, John Heatwole, Julie and Larry McGrane, Marie V. Melchiori, CGRS, Jeff Mellott, Gordon Miller, Jerry Ruhlen, Dr. Rebecca Torisky, and Dr. Joseph Whitehorne. In addition, a special thanks to Joanne Faber and Radha Sehgal, for their editorial assistance.

[Haworth co-indexing entry note]: "Quantity Feeding During the American Civil War." Torisky, Danielle M., Reginald F. Foucar-Szocki, and Jacqueline B. Walker. Co-published simultaneously in *Marriage & Family Review* (The Haworth Press, Inc.) Vol. 28, No. 1/2, 1998, pp. 69-91; and: *The Role of the Hospitality Industry in the Lives of Individuals and Families* (ed: Pamela R. Cummings, Francis A. Kwansa, and Marvin B. Sussman) The Haworth Press, Inc., 1998, pp. 69-91. Single or multiple copies of this article are available for a fee from The Haworth Document Delivery Service [1-800-342-9678, 9:00 a.m. - 5:00 p.m. (EST). E-mail address: getinfo@haworthpressinc.com].

KEYWORDS. Quantity feeding, Military feeding, Special diets 1861-1865

INTRODUCTION

Through examination and interpretation of 19th century military feeding manuals and other sources, surgeons' and nurses' reports, soldiers' and their families' letters, and diaries, this chapter provides a historic description of the food production, quality, and safety challenges facing those individuals who fed Union and/or Confederate soldiers during 1861-1865. This review will include a spectrum of circumstances ranging from more favorable in-camp quantity feeding to more adverse conditions such as on the march, in battle, wounded/sick in field or general hospitals. The impact of family influences on soldier food preferences has played a key role in morale and health. Whether this influenced whole groups enough to determine battle outcome is speculative but intriguing. At least one medical officer in his memoirs suggests that soldiers' health and diet did affect their performance in battle (Letterman, 1866).

Quantity feeding has always been an integral part of hospitality. Military life for extended periods of time away from family and loved ones poses a challenge for those given the responsibility to maintain the physical and psychological health of their charges. In the north, during the period 1861-1865, field officers known as purchasing commissaries of the U.S. Army's Subsistence Department were responsible for identifying and procuring food supplies from available markets. This included items to be issued to troops as rations, as well as special foods demanded by military hospitals (Risch, 1962). Detailed procedures were in place for requisitioning and issuing prescribed amounts of meat, bread, coffee, sugar, and other items, from chief to regimental commissary level. In regiments where a commissary was not appointed, the quartermaster sergeant assumed responsibility for both quartermaster and commissary duties (Risch, 1962). Unfortunately, army guidelines for actual preparation and cooking of rations into nutritious meals were not well-defined. Early in the war, equipment such as kettles and frying pans were issued to squads of six to ten men for the purpose of small-group cooking, but skill and talent in this area were inconsistent (Huston, 1966). Letters written from soldiers and their families to one another often mentioned camp food and how certain food items from home were missed. Recipe manuals for military use at this time reflect that in some instances a particular effort was made to provide home-like comfort and familiarity in menu choices and cooking methods. Such efforts appear to have met with mixed success.

EARLY INFLUENCES ON 19TH CENTURY QUANTITY RECIPES (RECEIPTS)

The Crimean War (1854-1856) and its accompanying sanitary horrors made urgent the development of quantity feeding kitchens, procedures, and food preparation methods designed to nourish the sick and to combat what was known to cause and spread disease from contaminated food and water. According to Cooper (1967), Florence Nightingale accompanied her mother on regular visits to care for the sick in their English church community. This was part of Nightingale's education, and it exposed her to food needs and practices of her neighbors. Her family-based observations and experiences were enhanced by her own study and training in food and chemistry, through visits to local institutions, and consultation with experts in medicine and related fields. She gained further experience in nursing, and in quantity food purchasing and production, while serving as superintendent of a London hospital known as the Establishment for Gentlewomen during Illness. This was a bold step for a woman in 19th century England, as nursing was not considered an appropriate occupation for a lady (Cooper, 1967).

Nevertheless, at the outbreak of Crimean War, she was appointed by British Secretary of War to the post of Superintendent of the Female Nursing Establishment in the English General Military Hospitals in Turkey. In 1854, she arrived with a team of 38 nurses in Scutari (Barrack Hospital), and immediately attended to the improvement of poor sanitary conditions and preparation of special (known as "extra") diets and the establishment of Extra Diet Kitchens. Before her arrival, it had taken 3-4 hours to serve a meal, and this limited to two the number of meals served per day for many soldiers. This was primarily due to poor organization, inadequate or inoperable cooking equipment, and inappropriate delivery and storage of food supplies that resulted in a menu of salted meat and a few vegetables. Soon several Extra Diet Kitchen facilities were established in the hospital.

A few months later she was joined by French chef Alexis Soyer, who made valuable contributions to food production and procurement of proper equipment in the general kitchen. Additional improvements were also made in other Crimean Peninsula hospitals by Nightingale and Soyer. Her organizational and administrative skills made her a sought-after resource both during and following the Crimean War. She was soon called upon to make recommendations to the British army in matters of hospital care, and at the request of Queen Victoria and the Minister of War, produced a report in 1858 entitled, *Notes on Matters Affecting the Health, Efficiency, and Hospital Administration of the British Army* (p. 7). While it was never published on a wide scale, and according to Cooper is a rare find today, its content is believed to have influenced the Royal Commission in its inquiry into army hospital regulations. This is reflected in their report, which included recommendations regarding the organization and flow of authority in hospital kitchens.

Cooper refers to two of 18 sections in this report which not only addressed army diet, but also appear to have foretold of challenges soon to be experienced by Union and Confederate armies in the feeding of vast numbers of soldiers. Highlights from these sections, Notes on the Dieting and Cooking of the Army, and Notes on the Functions of the Commissariat about the supply of Food for the Army, included this memorable quotation: "'The cooking for the Army has not advanced with the requirements of the times, in the art of preparing the greatest variety and best combination of the most nourishing food with rapidity and simplicity'" (Nightingale in Cooper, 1967, p. 7). This was followed by recognition of the lack of food production training of army cooks, reliance on individuals or small companies of men to cook for themselves, and poor equipment furnished to the army.

In 1859 Nightingale published *Notes on Nursing*. Its chapter "Taking Food" discussed the differing food needs of acutely versus chronically ill patients. The chapter "What Food" addressed the need for specific food groups such as vegetables. When the American Civil War began in 1861, Nightingale's advice was sought by the U.S. Secretary of War, and by an army captain who asked her to review a draft of Commissary instructions (Cooper, 1967). Direct quotes from *Notes on Nursing* can be found in both U.S. (Wittenmyer/USCC, 1862-65) and Confederate (Surgeon General, Army of Virginia, 1861) military cooking manuals.

In 1863, while the American Civil War was in progress, Nightingale contributed information to a two-volume published report on sanitary issues of the British army in India, which included the reminders that (1) the soldier's diet needed to be adjusted for different seasons and different climates and that year round rations did not reflect this need; (2) only a few soldiers showed awareness of the effect of the diet on overall health; (3) more vegetables should be consumed; and, (4) improperly cooked food made it difficult to digest. The implementation of her recommendations in India is believed to have played a part in reducing the death rate from 69 to 18 per thousand in the British army over a period of 10 years (Cooper, 1967).

This was "cutting edge" information for that time, and Nightingale's and Soyer's food preparation and sanitation principles were reflected in American army and medical feeding manuals (described below). To what degree and effectiveness this sanitation and dietary information was conveyed to and acted upon by the "common soldier" is questionable considering that the high proportion (more than half the total) of deaths during the Civil War were from diseases. Many of these deaths were attributed to diarrhea or dysentery due to bad food and/or water (Adams, 1952; Cunningham, 1958; Dammann, 1993; Letterman, 1866; Maust, 1994; Robertson, 1984). Exact figures differ from source to source; however, Dammann (1993) reported that for both sides 414,000 of 618,000 deaths during the war were due to disease. U.S. Army records list acute and chronic diarrhea, typhoid fever, and acute and chronic dysentery as responsible for the greatest number of deaths by disease. Others included typho-malarial fever, typhus, delirium tremens, scurvy, and venereal diseases (Dammann, 1993). Interpreting morbidity and mortality statistics from this period is difficult because many diseases occurred in combination with others, diagnosis was difficult, and reliable records were not always kept (Gillett, 1987).

Influence in the United States

The influence of Florence Nightingale is evident in Mrs. Annie Turner Wittenmyer's recipe collection (Wittenmyer/USCC, 1862-65). Mrs. Wittenmyer (1827-1900) was a school teacher in Keokuk, Iowa, when the Civil War began in 1861. She became Iowa's state sanitary agent in 1862, and was given permission by Secretary of War Edwin Stanton to visit Iowa soldiers to assess their needs in Kansas and Mississippi. Because of her reports and letters back to the Soldiers' Aid Societies, she was able to collect $136,000 in food and sanitary supplies which she distributed to sick and wounded soldiers.

Her activities in field hospitals, which traveled with the army, alerted her to the need of special diets for these men, who generally could not tolerate regular camp food and who often suffered malnutrition, which compounded the problems of their diseases and injuries. With the support of President Abraham Lincoln and Surgeon General Joseph Barnes–and in cooperation with the U.S. Christian Commission (USCC), the USO and the Red Cross–Mrs. Wittenmyer established hospital diet kitchens to better provide nutritious and easily digestible meals for the sick and wounded. Food donations procured by USCC made possible the inclusion of such items as fruits and vegetables, preserves, eggs, butter, sugar, and dried meat to the limited fare supplied by the hospital commissaries. Such foods were not only nutritionally valuable, but were also said to have provided psychological comfort for the suffering men.

Diet kitchens were under the authority of army surgeons, but generally were managed by USCC women, who provided letter-writing and other services for soldiers along with their special cooking duties. "Before the end of the war, more than one hundred diet kitchens were in service. During the last 18 months of the war, over two million rations were issued from the long lines of special diet kitchens. It is clearly believed these services saved the lives of thousands of soldiers," so state S. Jackson and G. Floyd in their introduction to the 1983 printing of Mrs. Wittenmyer's *Collection of Recipes for the Use of Special Diet Kitchens in Military Hospitals,* originally published between 1862 and 1865.

Soyer's Culinary Influence

As reference was made to Florence Nightingale in Wittenmyer's recipe collection, so were the recommendations of Chef Alexis Soyer cited in the "Culinary Department" and "Health Department" sections of Dr. Louis Le Grand's military manual for Union soldiers. While numerous recipes from Soyer's collection were featured for both regular (Le Grand, 1861, pp. 71-75) and hospital diets (pp. 96-98), Le Grand pointed out that many of Soyer's recipes would be too expensive for the U.S. Army, in their quantities of meat proportional to number of men served by one recipe. He thus included a section of recipes submitted by an "able and experienced American housewife" (Le Grand, 1861, p. 76), paying tribute to the ability of "good housewives" to employ greater "economy" in cooking, and by including a section of her recipes in the soldier's manual for the company cook (Le Grand, 1861, pp. 76-79). It is evident to present-day readers of the manual that he recognized the culinary competence of women, and considered the contribution of this anonymous housewife as indispensable information for use in feeding. More than serving to convey practical food preparation instructions to the literate soldier, the inclusion of this recipe section in the soldier's manual also suggests an importance placed upon family and home reminders, perhaps to maintain the morale of Union soldiers. Le Grand also gave Chef Soyer credit for contributing to the troop morale during the Crimean War, stating, "He instituted a thorough system in the culinary department, and, by his excellent arrangements and thoroughly scientific principles of preparing and mixing the food, produced a most astonishing change in the comfort, health and happiness of the entire [British] army" (LeGrand, 1861, p. 71).

Tripler and Blackman (1861) in their *Handbook for the Military Surgeon,* Chapter II on "Military Hygiene" also praised Soyer, and included quantity recipes (called "receipts" in the 19th century) from his then-recently published collection for the British Army. Some of these included Soup for Fifty Men, Stewed Salt Beef and Pork for One Hundred Men, Coffee a La Zouave for Ten Men, and Tea for Eighty Men. His hospital recipes included Beef Soup, Beef Tea, and Plain Boiled Rice, versions of which are found in the Wittenmyer collection. As shown in the recipes for beef tea given in Table 1, there are differences between Soyer and Wittenmyer's versions regarding cooking styles, procedures, and specific ingredients and proportions–the latter possibly reflecting differences in rations and expected food availability. Mrs. E. F. Haskell's (1861) household recipe, found in Chapter IV, "Cooking for the Invalid," of her *Housekeeper's Encyclopedia,* is included in Table 1 to show that beef tea was also used in feeding the sick on the home front.

TABLE 1. Quantity and Household Recipes for Beef Tea

Beef Tea–Quantity Recipe from Soyer as Cited in Tripler and Blackman (1861)

Cut 3 lbs. of beef into pieces1 the size of walnuts, and chop up the bones, if any; put it into a convenient-sized kettle, with ½ lb. of mixed vegetables, such as onions, leeks, celery, turnips, carrots (or one or two of these, if all are not to be obtained); 1 ounce of salt; a little pepper; 1 teaspoonful of sugar; 2 oz. of butter; ½ pint of water.

Set it on a sharp fire for ten minutes or a quarter of an hour, stirring now and then with a spoon till it forms a rather thick gravy at bottom, but not brown; then add 7 pints of hot or cold water, but hot is preferable; when boiling, let it simmer gently for an hour; skim off all the fat, strain it through a sieve, and serve. (p. 19)

Beef Tea–Quantity Recipe from Wittenmyer (1862-65)

Mince four pounds of beef very fine, and pour over it one pint of cold water. Boil it hard for five minutes, skim it well and pour it out through a colander. When perfectly cold, strain it through a cloth, and season with salt. (p. 10)

Beef Tea–American household recipe from Haskell (1861) for Comparison with Quantity Recipes

Cut up a pint of juicy sirloin beef in small bits; put it in a quart bottle, with half a pint of cold water; cork and wire firmly, and boil fifteen minutes; then press the meat, salt the tea, and use it as directed by the physician. (p. 397)

HARDTACK FOR HUNDREDS:
CHALLENGES OF FEEDING THE ARMIES

Typical rations for Union and Confederate soldiers, as listed in Tables 2 and 3, assumed a "best-case scenario," more likely to occur when troops were not engaged in battle, and located near sources of production and supply. Meat quality and safety could not be guaranteed; in the case of the Union army, meat shipped frozen by northern meat packers could arrive at an army depot in a southern location that had no means of refrigeration for safe storage (Huston, 1966). Soldiers on the march were issued fresh beef, since herds of cattle for this purpose followed the moving army; however, the flavor of this beef was poor, due to the long marching of the animals with minimum forage and rest (Huston, 1966). As the war progressed from 1861 to 1865, intended allotments per soldier (e.g., 20 ounces fresh

TABLE 2. Typical Union Army Rations and Associated Slang Terms*

Hard bread or Hardtack biscuits
Lard
Sugar or molasses

Coffee   subtle poison, Lincoln's coffee–in other words, the "real" stuff; an unpopular extract of coffee mixed with milk and sugar was issued for a short time in the field but rejected, this early attempt at instant coffee

Beef or dried/salted meat

          "mule" referred to bad meat; of course, in real bad times,
          mule referred to . . . mule!
          . . . or mutton, pork, bacon, fish

Desiccated ("desecrated") vegetables

          boiled hay, baled hay, brick, fodder, son-of-a-seadog–this was federal effort to include a scurvy-preventive (antiscorbutic)–potatoes, onions, others . . . or beans, rice, hominy, canned/fresh (?) veg if available

Vinegar, salt, pepper
Flour or soft bread or cornmeal (if not hardtack)
Baking powder (needed in the field)
Soap, candles

*Sources: Kory, 1993; Lyman, 1994; Price, 1961; Risch, 1962; Robertson, 1984.

TABLE 3. Typical Confederate Army Rations and Associated Slang Terms*

Cornbread or raw cornmeal
    . . . or flour or hard bread

Fresh pork or bacon or bacon fat or lard
Fresh or salt beef (also subject to being "mule"/spoiled)
Rice
Sugar
Molasses
Vinegar
Salt
Beans
Peas (when available)
Dried fruit (when available)

Fresh vegetables (when available)
    some were also encouraged to eat wild onions to prevent scurvy

Coffee or coffee substitutes
    peanut, sweetpotato, peas, corn, chicory, wheat, okra seed ("seedtick" coffee)

Soap, candles

---

*Sources: Price, 1961; Lyman, 1994; U.S. National Archives, 1863; Robertson, 1984.

or salted beef; 12 ounces hard bread) were not guaranteed, and some items on the official ration list could rarely be obtained (Kory, 1993). Thus, depending on engagement of troops, status of railroads and other supply routes, commissary error (Kory, 1993) and other factors influencing delivery of food and cooking supplies, troops on both sides could find themselves in either feasting or starving conditions. Table 4 details Vitamin C and A deficiencies known to have occurred among the military population of both sides, which were associated with lack of fruits and vegetables.

The dependability of obtaining complete rations appears to have been questionable–and limited in variety even if all listed menu items were available. Lack of fruits and vegetables in the soldier's diet was known by both Union and Confederate armies to threaten his health. When this was combined with sleep deprivation and other physical and emotional stresses inevitable on the march and in battle–in the view of some medical officers–poor diet also affected troop morale and preparedness. Dr. Jonathan Letterman, who reported to General McClellan in June 1862 as Medical

TABLE 4. Vitamin Deficiency Diseases and Associated Symptoms Reported to Occur Among Union and Confederate Soldiers*

Scurvy (Vitamin C)
- Bruise easily (upon pressing skin with finger)
- Gums bleed, lose teeth
- Lose hair
- Unable to walk
- Slow wound healing
- Greater likelihood of secondary hemorrhaging (w/surgery)
- Poor resistance to infection
- Considered by both Confederate and Federal medical officials as a threat to strength of armies

Night Blindness or "Gravel" (Vitamin A)
- Poor vision in dim light / nighttime
- Poor recovery from flash of bright light, especially in darkness
- Especially a problem w/Confederate soldiers suffering from fatigue, lacking green, yellow, and orange vegetables and fruits, and w/overexposure to sun

*Sources: Brockett & Vaughan, 1867/1993; Cunningham, 1958; Letterman, 1994/1866; Lyman, 1994; Robertson, 1984; Sizer & Whitney, 1994.

Director of the Army of the Potomac, observed in his memoirs the psychological effects of scurvy when he wrote

> causes which give rise to it undermine the strength, depress the spirits, take away the courage and elasticity of those who do not report themselves sick, and yet are not well. They do not feel sick, and yet their energy, their powers of endurance, and their willingness to undergo hardship, are in a great degree gone, and they know not why. In this way the fighting strength of the army was affected to a much greater degree than was indicated by the number of those who reported sick. (Letterman, 1866, p. 7)

The power of disease to reduce total fighting forces was recognized earlier by Dr. Henry Bellows, President of the U.S. Sanitary Commission, who asserted that disease and filth posed greater danger to men than did the battlefield itself. Following a tour of Union encampments he observed unsanitary conditions, poor group and personal hygiene, lack of ability of soldiers to properly nourish themselves, and an alarming prevalence of dysentery. "It is before these inglorious but deadly foes that our brave boys will flinch; before their unseen weapons that they will fall!" he wrote (USSC, 1864, pp. 10-11).

What options were available to soldiers then, in order to supplement a high-starch, high-fat ration? Company cooks were encouraged to save unused rations, resell them and accumulate a "company savings" or "slush fund" (Kory, 1993) to be used for buying other foods or cooking equipment from local farmers, or from merchants known as sutlers who followed the armies. Individual soldiers could also buy food from sutlers. These independent merchants offered a variety of food and nonfood items such as produce and tobacco, but had a reputation for charging inflated prices for their wares, and food quality and safety were not guaranteed in this market (e.g., some were reported to have sold spoiled meat). Sutlers themselves risked capture by the opposing force if they were too close to the battle. Confederate surgeon Spencer Welch reported in a letter to his wife that relief from months of scant food supplies had been afforded when his brigade caught up with "sutlers stores and trainloads of flour and meat, and we captured a few prisoners. I went into a sutler's tent and got three days' rations of ham, crackers and salt" (Welch, 1862, pp. 61, 65, 69). Dr. Welch in letters to his wife made numerous references to long marches, inadequate amounts of rations, and conditions of hunger in his 13th South Carolina Volunteers (McGowan's) brigade.

Foraging for supplemental food was another option, but not always an approved one. Some officers forbade their men to forage from local families' land, and soldiers were expected to pay for any food obtained from farmers. However, occasionally families found themselves unwilling providers of livestock and produce for their own or the opposite army. An example of this was described by Welch (1862, pp. 66-67) when soldiers were driven by hunger to steal food. Food shortages and hunger were particularly a problem for Confederate troops. Many areas of the South were affected by naval blockades preventing goods from being imported, and problems in transporting food within the Confederacy (Massey, 1952; Mescher, 1994), due to shortages of rail cars, carts, wagons, and even horses and mules to pull them (Massey, 1952).

This was especially felt in the Chimborazo Hospital in Richmond (Pember/Wiley, 1954). Dr. Frances Porcher was given leave from active duty as a field surgeon by the Confederate government in order to compile a 601-page volume (Porcher, 1863) which catalogued edible, medicinal and otherwise useful flora which was native to the Southern states. This was an effort to encourage resourcefulness in the wake of anticipated shortages of food, medicine, and other goods needed for daily living. These shortages would affect not only troops, but civilians too, as the Confederacy channeled many resources to support its army. One Southern homemaker wrote in her diary about struggling to provide her family with adequate food, coping with harsh winters that would freeze (and eventually rot) potatoes stored in the attic or basement; and, about prizing occasional treats of sugar and real coffee (McDonald, 1875).

This excerpt from an August 9, 1862 diary entry from Confederate surgeon Caleb Dorsey Baer described the hardship of limited and poor quality food:

> Up to this time, from their arrival on Cow-Skin Prairie, our army had lived upon what ever could be obtained in the country, part of the time upon Rye ground but not bolted, and upon cornmeal so sour that the livestock would not eat it–with this they had only beef and no salt to season any of their food. They then commenced using roasting ears and made green corn soup, composed of the green corn cut from the cob and boiled with a piece of beef [sic] this was their diet until the Battle of Wilson's Creek and their arrival at Springfield. (Baer, Civil War Diary)

It was little wonder that ailments of the stomach and bowel became so common in Civil War army camps.

Lack of cooking skills and poor sanitary practices among soldiers themselves was recognized to be a common problem in both Union and Confederate camps. Warnings abounded in cooking manuals by Wittenmyer (1862-65), Le Grand (1861), and Tripler/Blackman (1861) to wash hands, reduce fat and grease in cooking, cook thoroughly, boil water and other liquids, and to follow other practical sanitary and culinary tips to prevent indigestion and foodborne illness. However, some combination of (1) failure for this information to reach many company cooks and individual soldiers, (2) lack of cooking skills among many soldiers (including knowledge of the need to *cook* dried beans and grains before eating them), and (3) the unfortunate abundance of contaminated food with the lack of discernment as to whether to chance eating it after cosmetically "fixing" it up, led to many unnecessary cases of diarrhea, dysentery, and other ailments that frequently proved fatal. Union Captain James Sanderson admonished in his preface to cooking instructions that "Cleanliness is next to Godliness, both in persons and kettles; be ever industrious, then, in scouring your pots" (p. 4). He continued later, "Remember that beans, badly boiled, kill more than bullets; and fat is more fatal than powder. . . . Skim, simmer, and scour, are the true secrets of good cooking" (p. 5).

Dr. J. Letterman, from the army of the Potomac, developed recommendations on quantity feeding regarding causes of scurvy and other diseases that reflected his awareness of the importance for not only appropriate food supplies, but the need for preparation in quantity to prevent foodborne illness. The following is an extract from his July, 1862 letter to Brigadier-General S. Williams, which became published in the form of orders to the army: "I recommend that an abundant supply of fresh onions and potatoes be used by the troops daily for a fortnight, and thereafter at least twice a week, COST WHAT THEY MAY; that the desiccated vegetables, dried apples or peaches, and pickles, be used thrice a week; that the food be prepared by companies and not by squads; and that these be two men detailed from each company as permanent cooks to be governed in making the soups, and cooking by the enclosed directions . . ." (Letterman, 1866, pp. 12-13). He continued to insist upon such other practices and arrangements as proper shelter; air circulation; and, better sanitation which for the kitchens also meant digging refuse pits. Additionally, he stated the need for a reasonable balance of drill and rest, a meal schedule to optimize rest and nourishment, and the inclusion of breakfast before a day's march–even "if only a cup of coffee" (p. 13)–upon rising from an adequate night's sleep.

Letterman's memoirs showed that he was plagued not only with lack of supply of fresh vegetables and other antiscorbutics, but often with inefficient delivery. In one instance, large quantities of produce were ordered by the commissary; however, when the food arrived, it was left on the wharf to spoil, due to a lack of staff on hand to transport it to its proper destination. Letterman was just as quick to report reductions in the number (lists) of sick men in instances when he could successfully supply these foods to the troops.

Frustration was also felt at the field hospital level. Another doctor recognized failures in the quantity feeding system and reported taking firm steps to correct them. Major Albert G. Hart, surgeon with the 41st Regiment of Ohio Volunteers, defined the critical problem facing him as a surgeon as that of "obtaining and preparing a suitable diet" for hospitalized soldiers (Hart, n.d., p. 23).

Upon discovering both a lack of proper kitchen procedures and poor accountability among field hospital cooks, and their refusal to accept skilled help from two women trained by the U.S. Sanitary Commission who were present and offering assistance, Major Hart took command of the kitchen and placed the USCC women in charge. Any defiant cook who tested his authority with disobedience was sent back to the war front. He reported that this took only two instances for that type of behavior to be squelched. He realized that special diets were being blindly ordered by surgeons without knowledge of what food items were available from the commissary, so he developed a form of hospital cycle menu that he called a "bill of fare." Its design was not unlike present-day hospital selection menus sent to patient rooms with trays, based on available supplies, to be used by surgeons from which to order their patients' diets. "This bill of fare was changed every few days, and the diet for all patients was much improved" (Hart, n.d., p. 36). Additionally, he was concerned with the difficulty hospital patients would have eating hardtack bread, so he persuaded a civilian woman to teach one of his cooks how to bake fresh, soft, salt-rising bread using a Dutch oven the army had confiscated. Thus, a determined Hart injected a measure of discipline and order into an otherwise inefficient field hospital kitchen.

Similar confusion existed in Confederate hospitals, especially at the war's beginning. A checklist for inspectors of hospitals shows that, at least in writing, there was attention paid to sanitary conditions of the kitchen and latrine areas, quality of food, supply of antiscorbutic foods, and recordkeeping of diet prescriptions (Guide for Inspection).

On the Union side, an account from the diary of a surgeon in McClellan's Army of the Potomac speaks of frustration with military bureaucracy and the impact of petty infighting about food and medical care as the 5th Regiment of Wisconsin Volunteers prepared to march to battle in the mid-Atlantic area. Dr. Alfred Castleman, a surgeon with the regiment, had carefully trained his nursing staff in the proper lifting of wounded men from battlefields, and in the physical handling of sick and wounded men. These personnel were also trained in the preparation of food for special diets. After a group of soldiers presented a gift of an engraved sword to Dr. Castleman, in gratitude for humanitarian actions and relief work for his staff during a bitter winter season when many of the staff were too sick to perform their duties, ten of them were relieved of duty by the Brigadier General who claimed they had violated army rules. Castleman was unsuccessful in appealing the decision, and became disillusioned with his superiors and the army in general. As the Army of the Potomac prepared to move after a long period of inactivity under General McClelland, and as seven inexperienced privates reported to Castleman as replacement nurses, the discouraged surgeon wrote:

> This morning as my newly appointed nurses came in, I was utterly
> disheartened. There is not a man amongst them who can make a toast
> or broil a chicken; yet the sick must depend on them for all their

cooking . . . Not one has ever dispensed a dose of medicine, and yet I must depend on them for this duty. (Castleman, 1863)

Role of African Americans in Quantity Feeding of Troops

It should be noted that while feeding manuals included recipes for large numbers of men, there were other recipes for smaller quantities. If a soldier, or former slave, with cooking experience could serve as company cook, then larger numbers of men could be fed (Huston, 1966). Kory (1993) said that soldiers in camp seldom cooked in groups greater than ten. She added, however, that an act of Congress in 1863 enabled Northern armies to enlist African Americans to cook for much larger groups of men. "It was hoped by the civilians at home that the proper preparation of food would cut down on disease among the ranks" (Kory, 1993, p. vi). George Anna Woolsey, a U.S. Sanitary Commission staff nurse, spent three weeks in Gettysburg following the three-day battle. In her account of these three weeks, she stated that African American men were with the Commission performing large-quantity cooking of soup and coffee under her supervision (Woolsey, 1863/1993).

Susie King Taylor was a freedwoman and former Georgia slave who offered more than three years of volunteer service for the 33rd U.S. Colored Infantry. In her own account of her army life was a passage referring to food preparation:

A mess-pan is made of sheet iron, something like our roasting pans, only they are nearly as large round as a peck measure, but not so deep. We had fresh beef once in a while, and we would have soup, and the vegetables they put in this soup were dried and pressed. They looked like hops. Salt beef was our stand-by. Sometimes the men would have what we called slap-jacks. This was flour, made into bread and spread thin on the bottom of the mess-pan to cook. Each man had one of them, with a pint of tea, for his supper, or a pint of tea and five or six hard-tack. I often got my own meals, and would fix some dishes for the non-commissioned officers also. (Taylor, 1902, pp. 28-29)

During the war, other black freedwomen could work in hospitals in exchange for food, clothing, and a small salary, "but most supported themselves as domestics, washerwomen, seamstresses, and vendors, selling their goods and services to the troops and the few whites who resided in the area. Good cooks were often patronized by soldiers and freedmen's aid society teachers and agents" (Walker, 1991, p. 16). Troops tended to ignore warnings from their officers not to consume "chicken fixins" prepared by black vendors. However, one officer admitted, "The [Negro] shanties were . . . besieged by our hungry boys, and the black 'aunties' and their daughters were soon driving a good business in supplying the soldiers with hoecake" (Haines, 1863 as cited in Walker, 1991, p. 16).

Freedmen were reported to have made significant contributions to the U.S. Army's foraging efforts for livestock and hospital supplies. They "frequently led foraging parties to places where supplies, necessary for the Department were obtained. In this way, boat loads of pine and oak wood for the hospitals and Government offices, a steamboat load of cotton in bales for the protection of the gun boats, and numbers of horses and mules, with forage for the Commissary's Department cattle, swine, and sheep were obtained at no other cost than the small wages of the men. Without doubt, property far exceeding in value all that was ever paid to the blacks, was thus obtained for the Government" (Colyer, 1864, p. 30).

Several diaries or letters have cited individual African Americans whose ingenuity or skill proved valuable in providing food in hospital or camp. Phoebe Pember wrote of Jim, "a small black boy," who acted as message-carrier, procured kitchen equipment and cooked food, as Pember struggled to establish her hospital kitchen at Richmond's Chimborazo Hospital with very few resources (Pember/Wiley, 1954, p. 19). Confederate surgeon Spencer Welch made several references to his "servant Wilson," who helped him forage and cooked for him during the 1862 Peninsula Campaign in the aftermath of a battle at Ox Hill (Welch, 1862, pp. 71-72).

COMMISSIONS, COMMUNITY GROUPS, AND FAMILIES AS SUPPLIERS OF FOOD FOR THE ARMIES

Ladies' Aid Societies in both the North and South, independent male and female volunteers, local sewing circles, and such organizations as the U.S. Sanitary Commission and U.S. Christian Commission all played roles, and often worked together, in bringing food and family-like comforts to men in the armies. Dr. Hart not only praised the participation of the USSC women in his hospital kitchen, but noted that a Northern Ladies' Aid Society "filled a thousand gaps left by the Medical Purveyor's Department, and gave the surgeons untold help on the field, in the regiments, and in the hospitals" (Hart, n.d., p. 39). The Christian Commission, as described earlier, often worked in conjunction with the U.S. Sanitary Commission. The latter was formed for the purpose of providing medical and sanitary supplies, personnel, and advice to the Army Medical Department, and was received with mixed reactions, ranging from welcome to resentment, by army medical staff (Gillett, 1987). Among its areas of focus, the USSC included "the proper provision of cooks, nurses, and hospitals . . . " (USSC, 1864, p. 7). Like the Christian Commission, it also provided letter-writing and reading materials and services, and articles of clothing. There also existed a Western Sanitary Commission which operated in a similar manner, but primarily west of the Mississippi River.

Given the overlapping activities among the three commissions, and occasional close proximity to one another, there were inevitably some feelings of rivalry among them. Despite this, there are accounts of their cooperation with each other and the army; Maust (1994) wrote that the Christian Commission was more than well-received by the Second U.S. Corps Hospital in Gettysburg in July, 1863, where they were a critical "disaster relief" source of emergency food, personnel, and medical supplies following the three-day battle. One USCC member later wrote of the army's accommodating actions during this crisis: "To get at these different hospitals was no little work, and then to get goods to them would have been impossible, but through the kindness and promptness of Col. Rankin, quartermaster, who furnished us wagons and ambulances on call, and thus enabled us daily to send out wagon loads to the different hospitals" (Cross, 1865 in Maust, 1994, p. 71).

Both Christian and Sanitary Commissions served as channels through which families and communities could send food, clothing, and other items in large quantities to the army; each developed systems of transporting goods via rail or other means to locations where needed. The Sanitary Commission was known for its Sanitary Fairs, where food and other contributions were collected for the war effort. USSC nurse George Anna Woolsey praised communities back home for sending what they could to areas engaged in battle. Woolsey, in a letter to a friend, described the three weeks spent by her and her mother treating the wounded at Gettysburg: "No men were turned back. You fed and you sheltered them just when no one else could have done so; and out of the boxes and barrels of good and nourishing things, which you people at home had supplied, we took all that was needed. Some of you sent a stove (that is, the money to get it), some of you beef stock, some of you the milk and fresh bread; and all of you would have been thankful that you had done so, could you have seen the refreshment and comfort received through these things" (Woolsey/Johnson, 1863/1993, p. 117).

In the South, Phoebe Yates Pember, employed as matron of the Confederate Chimborazo Hospital in Richmond, Virginia, was grateful for private donations of food and clothing to the hospital. "Immense contributions, coming weekly from these sources, gave great aid, and enabled us to have a reserved store when government supplies failed" (Pember/Wiley, 1954, p. 40). Regarding family visitors, Pember reported from a less favorable perspective in her diary that visits were made–and occasionally long hospital stays imposed–by some to loved ones who were recovering in the hospital. Sometimes these families would bring inappropriate food, contraindicated for the medical condition of the patient; even in times of shortage, they expected to use the scarce fuel resources and kitchen facilities of the hospital to prepare the foods they brought. In Pember's situation, dealing with such "intruding" families easily taxed her efforts to maintain a well-ordered nursing and feeding system for recovering soldiers (Pember/Wiley, pp. 65-68). Otherwise, in the Confederacy, Ladies' Aid Societies, other women's groups, and families themselves were known to be extremely active and fervent in their efforts to support war efforts, sending food and clothing to soldiers and making bandages for the army.

North and South, families responded to complaints from their enlisted loved ones about scant and/or poor-quality rations, and requests for home favorites. Family care packages may also have acted as a long distance food service for smaller units of men. Sometimes, there was an unwritten code among soldiers that if one man received a food care package from home, he would share it with others as might be possible in his unit, depending on the amount sent–especially among neighbors and friends in the same unit. The latter was believed to be true for the 52nd Regiment Virginia Infantry (Pegram's Brigade): "If neighborhood men shared with each other it was understood the favor would be returned" (Miller, 1994).

Confederate soldier Jesse Rolston, Jr., of the 52nd Virginia Infantry wrote to his wife Mary Catherine requesting vegetables be sent to him at camp, "and in an earlier letter he was out 'picking greens.' Jesse may have realized these were lacking in his camp diet" (Miller, 1994, p. 46). He frequently asked for butter and apples (spelled by Rolston as "appels") to be sent whenever possible, and identified that rations were very meager. Hunger appears to have been a great problem among the men in Rolston's camp. There were also many references to deliveries made back and forth between husband and wife in "the box," through various friends, neighbors, or even absent-without-leave comrades. He would send items for her and the children in the box, and receive back from her such things as blankets, clothing and food in the same box. Some articles sent by Rolston to his family were tin cups, britches, socks (to be mended and/or washed?), nails, rice, coffee (this was a premium item in the blockaded South), and cotton cloth. Rolston complained in his letter of October 28, 1863, that in the face of inflated apple prices offered by sutlers, "meat and bread is all we draw from these days" (Miller, 1994, p. 50). His letter written November 14, 1863, indicated that he did receive "the butter you sent and appels [sic] too" (p. 51). These deliveries were apparently not made free of charge, since Rolston offered to send money to his wife to "pay for going and coming" (p. 53). Other requests came for pies, apples, potatoes, and for her to "put a mess of cornmeal in if you can. I'd [sic] love some corn bread to eat" (p. 56).

Jesse's wife was not the only one who sent food to the camps; this was evident in an earlier letter of April 8, 1863, in which he commented that they were "living fine" because two soldier friends had received "boxes of provisions from home and it tasted good" (p. 31). In the same letter, however, he said that as much as he would like to receive a box from Mary Catherine, he warned her only to send it *with* someone to avoid the risk of having it stolen while en route to him.

A letter dated October 9, 1864, from Rome, Georgia, written by a Union soldier identified only as Matt to his wife Sallie, speaks clearly of a husband's and father's concern and provisions for his family to have adequate food back home (please note errors due to transcription and/or original writer): "Sallie, as near as I can learn from Northern papers, everything in the shape of provisions if [is?] not likely to fall in price for the next nine months. I think it would be economy [sic] for you when you get that $100.00 to engage and pay for as much wheat and corn as you may need till next harvest. Get it of [sic] some farmer, as you need it but pay him now. I would advise you to make free use of Graham and corn bread, being cheaper and more wholesome. At All. Coll. Geo. [a local market?] Isaac and I used to get Graham bread made of Rye and wheat ground together half & half. It makes very wholesome bread. Be sure and have a good supply of Fruit, Peaches & Apples. Do your best to supply the children with a proper diet" (Letters, 1862-65).

CONCLUSION

This chapter has only begun to describe a period of great turmoil in the homes, hospitals and camps of a country engaged in civil war. While much was beginning to be known about how to prevent the spread of disease through proper hygiene and sanitary measures, many factors combined to create obstacles to proper feeding and adequate health care for thousands of American soldiers, both North and South. It is critical for present-day family, health care, and hospitality professionals to study the brilliant efforts, instances of ingenuity and team work–especially between parties of different backgrounds and approaches–of the 19th century Americans as many did try to work together to relieve the devastation and suffering being visited upon soldiers and their families. *Cooperative effort* between men and women, between civilian and military populations, between races of people in our country, and within the military organizations themselves, helped in overcoming obstacles to providing nourishment and proper medical care for soldiers. As many of us in the family, health, human service, and hospitality professions find ourselves in competitive, high-stress work environments, we can learn much from the insights related to team work, cooperation, and family support that can be gained by studying a difficult and challenging portion of our professional and human history.

AUTHOR NOTE

Danielle M. Torisky received her Bachelor of Science degree in Home Economics/Nutrition and Fine Arts at Seton Hill College in Greensburg, PA, and her Master of Science and Doctor of Philosophy degrees in Community/Public Health Nutrition at Virginia Tech in Blacksburg, VA. She teaches at graduate and undergraduate level; courses include Sports Nutrition, Nutrition for Wellness, Computer Systems in Food and Nutrition, Quantity Food Service, Quantity Food Production, and Nutrition Education/Counseling. She has also taught Current Topics in Food. Special areas of research interest include Civil War food and medical history with focus in the dietetics area; use of multimedia technology in nutrition education; nutrition education and special nutrient needs of developmentally disabled individuals and their families; nutrition and behavior; and related projects which combine service and research in community and worksite settings.

Reginald "Reg" Foucar-Szocki grew up in Hospitality industry in Western New York. His formal education includes a bachelor's degree from Michigan State University in Hospitality Management, a master's degree in Vocation Education from SUNY Buffalo and his doctorate in Adult Education and Human Resource Management from Syracuse University. He is a colleague of the Creative Education Foundation, an active member of CHRIE and has a national reputation in the area of Creativity, Problem Solving and Experiential Learning. His most recent book co-authored with Dr. Jack Samuels, *Guiding Your Entry into the Hospitality & Tourism Mega-Industry,* is a guidebook for internship in the hospitality industry. A strong believer in learning by doing, Dr. Foucar-Szocki interns every second summer. Those companies include ARAMARK, Pizza Hut, CHRIE, the Greenbrier and Marriott. He lives in the beautiful Shenandoah Valley of Virginia with his wife, Diane, and two wonderful children, Jonathan and Katy, and dog, Tazzle.

Jacqueline B. Walker is an active scholar in the area of Civil War, Emancipation, and Reconstruction experiences of American slaves and freed people. A native of East Orange, New Jersey and graduate of Douglass College of Rutgers-The State University of New Jersey, she received her MA and PhD degrees in American History, from Duke University in Durham, North Carolina.

REFERENCES

Adams, GW (1952). *Doctors in blue: The medical history of the Union Army in the Civil War.* NY: Henry Schuman, 1952.

Baer, CD (n.d.) "Civil War Diary of Caleb Dorsey Baer"–unpublished manuscript in the possession of F. Terry Hambrecht, National Institutes of Health, Bethesda, MD 20892.

Brockett, LP, & Vaughan, MC (1867). *Women at war: A record of their patriotic contributions, heroism, toils and sacrifices during the Civil War.* Reprinted edition 1993 by Longmeadow Press, Stamford, CT; originally published in 1867 by R.H. Curran, Philadelphia, PA.

Castleman, AL (1863). *The Army of the Potomac–Behind the Scenes.* Milwaukee: Strickland & Co. Excerpt from original reprinted in Straubing, HE (1993). *In Hospital and Camp–The Civil War Through the Eyes of its Doctors and Nurses.* Harrisburg, PA: Stackpole Books, pp. 39-57.

Colyer, V, (1864). *Report of the Services Rendered by the Freed People to the United States Army, in North Carolina, in the Spring of 1862, after the Battle of New Bern.* New York: Published by Vincent Colyer, 1864.

Cooper, LF (1967). Florence Nightingale's contribution to dietetics. In *Essays on history of nutrition and dietetics,* compiled by Beeuwkes, AM, Todhunter, EN, and Weigley, ES. Chicago: American Dietetic Association, pp. 5-11.

Cunningham, HH (1958). *Doctors in gray: The Confederate Medical Service.* Baton Rouge: Louisiana State University Press.

Dammann, G (1993). *Pictorial Encyclopedia of Civil War Medical Instruments and Equipment. Volume 1.* Missoula, MT: Pictorial Histories Publishing Company, 1993.

Guide for Inspection of Hospitals and Inspector's Report. In Parrish, TM & Willingham, RM (n.d.) *Confederate Imprints: A Bibliography of Southern Publications from Secession to Surrender.* Item 1969. Austin, TX: Jenkins Publishing Co.

Gillett, MC (1987). *The Army Medical Department 1818-1865.* Army Historical Series. Washington, DC: Center of Military History, United States Army.

Hart, AG (n.d.). *The Surgeon and the Hospital in the Civil War.* Reprinted 1987 by Olde Soldier Books, Inc., Gaithersburg, MD.

Haskell, EF (1861). *The Housekeeper's Encyclopedia.* New York: D. Appleton and Company. Original work contained in Shep, RL, ed. (1992). *Civil War Cooking: The Housekeeper's Encyclopedia.* Mendocino, CA: RL Shep, p. 397.

Huston, JA (1966). *The Sinews of War: Army Logistics 1775-1953.* Washington, DC: Office of the Chief of Military History, United States Army.

Kory, ES (1993). *1862 Manual for Army Cooking.* Norristown, PA: Norristown Press, pp. i-xx.

Le Grand, L (1861). *The military handbook, and soldier's manual of information.* NY: Beadle & Co.

Letterman, J (1866). *Medical recollections of the Army of the Potomac.* Knoxville, TN: Bohemian Brigade Publishers, 1994 (originally printed by D. Appleton & Co., New York, 1866).

[Letters from Civil War Soldier, 1862-1865]. MS96-005. Blacksburg, VA: Special Collections Department, University Libraries, Virginia Tech.

Lyman, D (1994). *Civil War Wordbook*. Conshohocken, PA: Combined Books, Inc.

Massey, ME (1993). *Ersatz in the Confederacy–Shortages and Substitutes on the Southern Homefront*. Columbia, SC: University of South Carolina Press. (Originally published in 1952 by USC Press.)

Maust, RR (1994). The Union Second Corps Hospital at Gettysburg, July 2 to August 8, 1863. *Gettysburg: Historical Articles of Lasting Interest.* January 1, 1994; Issue #10; pp. 53-101.

McDonald, Mrs. Cornelia (Peake) McDonald (1875). *A Diary with Reminiscences of the War and Refugee Life in the Shenandoah Valley, 1860-1865*. Annotated and supplemented by Hunter McDonald, Nashville, TN: Cullow & Ghertner Co., 1934.

Mescher, V (1994). *"Making Do" or Substitutions of Scarce Items During the Civil War*. Burke, VA: Nature's Finest and the author.

Miller, JD, ed. (1994). *"Until Separated by Death"–Lives and Civil War Letters of Jesse Rolston, Jr. & Mary Catherine Cromer*. Bridgewater, VA: Good Printers, Inc.

Pember, PY (1862-1865). *A Southern Woman's Story–Confederate Life in Richmond*. Wiley, BI, ed. (1954). Marietta, GA: Mockingbird Books, McCowat-Mercer Press, Inc.

Porcher, FP (1863). *Resources of the Southern Fields and Forests*. Charleston, SC: Steam-Power Press of Evans & Cogswell. Reprint edition 1970 by Arno Press, Inc. and the New York Times, New York.

Price, WH (1961). *Civil War Handbook*. Fairfax, VA: L.B. Prince Co., Inc. and Staunton, VA: Virginia Publications. Civil War Research Associates Series, p. 11.

Risch, E (1962). *Quartermaster Support of the Army: A History of the Corps*. Washington, DC: Quartermaster Historian's Office, Office of the Quartermaster General.

Robertson, Jr., JI (1984). *Tenting tonight: The soldier's life*. Alexandria, VA: Time-Life Books, Inc., pp. 85-88.

Sanderson, JE (1862). *Camp Fires and Camp Cooking; or Culinary Hints for the Soldier*. Washington: Government Printing Office. Published for Distribution to the Troops. Headquarters "Army of the Potomac," pp. 1-14. (Reproduction of original work, in Kory, ES (1993). *1862 Manual for Army Cooking*. Norristown, PA: Norristown Press.)

Sizer, FS, & Whitney, EN. (1994). *Nutrition Concepts and Controversies*, 6th ed. Minneapolis/St. Paul: West Publishing Co., pp. 216-220, 238-242.

Surgeon General, Army of Virginia (1861). *Directions for Cooking by Troops, in Camp and Hospital, Prepared for the Army of Virginia, and Published by Order of the Surgeon General: With Essays on "Taking Food," and "What Food," by Florence Nightingale*. Richmond, VA: J.W. Randolph. Laramie, WY: 1991 reproduction copy by Sue's Frou Publications.

Taylor, SK. *Reminiscences of My Life in Camp with the 33rd United States*

Colored Troops Late 1st S.C. Volunteers. Boston: Published by the Author, 1902. Reprint edition 1968 by Arno Press, Inc., and the New York Times, New York.

Tripler, CS, and Blackman, GC (1861). *Handbook for the Military Surgeon*, Chapter II. Military Hygiene–Preservation of Health of Troops in Campaign. Cincinnati: Robert Clark & Co., Publishers, pp. 10-22.

United States Sanitary Commission (1864). *The Sanitary Commission of the United States Army: A Succinct Narrative of its Works and Purposes.* New York: USSC. Reprint edition 1972 by Arno Press, Inc. and the New York Times, New York.

United States National Archives (1863). RG 109 War Department Collection of Confederate Records: M437 Letters Received by the Confederate Secretary of War. Roll #105. Item 59-N-1863, frames #720-730.

Walker, JB (1991). "New Bern, North Carolina: The Organization of Black Labor Behind Union Lines." Paper presented at the Annual Meeting of the Organization of American Historians, Louisville, KY, April 11-14, 1991.

Welch, SG (1911). *A Confederate Surgeon's Letters to His Wife.* New York & Washington: The Neale Publishing Co. In Straubing, HE (1993). *In Hospital and Camp: The Civil War Through the Eyes of its Doctors and Nurses.* Harrisonburg, PA: Stackpole Books, pp. 58-73. (NOTE: Straubing states on p. 59 that Welch's letters were "edited to omit personal matter.")

Woolsey, GAM (1863). *Three Weeks at Gettysburg.* In Johnson, CF, ed. (1993). *Gettysburg: Historical Articles of Lasting Interest.* July 1, 1993; Issue #9; pp. 116-121.

Wittenmyer, Mrs. Annie (under the auspices of the US Christian Commission). *A collection of recipes for the use of special diet kitchens in military hospitals.* Mattituck, NY: JM Carrol & Company, Mattituck & Bryan, 1983 reprinting of document originally published between 1862 and 1865.

PART II:
HUMAN RESOURCE ISSUES
IN THE HOSPITALITY INDUSTRY

The American Attitude
Toward Hospitality Service Employment

Nancy Loman Scanlon

SUMMARY. As one of the major sources of employment in the United States, 10.1 million employees in 1995 (AHMA 1997, 1), with expected employment of over 14 million by the year 2005, it is important that the perception of 'being employed' in a hospitality-related job conveys a positive connotation. This article seeks to identify the root causes of the less-than-positive American attitude toward hospitality service employment and to present the results of recent research that identifies ways in which employers can meet the needs of prospective employees to provide meaningful and satisfying workplaces. *[Article copies available for a fee from The Haworth Document Delivery Service: 1-800-342-9678. E-mail address: getinfo@haworthpressinc.com]*

Nancy Loman Scanlon is a PhD candidate at the University of Delaware, 460 West Chestnut Hill Road, Newark, DE 19713.

[Haworth co-indexing entry note]: "The American Attitude Toward Hospitality Service Employment." Scanlon, Nancy Loman. Co-published simultaneously in *Marriage & Family Review* (The Haworth Press, Inc.) Vol. 28, No. 1/2, 1998, pp. 93-107; and: *The Role of the Hospitality Industry in the Lives of Individuals and Families* (ed: Pamela R. Cummings, Francis A. Kwansa, and Marvin B. Sussman) The Haworth Press, Inc., 1998, pp. 93-107. Single or multiple copies of this article are available for a fee from The Haworth Document Delivery Service [1-800-342-9678, 9:00 a.m. - 5:00 p.m. (EST). E-mail address: getinfo@haworthpressinc.com].

KEYWORDS. Service employment, Hospitality employment, Service attitude

INTRODUCTION

It is the purpose of this article to discuss the foundation of the generally negative attitudes of the American public toward hospitality service-oriented job positions and to examine the changing economic base of the United States and the need for recognition of the present and future importance of employment in this service sector. If the potential of the rising service economy in the United States is to be fully realized on a national scale, the need for creating an attitude of support and acceptance of hospitality job positions must be brought to the attention of the general public.

As the twentieth century comes to a close, the American public is slowly developing an awareness that the economy of the United States no longer rests on the bumpers and hubcaps of the automobile industry, the turbo engines of airplane manufacturers or Pittsburgh's roaring steel mills. Generations of Americans consider honorable and worthy employment to be deeply rooted in the ability of men and women to physically produce material goods on which is placed an established value. The production of these goods generates incomes to support families as well as the tax revenues and resources upon which cities and towns depend for their existence. The prevailing attitude toward work is that labor should produce tangible goods which can be tallied and valued as part of an individual's ability to contribute to the well-being of their home and community.

The dawning revelation that 'service' industries have overtaken the primary position that manufacturing industries have historically held in the American economic mosaic is being met with disbelief and recoil. 'Service,' with its connotation of subservience, as the foundation of the American workforce conflicts sharply with the traditional image of 'independence' harbored by a large percentage of the United States population. The perception of society as a whole regarding the status accorded to hospitality 'service' jobs is also a major factor in the development of a negative view toward hospitality employment. Wood (1993) discusses the issues surrounding the effect that the perception of status in relationship to willingness to work has on hospitality industry employment. He contends that lodging and foodservice employment is perceived as being "relatively low in status, mainly because of the personal service nature of the work involved and second, many who work in the industry belong to social collectivities of relatively limited social esteem and status, such as women, the young, and members of ethnic minorities" (Wood 1993, p. 1). The following discussion hopes to argue that this and other historical elements contribute to the negative perception of hospitality-related employment in the United States.

HISTORY OF THE AMERICAN SERVICE 'ATTITUDE'

American history reveals the roots of the conflict between these two forms of labor: *service* and *manufacturing*. The French historian and political theorist Alexis de Tocqueville toured America in the 1830s and in 1835 published his observations of American society and culture in the book *Democracy In America*. His notes on the American attitude toward 'service' positions reveal the considerable differences in attitude between those of the 'New Republic' and France of the Old Regime:

> Tocqueville observed that in democratic societies such as the young American nation, these relationships [between master and servant] were characterized by aloofness and indifference on both sides. In aristocratic societies, despite the greater social difference between master and servant, time ultimately binds them together. They are connected by a long series of common reminiscences, and however different they may be, they grow alike. (Maza, 331)

A large part of the immigrant population that left Northern Europe in the late nineteenth and early twentieth century did so to flee bonds of servitude. America offered the opportunity for individuals to become independent land-holders. Although many, primarily women, entered into household service as a means of immediate income, this form of labor was a way to independence, not a life-long bondage.

Much of the aversion by Americans to the concept of a service-oriented job is a failure to understand the history and traditions that accompany service-related positions in European society. To be 'in service' was to put oneself in a position of obligation toward an employer and to provide menial functions in support of an employer's welfare, tasks which are similar to those that have been performed for centuries. In contrast, manufacturing jobs contribute to the success of a company, require physical skill and varying levels of technical knowledge and aid corporations in the advancement of industrial technology and mankind's well being. Manufacturing labor has been more highly revered for these reasons.

HISTORY OF EUROPEAN SERVICE: 1700s

The history and traditions of the staff positions for hotels and restaurants find their roots in eighteenth century France and England. The

French Revolution is principally responsible for the emergence of the commercial hotel. Until that period in European history those who traveled stayed in either rudimentary inns and taverns or the chateaus, estates and 'hotels' of acquaintances, according to their social station. At the close of the Revolution two major factors produced a demand for the commercial hotel. The first was the flight from France by the French aristocracy leaving their homes and service staff behind. The second was that the new bourgeoisie, lacking the resources of the former aristocracy, required public accommodations considerably above the standards that inns and taverns offered. From the ruins of the 'hotels,' or residences of the French aristocracy, rose the public houses of Paris. "On the eve of the French Revolution in 1789 there were about two million servants in France; therefore one out of every twelve French men and women earned his or her living as a domestic" (Fairchilds 1984, 4). From these two million came the original staffs of the emerging commercial hotels and restaurants of Paris.

THE CHANGING SERVANT CLASS OF FRANCE IN THE 1700s

Prior to the 1700s it was the custom in the aristocratic houses of Europe for young men from lesser ranking families to join the household of a noble family in order to learn the manners of the day, to be educated, and to find themselves employment. By the 1700s, however, in both England and the Continent, this custom had given way to the practice of using members of the household service staff to fill the positions of butlers, footmen and such. Among the household service positions found in Paris in the late 1700s were *homme de confiance* (secretary and/or accountant); *gens de livree* (accompanied and transported household members and regulated the admittance of guests into the house); *portier* (admitted visitors and took deliveries); *femme de charge* (head housekeeper); *maitre d'hotel* (manager of food preparation and service) and *officier* (wine, silver and linen steward and often the pastry chef). With these positions came a type of social prestige and financial rewards.

House servants now found themselves cast in a social role that often separated them from lower class society as a whole:

> The lower classes resented domestics for the violence that they often exercised on behalf of their masters, and for the power their control of their masters' purse often gave them over tradesmen and shopkeepers. And they disliked them for their own sakes as well. They resented their fine clothes and superior manners, their relatively high

salaries, their abundant leisure time, and the security they enjoyed of having their food and lodging always provided for them. But above all they resented their arrogance, their bland assumption that their association with les grands and their knowledge of the ways of the fashionable world made them superior to a mere artisan or laborer. . . . Servants were, after all, mere lackeys who had surrendered the independence that was the birthright of a free man to put themselves under the yoke of a master. (Fairchilds 1984, p. 45)

The changing face of French politics also altered the nature of the traditional definition of the servant. Prior to this period, the traditions of domestic service and the relationship between master and servant were based on the feudal system and rooted in the Middle Ages. A patriarchal hierarchy brought the servant under the care of the 'master' who became responsible for their overall well-being:

The major blow to the character of domestic service came with the emergence among the nobility and the office-holding bourgeoisie of a new style of family life . . . transforming the very purpose of their servant keeping . . . [with] the emergence of the modern affectionate family. . . . Thus in the last decades of the Old Regime the servant was expelled from the family circle. He ceased to be the "adopted child" of a patriarchal family and became instead a stranger, someone hired to do housework or personal service in return for a wage. (Fairchilds 1984, p. 17)

This shift is paramount in the transition of attitude from loyal retainers to independent hirelings on the part of the service staff. "A servant's work was no longer a duty he owed to his master; instead it was a commodity of his own which he could exchange for cash. Servants ceased to be members of patriarchal households and took their place in the ranks of working classes" (Fairchilds 1984, 17). This change in attitude coincided with the rise in the bourgeoisie class and the need for public houses offering accommodations and service that was considerably above the standards that inns and taverns offered.

THE FOUNDATIONS OF THE HOTEL AND RESTAURANT INDUSTRY

With the demise of the nobility in France the domestic servant was left in the position of being highly skilled in the running of the households of the upper classes and little else. Some individuals chose to apply these skills in entrepreneurial ventures:

> On the 17 July, 1789 the Prince de Conde leaves France and goes into exile, with the result that a whole Pleiad of superb artists–are thrown out of work. Before the year is out Robert [maitre d'hotel to the Prince de Conde] opens a restaurant. . . . At his restaurant on the rue de Richelieu, Robert gathers together the former staff of the Hotel de Conde. (Aron 1975, pp. 18 to 19)

As the bourgeoisie class rose and the nobility shifted to a much less formal life style many skilled domestics became entrepreneurial hoteliers and restauranteurs. Fairchilds (1984, p. 59) discusses how this opportunity created an attitude different from the typical member of the lower classes as being "a passion for social mobility, a devotion to making money and a willingness to take risks to make their fortunes."

In England, in the middle of the eighteenth-century:

> a career of service might . . . enable a servant to secure some employ-ment or set up in some business that ranked above service in the hierarchy of occupations, or entitle him to a greater degree of respect than he had received before he entered service; it might even bring him financial independence. . . . One occupation stands out as having been especially favored. A great many domestics became keepers of public houses. . . . A compelling explanation for their preference is that the skills and training required for service were also ideal equip-ment for tavern keeping. . . . Writing in 1777, a newspaper corre-spondent [Morning Post, June 4, 1777] observes how "The menial servant tired of his Masters company, and mid-night revels, becomes the landlord of a smug public house. (Hecht 1956, 188 to 189)

The Gentleman's Magazine of 1797, makes the following comments on the job positions found in 'public houses':

> When we consider who are the sort of persons who occupy public houses of every sort, from the best inn on the Bath road to the lowest small-beer pothouse, or hedge ale-house, they are servants of all descriptions; the butler and the housekeeper, the footman and the lady's maid, the coachman and the cook, . . . all direct their settle-ments for life to a public house.
> The George Inn at Warminster was taken in 1774 by Simon Hay-ward, who had been butler to Edward Southwell. The Red Lion Inn

at Bagshot was taken in 1780 by Peter Harvey, who had formerly been cook to the Duke of Bolton. The White Swan Inn Alnwick was occupied by a man named Wilson, who at one time had lived as footman in the Hervey family. The Fountain Inn at Biggeswade was opened in 1790 by J. Scarborough, who had served as butler to the Duke of Chandos. (Hecht 189 to 191)

The turn of the nineteenth-century saw the development of the commercial hotel in both Europe and America. By the mid-1800s, the grand hotels of Europe were in their infancy. Cesar Ritz became the first great hotelier, soon joined by Richard D'Orly Carte with The Savoy Hotel in London. Great American hotels such as The Astor House in New York City in 1834, followed by The Parker House in Boston in 1855, The Palace in San Francisco in 1875, The Del Coronado in San Diego in 1888 and in 1893 by The Waldorf Astoria, again in New York City, were appearing simultaneously to their European counterparts.

It is important to note that while the venue and manner in which professional service staff operated changed, the traditions of position and training did not. With the transfer of domestic servants to public houses and restaurants came the development of the apprenticeship training system for both 'back'- and 'front'-of-the-house positions. To advance from busboy to waiter to captain to maitre d'hotel it was necessary to serve under established mentors whose responsibility it was to train the individual in the prerequisites of a job position. At the completion of each position, successful training was acknowledged by the signature of the 'trainer' and the individual advanced to the next position in the dining room chain of responsibility and authority. Similar training procedures were followed for the kitchen. This tradition is still practiced in European hotel, restaurant and culinary technical education.

In America, however, formal traditions and training generally existed only in those hotels and restaurants that catered to the upper class. Staffed by European-born and trained general managers and maitre d' hotels, training in these hotels and restaurants was organized along the lines of the European apprenticeship system.

AMERICAN HOTEL AND RESTAURANT SERVICE EMPLOYMENT HISTORY

In addition to the 'grand' hotels, hundreds of small hotels and restaurants were opened to service the continually increasing ranks of the American commercial traveler who found the railroads a means of expanding American businesses:

> Within a few years [of 1830] the traveling salesman had become a recognized feature of American Life. . . . He became one of the chief mainstays of the hotel business, providing about seventy-five per cent of the transient business in those houses classified as commercial hotels . . . The Hotel Gazette of 1883 estimated that there were then more than two hundred thousand of them [commercial travelers] in the United States. (Williamson 1975, pp. 123 to 124)

The railroads answered the demand by building hotels and restaurants adjacent to the railway stations and staffing them with men and women anxious to move West or find employment away from the isolated farms of the Mid-West.

Long hours, poor working conditions, crowded dormitories and unethical managers and owners soon created a work environment that was regarded as menial and temporary. "By the 1890's [hotels and restaurants] employed a labor force of approximately a quarter of a million people" (Josephson 1956, 4).

> . . . immigrants, or sons of immigrants, coming largely from France, Germany, Switzerland, Italy and the Austro-Hungarian Empire. . . . Wages were certainly higher than in old Europe . . . But employers had a sharp eye for profits and drove their workers hard.
>
> The waiters, by custom, stood with their hands behind their backs . . . or ran their feet off for fourteen or fifteen hours bearing trays of food and drink. (Josephson 1956, 5)

Periodic recessions sent this pool of employment into the streets at a moment's notice. Insecure employment and poor working conditions did little to create an attitude of credibility regarding hotel and restaurant jobs. By the 1880s the unions emerged. The hotel and restaurant workers were not to be overlooked in the union movement. As a waiter working in Chicago and St. Louis in the 1870s and 1880s, Jere L. Sullivan was often required to do culinary and housekeeping jobs in addition to his regular duties. In protest Sullivan formed a waiters' union, the object of which was to emphasize the need for clearly defined craft or trade rules. "I organized a waiter's union so as to be able to belong to something. That was the Local Assembly of Waiters of St. Louis" (Josephson 1956, 11).

Registering complaints regarding abuses of time and wages, Julius Leckel, a union leader of the waiter's union in New York City wrote:

. . . unfortunately white slavery is still flourishing in various guises. One class of wage-earners still suffering from such bondage is, without doubt, the waiters' profession . . . the general public is unaware of the fact that waiters are often compelled to work fifteen hours and even longer, day after day, with hardly enough allowance of time to partake of the hastiest of meals. (Josephson 1956, 13)

With the emergence of the American Federation of Labor (AFL) a number of waiters' and bartenders' unions were chartered for New York City, St. Louis, Chicago, Indianapolis, Minneapolis and Denver and Boston.

The history of the Hotel and Restaurant Employees and Bartenders International Union AFL-CIO has been a series of successes and failures. By January 1934 the union in New York City was powerful enough to "take action against the Waldorf Astoria with waiters, busboys and cooks protesting at wages of $7.50 a week and tips (Josephson 1956, 227) . . . the movement broadened into a general strike against twenty-five New York hotels–the third in fifteen years" (Josephson 1956, 217). In St. Louis a strike of 5,000 hotel workers broke forth in the spring of 1937, headed by Kitty Amsler, the veteran leader of waitresses, and Jess Keller, head of the cook's local (Josephson 1956, 275).

The New York State Labor Department characterized these workers as:

the lowest paid of any service industry, their job security was practically zero and working conditions . . . universally bad. Sun rise to sunset marked their working hours for generations. Many never saw their families for days and days because they arose at such an early hour and worked such long hours for meager wages paid once a month . . . New York's giant hotel industry in 1937 was one of the largest industries in the country and was valued at a billion dollars in assets. (Josephson 1956, 281)

Union efforts in the 1930s and 1940s impacted significantly on both wages and benefits:

The New York State Department of Labor reported in 1951: In the twelve years of the Hotel Council's existence, New York City hotel workers' hourly wage rates have risen by a larger percentage than the pay of workers in most other industries, service or non-service. Waiters, from 17 cents an hour in January, 1939, to 55 cents, in June, 1950–an increase of 223%. Hotel maids, in the same period, from 26 cents to 78 cents, or 200%; service bartenders from 52 cents to $1.33, or 155%; elevator operators from 35 to 99 cents or 183%. (Josephson 1956, 283)

The significance of the changes in the working conditions for hourly hotel and restaurant employees over a 50-year period were summed up in the remarks of Hotel and Restaurant Employees and Bartenders International Union President, Hugo Ernst:

> The memories live for me again of the days at the turn of the century when I first went to work as a bus-boy in a hotel at $4 a week, for fourteen hours a day, seven days a week. The waiter of today with his guaranteed wage, fixed working hours, security of his job from tyrannical employers–under union protection–has no idea of the conditions we "old-timers" worked under, or the wages we got–if any. Or the fear of being fired at a moment's notice . . . Those days are gone forever. (Josephson 1956, intro.)

By the 1970s the union was extremely powerful with its largest membership ever. By instituting many human resource policies in response to employee needs and demands, hotel companies have reduced the number of issues that created a strong hotel and restaurant union membership throughout the United States. In the 1990s this same union struggles for membership and survival.

THE FUTURE OF EMPLOYMENT
IN HOSPITALITY BUSINESSES

Hospitality businesses offer excellent career development opportunities for all levels of employment. Research recently released from the National Restaurant Association (NRA) (1996) shows that approximately three out of five salaried personnel currently employed in tableservice restaurants began their careers as hourly employees. The NRA data also note that thirty-seven percent of all adults in the United States have worked in the restaurant industry at some time during their lives. The industry has not been as successful in retaining employees as it has in developing those employees who have chosen to stay.

An established minimum wage for hourly servers, pension and profit sharing packages for fulltime employees and health and education benefits are now available to hourly as well as salaried workers in most hotel and restaurant companies.

Bell persons, room service waitstaff, banquet (catering) servers, maids, and other hourly staff employees have the opportunity today to work in supportive environments that recognize the value of longterm employees and seek to create an atmosphere that encourages job retention, low turnover rates and high guest satisfaction scores. It remains to the American public to see the value in such job positions. In 1996 the minimum wage was established at $4.75 per hour to be increased to $5.15 per hour in September of 1997 (NRA 1996).

Tip-based job positions are unfortunately often evaluated for financial return solely on the basis of the hourly wage. Prospective restaurant employees need to understand that even in a small, family owned casual restaurant a server, making a tip-based minimum wage of $2.50 per hour can realize over eight dollars an hour for their efforts. These estimates of potential hourly earnings change according to the caliber of the operation and average check. Banquet servers generally realize a percentage of the gratuity from the total bill for every function in which they work in addition to the hourly wage. Bell persons and other tipped service staff are compensated according to their individual entrepreneurial efforts and can often be extremely rewarding.

CREATING A SERVICE ATTITUDE

If the foodservice and lodging industries are to create credibility for job positions at both hourly and salaried levels, they must address the attitude of the American public toward working in this sector. The recent "Industry of Choice" survey of foodservice employees by the Educational Foundation of The National Restaurant Association, showed that the top four reasons for choosing employment in a foodservice job were:

- Location near home
- Flexible schedule
- Perceive that it will be a fun job
- Better pay and benefits

This same study indicated that the top four reasons for choosing to leave foodservice employment for a job position outside of the industry were:

- Better pay and benefits
- Better work schedule
- More enjoyable work
- Career advancement
  (Foodservice Industry Forum 1997, 6)

If one looks at the correlation between issues of work schedule and work environment the assumption can be drawn that the industry as an employer is not meeting the expectations of new hires. If we look at the original complaints of hospitality-related workers in the 1800s and 1900s quoted earlier in this paper we can perceive that while working conditions and financial return have changed significantly for the better, the negative issues of long hours, financial value for work and atmosphere of the work place still exist. While the overall work place may have changed dramatically, the attitudes of the workers in it have not.

The American Hotel and Motel Association (AHMA) reports that in 1995, United States domestic travelers spent over 421.5 billion dollars within the United States alone on travel related products such as transportation, lodging, food service and entertainment, ranking the overall travel and tourism industry third in revenue generation in the United States. A pattern of success must be established paralleling that of the merchant princes of banking and industry, recognizing the tremendous achievements that have been and will continue to be realized by hotel, restaurant and travel and tourism-related businesses.

The economic impact of the combined lodging and foodservice industries in the United States is significant to overall employment and spending. The National Restaurant Association reports that in 1995 the foodservice industry posted earnings of $320 billion and the American Hotel and Motel Association reports lodging industry earnings of $72 billion, for combined revenues of $392 billion. This represented the employment of 9 million employees in 786,664 foodservice operations (NRA 1997, 1) and 1.1 million employees in 46,000 lodging establishments throughout the United States to whom lodging and foodservice employment combined paid over $392 billion in wages and benefits in 1995 (AHMA 1997, 1). By the year 2005, the U.S. Department of Labor expects 1.899 million people to be employed in the lodging industry (AHMA 1997, 2). The foodservice industry is expected to see similar increases in employment.

CONCLUSION

As the American economy shifts from a manufacturing to a service-oriented industry base, the general public is becoming aware that their livelihoods may possibly be dependent on employment in the hospitality industry. For many Americans, whose prior work orientation has been focused on the physical manufacture of products which have a tangible value, 'service' oriented employment is difficult to accept.

Hospitality-related employment in the United States has a history quite different from that of European hotel and restaurant service. The attitude toward European hospitality service employment is based on the relationship between master and servant which originated in feudal society and as recently as the late 1800s, still bound both social classes together. Europeans fleeing these same bonds of servitude came to America to find independence.

American workers today often carry this same attitude of independence with them as they face the prospect of a service-related job. Early hotel and restaurant service employment history in the United States is marked by a trail of abusive employers who paid negligible wages and demanded 7-day weeks and 14-hour days. The rise of the unions helped to change these practices but could not erase the perceptions carried forward by the American workforce.

The lodging and restaurant businesses of the 1990s look to the year 2000 when employment demands will exceed 14 million people. To meet these ever-increasing needs, hospitality businesses are offering opportunities to both hourly and salaried workers which include competitive wages, benefit packages and flexible work schedules, along with interesting and challenging work.

In order to meet American service-related business labor requirements in the year 2005, American workers must adjust their perceptions of the value and prestige of service-related jobs. These jobs, which provide the financial rewards of wages, tips and benefits, are the stepping stones to supervisory and management positions in businesses that are and will continue to be the fastest growing sector of the U.S. economy.

Greater and greater numbers of U.S. companies are moving their manufacturing plants to third world countries where environmental regulations and government controls are looser and labor is far less costly and demanding. In our consumer-driven economy, the vast majority of job openings will continue to be in the service industry sector. For those individuals who recognize the possibilities, the hospitality industry offers one of the best opportunities for long-term employment and successful careers.

AUTHOR NOTE

Nancy Loman Scanlon designs and facilitates training programs with hotel and restaurant companies throughtout the U.S. She is the author of *Marketing by Menu, Catering Menu Management, Restaurant Management, Foodservice Management,* soon-to-be-released *Quality Service Guaranteed* and the producer of the interactive video training program, *Menu for Profit.* Nancy holds a bachelors degree from the University of Connecticut and a masters degree from the University of Delaware where she is currently a PhD candidate in the College of Urban Affairs and is a recipient of the Pacesetter Award from the Roundtable for Women in Foodservice. Nancy began her hospitality career with Hilton Hotels working in food and beverage related positions. In 1980 she joined Johnson & Wales University to teach restaurant management related courses while stepping aside from industry to raise a family. During her time with Johnson & Wales University she began writing text books for hospitality education and eventually formed Profit Enhancement Programs, a company that produces hospitality related educational programs, education. As the Director of Food and Beverage Services for Interstate Hotels, Nancy developed and implemented quality food and beverage service training programs for over 65 hotels throughout the united States.

REFERENCES

American Hotel & Motel Association (1997). "Lodging Profile," Washington: American Hotel & Motel Association.

Angelo, R. and Vladimir, A. (1994). *Hospitality Today: An Introduction*, 3d ed. East Lansing, MI: Educational Institute of the American Hotel & Motel Association.

Aron, J. P. (1975). *The Art of Eating in France*, Translated by Nina Rootes. New York: Harper & Row.

Fairchilds, C. (1984). *Domestic Enemies: Servants & Their Masters in Old Regime France.* Baltimore: Johns Hopkins University Press, 1984.

Foodservice Research Forum (1997). "Industry of Choice," Chicago: Educational Foundation National Restaurant Association.

Forrest, L. C. Jr. (1990). *Training for the Hospitality Industry*, 2nd. ed., Lansing, MI: Educational Institute of the American Hotel & Motel Association.

Hecht, J. J. (1956). *The Domestic Servant Class in Eighteenth-Century England,* London: Routledge & Kegan Paul.

Hibbert, C. (1975). *Daily Life in Victorian England*, New York: American Heritage Publishing Co.

Horn, P. (1991). *The Rise and Fall of the Victorian Servant,* Wolfboro Falls, NH: Alan Sutton Publishing Ltd.

Josephson, M. (1956). *Union House Union Bar: The History of the Hotel and Restaurant Employees and Bartenders International Union AFL-CIO,* New York, Random House.

Lundberg, D. E. (1979). *The Hotel and Restaurant Business*, 3rd ed. Boston: CBI Publishing Co.

Marshall, D. (1949). *The English Domestic Servant in History,* London, George Philip & Son, Ltd.

Maza, S. C. (1983). *Servants and Masters in Eighteenth-Century France*, Princeton, NJ: Princeton University Press.

Montagne, P. (1961). *The New Larousse Gastronomique*, edited by Charlotte Turgeon, translated by Marion Hunter with a preface by Robert J. Coutine, New York: Crown Publishers, Inc.

McCarthy, J. R. (1931). *Peacock Alley: The Romance of the Waldorf Astoria*, New York, Harper & Brothers Pub.

National Restaurant Association (1997). "1997 Restaurant Industry Pocket Factbook," Washington: National Restaurant Association.

Tannahill, R. (1973). *Food In History,* New York: Stein and Day.

Williamson, J. (1930). *The American Hotel,* New York: Alfred A. Knopf.

Wood, R. C. (1993, November). Status and Hotel Catering Work: Theoretical Dimensions and Practical Implications. *Hospitality Research Journal, 16,* 1-15.

Striking a Balance:
The Future of Work and Family Issues
in the Hospitality Industry

Judi Brownell

SUMMARY. This chapter reviews previous literature related to men and women in the hospitality workforce and summarizes the challenges they have confronted as they strive to develop careers while maintaining family commitments. Current trends such as globalization, diversity, and technology are described and their impact on the hospitality workplace assessed. Specific actions that progressive hospitality organizations have taken as they address the need for a more responsive and flexible workplace are presented. Finally, suggestions are proposed for how educators and practitioners might work together to assist employees in increasing their quality of life and in achieving family and work balance. It seems likely that fundamental shifts in the basic assumptions affecting employee policies are necessary before organizational attitudes and practices will result in greater work and family balance for service employees. *[Article copies available for a fee from The Haworth Document Delivery Service: 1-800-342-9678. E-mail address: getinfo@haworthpressinc.com]*

KEYWORDS. Family/work balance, Quality of life, Women and work, Family-friendly policies, Family/work benefits

Judi Brownell is Professor of Managerial Communication and the Richard J. and Monene P. Bradley Director for Graduate Studies at the School of Hotel Administration, Cornell University, Ithaca, NY 14853 (e-mail: jlb18@Cornell.edu).

[Haworth co-indexing entry note]: "Striking a Balance: The Future of Work and Family Issues in the Hospitality Industry." Brownell, Judi. Co-published simultaneously in *Marriage & Family Review* (The Haworth Press, Inc.) Vol. 28, No. 1/2, 1998, pp. 109-123; and: *The Role of the Hospitality Industry in the Lives of Individuals and Families* (ed: Pamela R. Cummings, Francis A. Kwansa, and Marvin B. Sussman) The Haworth Press, Inc., 1998, pp. 109-123. Single or multiple copies of this article are available for a fee from The Haworth Document Delivery Service [1-800-342-9678, 9:00 a.m. - 5:00 p.m. (EST). E-mail address: getinfo@haworthpressinc.com].

Hospitality leaders in the 21st century are projected to place increasing emphasis on describing a vision and communicating values. A central vision emerging from the recent emphasis on quality and employee empowerment is of a workforce that is committed and personally satisfied. A core value that accompanies these images relates to personal and professional balance. As hospitality leaders look to the future, it becomes readily apparent that a number of significant changes must occur to meet the needs of a workforce with new demographics and new requirements–one which is less willing to sacrifice family for professional careers.

This paper first reviews previous literature related to men and women in the hospitality workplace and the challenges they have confronted as they strive to develop careers while maintaining family commitments. The hospitality work environment itself is described in terms of how it contributes to work and family conflicts. The second section identifies critical trends such as the changing composition of the workforce, diversity, globalization, and technology and explores the impact these factors have on the hospitality workplace.

The third section of the paper describes how progressive hospitality organizations have responded to these challenges and outlines the obstacles that remain. Finally, a configuration of the vision, values, and behaviors appropriate to this new environment is proposed. Suggestions are made for the ways in which educators and practitioners can work together as change agents to enable all employees to achieve greater balance between family and work.

CURRENT CHALLENGES IN CAREER BALANCE

Management positions have historically produced significant challenges as employees have attempted to balance families and careers. The demands of a supervisory role and the requirements for job advancement have created significant obstacles for hospitality professionals who aspire to senior level positions. This is due, in part, to the nature of the hospitality workplace itself.

The unique characteristics of hospitality organizations make them among the most challenging for employees who seek to advance their careers while maintaining active involvement in family activities. Literature that addresses challenges in the hospitality workplace has established this industry among the most demanding (Brownell, 1994; Lobel, 1991; Campbell, 1988; Gregg & Johnson, 1990; Fulford & Herrick, 1994; Vallelian, 1995; Kelly and Kelly, 1994). What factors make the hospitality industry so demanding and so difficult?

Hospitality employees find themselves confronted with continuous crises and a great deal of daily uncertainty. Their role as service providers, however, demands that they present an appropriate emotional response regardless of the circumstance. In many instances, the hospitality culture itself contributes to interactions that family-oriented employees find stressful, as long and irregular hours cut into family time. Since promotions and job advancement frequently require relocation, many hospitality employees experience pressing financial concerns. Finally, issues affecting women in the workplace appear particularly significant to hospitality employees as they strive to balance work and home responsibilities. We examine several of these factors in greater depth below.

Uncertainty creates high levels of job stress. Service delivery in the hospitality industry is a matter of meeting guests' expectations and responding appropriately to unanticipated events. Problems arise in the kitchen that require immediate attention; twenty more guests attend the banquet than were expected; the computer creates serious over-booking problems; a guest slips and falls on the diving board. Due to this uncertainty and the reactive nature of service delivery, hospitality management is not a 9:00 a.m. to 5:00 p.m. job. Success in the industry demands long hours and requires a great deal of crisis management and problem solving. These factors combine to create a dynamic but often stressful and exhausting work experience.

Ashforth and Humphrey (1993) define *emotional labor* as the "display of expected emotions by service agents during service encounters" (p. 88), and argue that conforming to such expectations has a significant psychological effect. Few industries require the emotional labor that hospitality contexts require. Constant attention and monitoring of the display of emotions takes a particularly heavy toll on employees who already are experiencing the stress of family and work conflict. The server who must remain pleasant while an unreasonable customer complains about the food, or the front desk employee who listens without becoming defensive to a verbally abusive guest, expend a great deal of energy on the job. When they return home to an elderly parent or to a spouse who anticipates their full support and attention, balance may be particularly difficult to achieve.

In addition, hospitality environments can be characterized as "sexualized" (Gutek, Cohen, & Konrad, 1990). The nature of work in the hospitality industry is likely to take employees into settings traditionally associated with gender-linked behavior–bars, bedrooms, and lounges. Many employees work in close proximity to one another on long and irregular shifts, often including evening and night time hours. Kitchens, in particular, have been identified as arenas where sexual overtures such as pats on the bottom, winks, and terms of endearment are commonplace. In addition, men and women are often hired, in part, because of out-going personalities and physical attractiveness. In many instances, required dress or uniform also accentuates gender stereotyping and sexuality. This combination of work environment and personal characteristics makes hospitality employees' work experience unlike any other (Ostroff, 1993).

Financial concerns are also key for employees with family responsibilities. Wages in hospitality organizations, particularly for hourly employees, are generally below those found in other types of industries. This makes expenses associated with child care and other family necessities particularly stressful. Promotions and the accompanying raise in pay for hospitality employees, more than for those in other service sectors, are likely to require relocation. Advancement often means leaving familiar towns, schools, and relatives to move across the country to a property that offers increased job opportunity. It is not unusual for an individual to move three or more times on the path from department head to general manager. The adjustments required on each relocation are difficult for an individual, but can be especially disruptive to families (Fierman, 1990; Barker, 1995; Glasgow, 1995; Lorenzini, 1994).

Over the last few years gender issues in the hospitality industry also have been addressed. Women traditionally have assumed substantial family responsibilities such as child care and household chores. Consequently, the hospitality literature throughout the 1970s and 1980s often focused on the challenges they confronted in balancing home and careers as they entered the workplace (Lobel, 1991; Snyder, 1993; Williams & Hunter, 1992).

One recurring concern for women in hospitality management has been the difficulty in developing work-related social networks. Informal work-related conversations often take place in contexts that are difficult or inappropriate for women, preventing them from establishing the relationships necessary to gain credibility or to close important deals. Upwardly mobile employees spend longer hours at the office, meet late in the afternoon, and socialize on the golf course or during happy hours after work (Mann, 1989, 1995; Brownell, 1993b; Duarte, 1992; Ibarra, 1993). While such practices make it difficult for all those who must balance their work and their family, they make it particularly challenging for women with significant family responsibilities to compete for recognition and promotions.

Employees realize that there are opportunities for them to advance in this rapidly growing industry, but they often feel that the requirements–long hours, stress, loss of quality time with their families–are not worth the potential benefits of a hospitality career. They recognize opportunities for success, but they are beginning to ask, "At what cost?"

The hospitality literature is now rich with first-hand accounts of men and women, at all levels, who have pursued careers while attending to family concerns (O'Dwyer, 1992; Stephens, 1992; Umbreit & Diaz, 1994; Withiam, 1992). From the owners of several Pizza Factory franchises (O'Neal, 1992) to the 1994 President of CMAA and Club Manager Norman Spitzig, Jr. (Finan, 1995), to women at the top (Brewton, 1994), the struggles inherent in work and family roles are vividly portrayed. And these work vs. family conflicts are not going away. Trends of the 21st century are likely to increase, not reduce, the work and family tensions that have been building for several decades.

TRENDS THAT AFFECT WORK AND FAMILY

A number of trends will bring their full force to bear on family and work relationships within the next decade. Among them are demographic shifts such as increasing numbers of women in the workforce, dual career and single parent families, and a growing number of workers who are responsible for the care of an elderly relative. In addition, increasing diversity, the globalization of the industry, and technological advances will affect the nature of the hospitality work environment and the types of accommodation that will need to be made to ensure balanced lives for all employees.

The number of women in the workplace in general, and the hospitality workforce in particular, is increasing steadily. The 1990 Bureau of Labor Statistics report indicated that well over half of the hospitality workforce was female. That number will continue to rise. By the year 2000, it is projected that seventy-five percent of all families will be dual career. As women become more successful in their professions, working fathers will have a greater interest in making it easier for their wives to balance work and family life (Thornburg, 1993; Smith, 1990).

It would be misleading, however, to assume that family and work balance is a woman's concern. Kelly and Kelly (1994) report that eight out of ten employees would choose a position that provides time for their families over fast-tracked career advancement or better salaries. Over half of all men typically report that they experience family and job conflict. The problem, several authors propose, is that organizational cultures have traditionally discouraged men from voicing their concerns or acknowledging the stress they experience from work and family conflicts. As Schachner (1991) notes, no longer is it appropriate to talk of a "mommy track";

what progressive companies must now consider is a "parent track" (p. 3). The problems of making time for family responsibilities are especially profound for the increasing numbers of single parents in the hospitality workforce.

While working Americans have always looked ahead at managing relationships that affect their spouse and their children, new demographics now require them to look back as they become primary care givers to their parents as well. The number of those in mid-career who must be concerned with the welfare of an aging family member is increasing steadily (Umbreit & Diaz, 1994). The costs of managing family relationships across generations makes home life particularly stressful for those in the middle.

As employees work longer, and as retired workers reenter the workforce, attention to life stages is a particularly critical concern. Although single parents, teenagers, and the elderly may work side-by-side, their personal needs may vary dramatically. While a mother of infants may value flexible time so that child care needs can be met, the father of a high school senior is more likely to seek additional compensation to pay for anticipated college expenses. Older workers may place more emphasis on working conditions, seeking jobs that provide comfort and a healthy work environment. In addition, diversity will continue to characterize the hospitality workforce. Organizations will need to reexamine their policies with regard to ethnic groups, women, employees with disabilities, and others with special needs.

The trend toward globalization also has consequences for families as they are forced to relocate in foreign environments. The added stress and expense of establishing a home in another culture can be devastating to couples or families who are willing, but may find themselves unable, to adjust to drastic changes in lifestyle. Yet, the globalization of the hospitality industry increases the likelihood that an employee's professional success will require relocation abroad. The impact of this movement on families is significant.

Finally, increasing technology plays a role in organizational flexibility and in the company's ability to respond to employee requirements. While in some instances such advances may depersonalize the organizational environment, computerized workstations and other developments make new options available to those who require alternative work routines and more flexible work schedules. The need for all employees to work long hours or at a particular workstation is reduced; a variety of tasks may be performed at home when computers are linked and employees are on line. Work can more easily be shared when databases are established and readily accessed. Although guest contact will remain a critical aspect of service delivery, an increasing number of functions in the hospitality industry will likely be streamlined and automated. As the workplace becomes more complex and employees become more demanding, hospitality organizations find themselves under pressure to respond to these growing needs and changes.

The Impact of Work/Family Issues on Organizations

Work and family conflict is unhealthy both for individuals and for their organizations. Paris (1992) reports that employee stress from balancing personal and work responsibilities is likely to result in substantially reduced performance as employees suffer the consequences of anxiety and depression. As Moskel (1995) notes, "We're the only country where . . . having a baby creates so much stress" (p. 45). As we reach the point where over eleven million children under the age of six have mothers in the workforce, and where each employee with a child under thirteen misses an average of eight days each year due to child care problems (O'Connell & Bloom, 1987), family balance is becoming one of the most critical issues of the twenty-first century. As Sandroff (1989) put it, the entrance of thousands of women into the workforce cannot be treated as a "little blip on the horizon" (131).

Family problems that become workplace problems are threats to a company's competitiveness and profitability. While organizations may talk of sensitivity to employee needs, no company is likely to ignore its bottom line. Data from surveys (Paris, 1990) repeatedly lead researchers to conclude that the difficulties faced in managing personal and work responsibilities frequently result in reduced performance. Family and career balancing is particularly stressful when:

a. The time in one role makes it difficult or impossible to fulfill requirements of the other role.
b. Fatigue from participation in one role makes it difficult to fulfill the responsibilities of the other role.
c. Behaviors required in one setting are completely different from those required in the other situation (Milkovich & Boudreau, 1991).

Although recent reports (Paris, 1990) indicate that employers remain unwilling to assume primary responsibility for assisting workers with managing family responsibilities, progressive organizations are beginning to understand the strong link between work/family balance and productivity. Organizations of the future are likely to discover that their competitive edge is not in salary or facilities, but in their responsiveness to the growing emphasis on family concerns (Baum, 1991; O'Connell & Bloom, 1987). As employee values change, so must organizational policies and practices.

INNOVATIONS TO CREATE WORK/FAMILY BALANCE

Efforts to assist employees in establishing and maintaining work and family balance are characterized by two themes. The first is a rethinking of the nature of work and the creation of innovative options for employees with family commitments. The second is an increase in the employee's ability to control those factors that affect family and work balance. Increasingly, organizational policies are being developed that delegate more responsibility to individuals for the management of their work life, and give them greater freedom and flexibility in choosing the way in which their work is accomplished.

During the past decade, progress toward family-friendly policies in the United States has been made at both the governmental and organizational levels. Twenty-seven states have enacted family or parental leave laws. Companies with family leave policies report lower absenteeism and reduced turnover (Caro, 1992; Mason, 1993; Gatton, 1994). As Vest and Mermen (1992) suggest, organizations must begin to acknowledge the manner in which both men and women prioritize work-related attributes. It seems evident that hospitality companies that move into the 21st century with a competitive advantage will be bringing with them fundamental values of equity and quality of life.

Human resource managers can rise to new challenges by developing and implementing work policies that address family needs (Brislin, 1992). Those employers who have offered such support report that they are satisfied that these policies are effective tools in the recruitment and retention of employees, in reducing employee stress, and in reducing absenteeism (Paris, 1990). Accommodations and policies reflect the growing emphasis on flexibility and responsiveness to individual needs toward the goal of increasing quality of life. Such options include:

- *Flextime:* Employees are required to be present for a specified core period, but the remainder of required hours may be scheduled to accommodate personal needs such as child care or appointments.
- *Part time:* Those with family responsibilities may opt to work less during certain periods of their professional careers.
- *Job sharing:* A type of part time work where two employees combine efforts to fulfill the responsibilities of one position.

- *Eldercare:* Time off to attend to the needs of parents and aging family members is perceived as a legitimate request.
- *Family leave:* Policies that make it possible to take time off from work to attend to pressing family issues with minimum negative impact on the individual's established career.
- *Compressed workweek:* Options that allow the employee to work the same number of hours in longer periods, as in electing to work four ten-hour days rather than five eight-hour days.
- *Home work:* Accommodations are made for employees to do a portion of their work at home.
- *Day care assistance:* Organizations assist with day care, either by offering it on-site or by sponsoring this service to make the care of children less stressful for employees.
- *Married unaccompanied policy:* A company pays a lump sum to cover trips to visit the spouse if family members are left at home while the employee works abroad.

Although hospitality organizations have not consistently been on the cutting edge of developing and implementing family-friendly policies, there has been significant recent response to employees' need for a more sensitive and responsive workplace. Two particularly vivid examples of how the hospitality industry has taken initiative in recognizing employees' need for work and family balance are the efforts of Marriott and Choice Hotels.

Under the leadership of Donna Klein, Director of Work and Family Programs for Marriott, the Central Atlanta Hospitality Childcare, Inc., is creating a large child care facility to meet the needs of nearly 2,000 hotel employees. This nonprofit consortium has been described as a family services center; its features include computer instruction, shared mealtimes, a get well facility for ill children, and parent/child aerobics classes (Wagner, 1994).

In similar efforts to accommodate the needs of those with families, Choice Hotels International created a "sick bank" which allows hospitality workers who have used all of their sick leave to tap into time off donated by other employees. In addition, Choice now allows a full time employee to apply for a leave of absence after he or she has been employed with the company for just thirty days.

Other examples of hospitality organizations that have listened to employees' family concerns, and then made accommodations, include Hampton Inns, a company that has reexamined and broadened its personal, medical, and maternity leave policies. The Opryland Hotel in Nashville, Tennessee, runs a day care center that accommodates infants of six weeks as well as older children. Sliding scale payment for Opryland employees further assists in providing a family-sensitive service.

In his discussion of how hospitality organizations have responded to the growing need for work and family balance, Caro (1992) cites Holiday Inn Worldwide, Handlery Hotel in San Francisco, the Equinox Hotel in Vermont, and Hospitality Franchise Systems as examples of large and small organizations that are making significant gains in providing benefits that address the needs of the growing number of employees concerned with family issues.

Obstacles to Change

> When people came to work and said, "We've got automobiles," employers said, "Oh, we've got to build some parking lots." When Americans became diet-conscious, company cafeterias added salad bars. So why . . . have companies been slow to accommodate the family needs of the two-career couples who have flooded the work force over the past 15 years?
>
> –Sandroff, 1989, 126

Whatever the visible efforts, key concerns remain regarding the bottom line impact and the lasting effects of family-friendly policies. Martin (1988) has criticized such programs for their lack of integration, and has described the majority of change efforts as "piecemeal." He notes that, too often, no accompanying shift is made in management philosophy or in decision-making models; hence, there is little organizational support for these new initiatives. In addition, it is frequently the case that middle managers and line supervisors are not involved in the change effort, and consequently are unwilling or unable to communicate policies effectively or to implement initiatives in a holistic fashion.

Another significant obstacle to change is the strong preference within the hospitality industry for face time. As Mason (1992) explains, the prevailing assumption is that ". . . if you are present at work for 40 hours a week, at your desk shuffling papers, you are accomplishing work" (p. 8). The key message that must be communicated is difficult to convey: Productivity, and hours present on the job, are not the same. In fact, several research reports indicate that flexible arrangements positively affect productivity, morale, and employee retention (Catalyst, 1993).

In addition, hospitality leaders need to understand that individuals alter their priorities through various life stages. Employers must make it possible for talented employees to leave the fast-track for intervals and then return when they are prepared to resume the intensity required to achieve professional advancement. Basic assumptions about the nature of work and how it is accomplished must be adjusted to keep pace with the needs of a new workforce which is reluctant, or unwilling, to sacrifice family for career success.

CREATING TOMORROW'S ORGANIZATIONS: A PARTNERSHIP

There is general agreement that the first step in creating responsive organizations is to recognize that the move toward balance requires a fundamental change in the mind set and basic assumptions about the workplace (Mason, 1992). Although policies are important, they are the easy first step in a long and complicated change process. Educators and hospitality leaders alike have an important role in facilitating the attitudes and practices that will result in greater work and family balance for service employees (Box 1).

Educators set the groundwork for change. The future generation of hospitality managers is in today's classroom, and educators need to take advantage of the opportunity to influence tomorrow's organizational policies and practices. In addition to providing a sound background in human

---

Box 1

Educators and Leaders as Change Agents

Educators Foster:

　　Innovation
　　Empathy
　　Effective Listening
　　Flexibility
　　Problem-Solving Skills

Hospitality Leader Practices:

　　Communicate Vision
　　Role Model Attitudes and Values
　　Develop Organizational Policies
　　Ensure Policies and Practices Support Values

---

resources management, educators must encourage innovation and instill empathy for employees who have special needs. Solutions to family and work issues require "out of the box" thinking as managers confront employees who have multiple needs. No one solution can accommodate the variety of issues that arise as the workforce becomes more diverse and more demanding. In addition, future hospitality professionals will benefit from an education that teaches them to recognize and value multiple perspectives. Effective leaders will be careful listeners, characterized by their open-mindedness and problem-solving skills.

To manage effectively in the new work environment, hospitality leaders must "walk the talk"; they must model key attitudes and behaviors. Tomorrow's leaders also need to have a clear vision of the kind of organization they want to create and the core values that distinguish it from earlier models. Before the hospitality industry can move ahead on family and work issues, values such as respect for individual differences, acknowledgment of the importance of both physical and mental health, and acceptance of innovative practices must be embedded in the organizational culture. This is a leadership challenge.

As in any change effort, organizational strategies must be carefully developed. Such strategies must not only include the introduction of family-friendly policies, but must also identify the means by which family and work balance can be supported on a daily basis. All levels of management must share a concern for creating work environments where flexibility and accommodation are regular practices. This may require new ways of measuring performance and new configurations of job responsibilities.

Hospitality leaders must take seriously the need to address family and work issues as they strive to create high performing organizations. Human resources are an organization's competitive advantage, an advantage that will be lost by those unwilling to confront new values and paradigms for understanding the nature of work. As hospitality professionals in the most successful organizations anticipate their futures, they will envision standing among family members, looking forward to spending quality time with loved ones while simultaneously pursuing their careers with commitment and enthusiasm.

AUTHOR NOTE

Judi Brownell teaches graduate and undergraduate courses in organizational and managerial communication and participates regularly in executive education. Professor Brownell has designed and conducted training seminars for a wide range of hospitality, educational, and other work organizations on such topics as: quality customer service, communication skills for women in management, effective listening, conflict management, teambuilding and leadership, performance appraisals, business writing, and presentational speaking. Current research includes studies related to the communication of service quality, the career challenges women hospitality managers confront, and the mentoring practices of senior level managers. Professor Brownell has also identified the key components of managerial listening behavior and has completed a comprehensive survey exploring the specific communication practices of middle and upper-level hospitality managers. She is now studying the implementation of total quality management programs and is designing a model of the communication of service values throughout a hospitality organization and how it relates to employee decision-making and performance. Dr. Brownell is author of several business and communication texts, including *Organizational Communication and Behavior: Communicating for Improved Performance* (Holt, Rinehart, and Winston, 1989), and *Listening: Principles, Attitudes, and Skills* (Allyn and Bacon, 1996). She has published over fifty articles in such journals as *The International Journal of Contemporary Hospitality Management, The Cornell Hotel & Restaurant Administration Quarterly, The Hospitality & Tourism Educator, The International Journal of Hospitality Management, FIU Review, The Journal of Management Education, Communication Education, The Journal of Business Communication, Communication Quarterly, Supervisory Management, Journal of the International Listening Association,* and *The Journal of Business Education.* Professor Brownell serves on the editorial boards of five professional journals.

REFERENCES

Ashforth, B. E. & Humphrey, R. H. (1993). Emotional labor in service roles: The influence of identity. *Academy of Management Review, 18*(1), 88-115.

Ashforth, B. E., & Humphrey, R. H. (1993). Emotional labor in service roles: The influence of identity. *Academy of Management Review, 18*(1), 88-115.

Barker, J. (1995). Family ties. *Incentive*, Performance Supplement, 18-23.

Baum, H. S. (1991). Creating a family in the workplace. *Human Relations, 44*(11), 1137-1159.

Brewton, S. (1994). Taking care of businesswomen. *ASTA Agency Management, 63*(11), 32+.

Brislin, J. A. (1992). Resolving employee benefit administration with family-friendly work policies. *Employee Benefits Journal, 17*(4), 5-10.

Brownell, J. (1994). Women in hospitality management: General managers' perceptions of factors related to career development. *International Journal of Hospitality Management, 13*(2), 101-117.

Brownell, J. (1993a). Women hospitality managers: Perceptions of gender-related career challenges. *FIU Hospitality Review, 11*(2), 19-31.

Brownell, J. (1993b). Addressing career challenges faced by women in hospitality management. *Hospitality & Tourism Educator, 5*(4), 11-15.

Campbell, K. E. (1988). Gender in job-related networks. *Work and Occupations, 15*(2), 179-200.

Caro, M. R. (1992). Family leave is not going away. *Lodging Magazine, 18*(4), 28-31.

Duarte, A. (1992). Trends: Women execs go for the greens: More women professionals are taking up golf to boost their climb up the corporate ladder. *Meetings & Conventions, 27*(8), 32-33+.

Fierman, J. (1990, July 30). Why women still don't hit the top. *Fortune,* 40-62.

Finan, T. (1995). Family Man. *Club Management, 74*(2), 42-44+.

Fulford, M. D., & Herrick, A. T. (1994). Women at work in hospitality: Fair notice for the nineties. *Hospitality Tourism Educator, 6*(4), 25-28.

Gaston, J. R. (1994). The family and medical leave act of 1993. *Bottomline, 9*(5), 24-27.

Glasgow, F. (1995). Mobility matters. *Resident Abroad,* 20-23.

Gregg, J. B., & Johnson, P. M. (1990). Perceptions of discrimination among women as managers in hospitality organizations. *FIU Hospitality Review, 8*(1), 10-22.

Gutek, B. A., Cohen, A. G., & Konrad, A. M. (1990). Predicting social-sexual behavior at work: A contact hypothesis. *Academy of Management Journal, 33*(3), 560-577.

Ibarra, H. (1993). Personal networks of women and minorities in management: A conceptual framework. *Academy of Management Review, 18*(1), 56-87.

Kelly, J. R., & Kelly, J. R. (1994). Multiple dimensions of meaning in the domains of work, family, and leisure. *Journal of Leisure Research, 26*(3), 250-274.

Lobel, S. A. (1991). Allocation of investment in work and family roles: Alternative theories and implications for research. *Academy of Management Review, 16*(3), 507-521.

Lobel, S. A., & St. Clair, L. (1992). Effects of family responsibilities, gender, and career identity salience on performance outcomes. *Academy of Management Journal, 35*(5), 1057-1069.

Lorenzini, B. (1994). Marketing & mobility = magic. *Restaurant & Institutions, 104*(17), 48+.

Mann, S. (1995). Politics and power in organizations: Why women lose out. *Leadership & Organization Development Journal, 16*(2), 9-15.

Mann, B. C. (1989). Networking in the '90s: Managers share their communication strategies. *Club Management,* 23-26.

Martin, A. W. (1988). Work restructuring in the 1990s. *ILR Report,* March, 6-11.

Mason, J. C. (1993). Publication promotes sharing of work-family policies. *HR Focus, 7*(2), 10.

Mason, J. C. (1992). Flexing more than muscle: Employees want time on their side. *Management Review, 81*(3), 6-9.

Milkovick, G. T., & Boudreau, J. W. (1991). *Human resource management.* Boston: Richard Irwin, Co.

Moskal, B. S. (1995). Promotions: Who gets them and why. *Industry Week, 244*(5), 44-47.

O'Connell, M. & Bloom, D. (1987). *Juggling jobs and babies: America's child care challenge.* Washington, DC: Population Reference Bureau, 1-54.

O'Dwyer, C. (1992). Special report: Opening doors and minds. *Lodging Magazine, 17*(9), 12-15.

O'Neal, T. (Sept 1992). Sandy Ollenberger: Full-time mother and full-time pizza operator. *Pizza Today, 10*(9), 16-18.

Ostroff, C. (1993). Relationships between person-environment congruence and organizational effectiveness. *Group & Organization Management, 18*(1), 103-122.

Paris, H. (1990). Balancing work and family responsibilities: Canadian employer and employee viewpoints. *Human Resource Planning, 13*(2), 147-157.

Sandroff, R. (1989). Why pro-family policies are good for business and America. *Working Woman, 14*(11), 126-131.

Schachner, M. (1991). Work/family benefits grow slowly. *Business Insurance, 25*(47), 3, 12-13.

Smith, M. T. (Jan 1990). Work and family: Fighting to have it all. *Money, 19*(1), 130-135.

Snyder, R. A. (1993). The glass ceiling for women: Things that don't cause it and things that won't break it. *Human Resource Development Quarterly, 4*(1), 97-107.

Stephens, B. (1992). Take that! *Food Arts, 5*(7), 34-38.

Thornburg, L. (1993). Workplace couples face mixed reactions. *HR Magazine, 38*(6), 43-46.

Umbreit, W. T., & Diaz, P. E. (1994). Women in hospitality management: An exploratory study of major and occupation choice variables, *Hospitality Tourism Educator, 6*(4), 7-9.

Vallelian, M. (1995). Still a rare breed: Moss Murray investigates how women fare in the quest for GM status. *European Hotelier,* 28-29.

Wagner, G. (1994). For Atlanta hotels, family is bottom line. *Lodging Hospitality, 50*(6), 10.

Williams, P. W., & Hunter, M. (1992). Supervisory hotel employee perceptions of management careers and professional development requirements. *International Journal of Hospitality Management, 11*(4), 347-358.

Withiam, G. (1992). A crack in the ceiling: Sills named president of colony resorts. *Cornell Hotel and Restaurant Administration Quarterly, 33*(1), 9.

African-American Women, Family and Hospitality Work

Angela L. Farrar
LaVerne Gyant

SUMMARY. Because of African-American women's overrepresentation in several hospitality-related occupations, hospitality research is uniquely positioned to make a significant contribution to understanding African-American women's work. This paper describes African-American women's participation as employees, managers, and entrepreneurs in the hospitality industry, as well as the multiple roles African-American families play in relationship to African-American women's domestic and hospitality work. *[Article copies available for a fee from The Haworth Document Delivery Service: 1-800-342-9678. E-mail address: getinfo@haworthpressinc.com]*

Angela L. Farrar completed the PhD in Hospitality and Tourism Management at Virginia Polytechnic Institute and State University. She is Assistant Professor in the School of Hotel, Restaurant, and Recreation Management at The Pennsylvania State University. Her research interests are in the racialization and gendering of hospitality management and education. Correspondence should be addressed to Angela L. Farrar at 201 Mateer, University Park, PA 16802-1307. LaVerne Gyant is currently Assistant Director of the Center for Black Studies and Assistant Professor of Adult continuing education at Northern Illinois University. She received both her master's and doctorate from the Pennsylvania State University. Her research interests include Africana women's studies and the participation and contributions of Blacks to adult education. She has published in the *Journal of Black Studies* and served as co-editor of *Threshold in Education*.

[Haworth co-indexing entry note]: "African-American Women, Family and Hospitality Work." Farrar, Angela L., and LaVerne Gyant. Co-published simultaneously in *Marriage & Family Review* (The Haworth Press, Inc.) Vol. 28, No. 1/2, 1998, pp. 125-141; and: *The Role of the Hospitality Industry in the Lives of Individuals and Families* (ed: Pamela R. Cummings, Francis A. Kwansa, and Marvin B. Sussman) The Haworth Press, Inc., 1998, pp. 125-141. Single or multiple copies of this article are available for a fee from The Haworth Document Delivery Service [1-800-342-9678, 9:00 a.m. - 5:00 p.m. (EST). E-mail address: getinfo@haworthpressinc.com].

125

KEYWORDS. Domestic service, Families, Tradition, Labor force, Entrepreneur

For almost four hundred years, domestic and commercial service work have been the predominant occupations for African-American women. However, the research on African-American women in these service occupations is relatively new, and in the case of hospitality service work, quite limited. By focusing only on either women or minorities, hospitality scholars and journalists have continually and consistently omitted African-American women, giving the appearance that *All the women are white, all the blacks are men* . . . (Hull, Scott, & Smith, 1982). With the exception of Cobble's (1991) historical description of African-American women's marginalized participation in hospitality labor movements, the work that has been done in this area seldom mentions the race of women included in discussions (e.g., Diaz & Umbreit, 1995; Garey, 1995) or in samples (for example, Brownell, 1993; Fernsten, Lowry, Enghagen, & Hott, 1988; Garey, 1996; Gregg & Johnson, 1990; Laudadio, 1988). Betters-Reed and Moore (1992a, 1992b) label this omission of African-American women from both management theory and practice the "whitewash dilemma, which has primarily evolved from an Anglo-American perspective" (1992a, p. 31). These omissions totally obscure the ways race differentially constructs the experiences of African-American and European-American women. While all women experience sexism and gender discrimination in domestic (Katzman, 1978) and hospitality service work (Brownell, 1993; Christensen, 1993), these experiences are qualitatively different for African-American and other women of color, who are also subjected to racism and racial discrimination (Dill, 1994; Farrar, 1996a; Howe, 1977; Romero, 1992).

Because of African-American women's overrepresentation in several hospitality and other service-related occupations (Brewer, 1993; Hacker, 1992), hospitality research is uniquely positioned to make a significant contribution to understanding African-American women's work. Additionally, all facets of the "multitiered system of employment" (Malveaux, 1986, p. 8) that characterize African-American women's work are represented in the hospitality industry, from managers in both traditional fields such as housekeeping and nontraditional jobs, including general management of entire hotel properties, to service workers, some of whom revolve between work and welfare. Focusing on African-American women in domestic and hospitality service work provides the opportunity to study the complex nature of phenomena which are generally studied in isolation: the public and private spheres; work and family; race, class, and gender.

Such a holistic, interactive approach allows us to more realistically study African-American women's lives in all their complexity. Finally, studying African-American women and their service work allows us to better understand the work of women and men of all races and classes, by adding another piece to the complex puzzle of interlocking relationships among race, class, and gender (Glenn, 1992; Zinn & Dill, 1994). Therefore, this paper has two purposes: (1) to describe the multiple roles–motivation, support, teachers, and sometimes employer-/organizationally-constructed barrier–African-American families play in relationship to African-American women's work; and (2) to describe the history of African-American women's work first in domestic service and their transition to being employees, managers, and entrepreneurs in the hospitality industry.

DOMESTIC AND HOSPITALITY SERVICE AS REPRODUCTIVE LABOR

Throughout history African-American women have worked in two interrelated spheres–one centered in their own private homes and communities, the other, the public world of paid or slave labor. African-American women have used these two spheres to nurture and advance the interests and well-being of their families and communities. While work in the private sphere was done for and most often earned African-American women the respect of their families and communities, work in the public sphere reinforced their subordinate status as women and as African-Americans (Jones, 1985). In both spheres, African-American women have traditionally performed the labor of social reproduction.

Glenn (1992) defines social reproduction as "the creation and re-creation of people as cultural and social, as well as physical, beings. . . . It involves mental, emotional, and manual labor" (p. 4). Food preparation, food service, and cleaning in the private homes of others (domestic service work) and in hotels, restaurants, and institutions (hospitality service work) are examples of public social reproductive labor. In a definition that is surprisingly similar to Glenn's (1992) definition of public social reproduction, Fisher and Bernstein (1991) describe the hospitality industry as being in the business of "the care and feeding of people who are away from home, . . . [by] providing facilities, food, and services to enhance the well-being of others" (p. 1).

Within the conceptual framework of social reproductive labor, we begin by discussing an integral part of African-American women's work experience: the multiple, interactive roles played by their families and communities. Next we turn our attention to the historical evolution from domestic service work, the earliest form of work that was widely available to African-American women, to African-American women's hospitality service work.

AFRICAN-AMERICAN WOMEN'S FAMILIES AND WORK

Franklin (1988) notes that within the African-American community "the family is one of the strongest and most important traditions" (p. 23). Despite obstacles, the African-American family has been a source of strength. It is viewed as an "institution of social solidarity and psychological security" which has served as "the underlying strength in the Black struggle for liberation and human dignity" (Nobles, 1974, p. 12). Contrary to the traditional mainstream view of inevitable conflict women face between their families and work, African-American families and communities have often served as a source of motivation, strength, support, and resistance against racial oppression for African-American women. At other times, the family has been transformed into a socially-constructed barrier to African-American women's workforce participation.

Providing financially for her family is often an African-American woman's primary motivation for working outside the home, regardless of marital status. Because of African-American men's limited employment opportunities, African-American women have a long tradition of working, and in many families they have been the only breadwinner (Collins, 1990; Lerner, 1992; Marks, 1993). As such they have often been faced with the total responsibility for meeting the family's physical, emotional, and financial needs (Jones, 1985; Lewis, 1989; Spaights & Whitaker, 1995). The income African-American women earned as domestic service workers allowed them to feed and clothe their children, to buy a house, to provide for college education, and to sustain their families in emergencies. Woodson (1930) stated

> men and children were fed and clothed with the earnings of the wife and mother who held her own in competition with others. Fortunate was the boy or girl who had a mother with the devotion which impelled her to give her life for the happiness of the less fortunate member of her indigent group. (p. 272)

By applying aspects of traditional African family life, which are centered around the principles of survival of the family and the Oneness of Being (Nobles, 1974), within the context of slavery and later oppression, African-American women and their families have survived, and in many cases thrived. Two such survival strategies have been interchangeable gender roles and flexible family structures (Nobles, 1974; Hill, 1972). This interchangeability and flexibility have made it possible for African-American women to meet the demands of home, work, community, and other responsibilities. Nobles (1974) and Staples (1973) noted that while the African-American woman has been a source of strength for the family, the critical issue within the family "is not whether it's female-headed or male-headed, but whether the survival of the family was maintained" (Nobles, 1974, p. 13).

Despite the belief that the African-American family was destroyed by slavery, they "have achieved a level of stability based on role integration. Males shared equally in the rearing of children–women participated in the defense of the family" (Staples & Johnson, 1993, p. 17). Even though employment for African-American men was limited and restricted, this did not stop them from seeking ways to provide for their families. Staples (1978), Nobles (1974), and Staples and Johnson (1993) found that many African-American fathers share in meeting family obligations. Their effort to maintain the family was evidenced by the commitment husbands and wives made to provide, care, support, and encourage each other and their children (Franklin, 1988; Nobles, 1974; Frazier, 1966).

In keeping the family and community together, African-American women have managed multiple roles–protector, provider, disciplinarian, homemaker, wife, mother (Jones, 1985; Lerner, 1992; Spaights & Whitaker, 1995). Managing these multiple roles has been difficult, but support provided through flexible family structures, along with the knowledge that these roles are necessary in the struggle for survival and equality has inspired African-American women. Lewis (1989) and Farrar (1996a) note that the sources of support working women receive include their partners, extended family, friends, and religion.

This trend continues today among African-American women who work in hospitality. For example, Darcus, an African-American woman who is a general manager at a corporate-owned, limited-service hotel property of a national chain describes how her family has helped her raise her daughter throughout a career that has included several re-locations because her employing organization requires that managers stay at the same property no longer than 18 months.

> One day [my daughter] asked me, what I would do if I got a promotion. I reminded her of my promise [that I wouldn't move until she graduates. That's five years from now]. She said it would be okay if we moved. Family and friends have made it work because they help out a lot. (quoted in Farrar, 1996b)

For many African-American women the extended family–grandparents, aunts and uncles, friends, and community–has served as a supportive force, whether they shared the same residence or lived nearby (Staples & Johnson, 1993). Via the extended family, African-American women have been able to work long hours while their children stayed with relatives, including the father, and/or friends. These support networks provide material and emotional assistance, thus allowing them to relieve some of the emotional and economic strains "associated with providing the basic necessities of food, shelter, and clothing" (Lewis, 1989). Historically, support was sometimes provided by older children who were responsible for the welfare of their brothers and sisters or who worked to supplement the family income. As one mother noted, "For two years my oldest child . . . has helped toward our support by taking in a little washing at home . . . For six months my youngest child . . . has been nursing and she receives $1.50 per week" ("More slavery," 1912, p. 198).

Despite the positive impact families play in relation to African-American women's work, European-American employers have often viewed African-American women's attempts to maintain their families and communities as political acts of protest (Jones, 1985). Because African-American women domestic service workers contributed much to the maintenance of European-Americans' families, European-Americans who employed domestic workers sometimes saw their employees' responsibilities to their families as an interruption of the employers' own economic and social welfare. Yet, African-American women viewed their actions as form of resistance, a way to "deprive European-Americans of full control over them as field laborers [and] domestic servants" (Jones, 1985, pp. 12-13). For example, African-American women often viewed the tasks they performed for European-American employers as being menial, while the employers often viewed the African-American women as being careless in their job performance. When the same task was done for her family and her community, her accomplishment received praise for the skillful, concerned, and generous way in which she completed it. As May Anna Madison, a domestic service worker describes,

> Now, they didn't work any harder for the white woman. As a matter of fact, they didn't work as hard for white people as they did for themselves. But when we worked for ourselves, everybody did what [s]he could do best and nobody bothered you. (Gwaltney, 1980, p. 173)

Unlike their European-American counterparts, African-American women rarely had the choice of working at home instead of entering the labor force (Harrison, 1989). Economic necessity required that they work to support their families. However, for those who could afford not to accept paid labor outside the home, their decision to stay home was often a sign of resistance to dominant race and gender ideologies that suggested African-American women were being lazy while their European-American women counterparts were fulfilling their domestic duties (Giddings, 1984). European-American men and women often saw African-American women's decision to work at home as African-American women trying to usurp privileges to which only a select few were entitled. Many African-American women who did stay home took in laundry, sold produce, or worked as seamstresses in order to supplement the family income. These jobs allowed them to be home with their children and, in rural areas, to help their husbands tend the land.

African-American women, enslaved and freed, sought to make sure their children resisted "the ruling race's" (Giddings, 1984; Jones, 1985) attempt to destroy the integrity of the family. They taught their children how to avoid punishment, cooperate with others, and to have a strong sense of self-esteem and faith (Collins, 1990). Many domestic workers saw their work in domestic service as "the means to put [their] children through" (Dill, 1980, p. 107) high school and college, thereby assuring their children the upward mobility racism and unequal opportunity had not allowed earlier generations to achieve.

Like their enslaved mothers and grandmothers, domestic service workers spent little time with their families, not by choice, but by their employers' insistence. "I frequently work from fourteen to sixteen hours a day. I am compelled . . . to sleep in the house. I am allowed to go home to my children . . . only once in two weeks, every other Sunday afternoon–even then I'm not permitted to stay all night" ("More slavery," 1912, p. 196). Other women recall how they met their children at the park, grocery store, or had them sneak to their workplace for a visit. The time these mothers spent with their children was precious. It was during these few stolen hours that African-American women shared family history, caught up on the family and school activities, sewed and cooked for their own families, and if there was time, took them to church or some other social activities.

Spaights and Whitaker (1995) have noted that children of domestic service workers faced a number of problems–delinquency, truancy, and illness. Many of these problems were alleviated when the mother switched from live-in to part-time or day work. In some cases this did not alleviate the problem, because they still worked fourteen to sixteen hours, often leaving home early in the morning. In their efforts to make sure their children stayed in school, met their court dates, went to the doctor/clinic, or to take care of a family member, some women lost their jobs for excessive absences.

Similarly, the culture of the modern-day hospitality industry often causes the family to serve as an obstacle because geographic and career mobility are generally considered prerequisites for success as a hospitality manager. Much like the European-American women studied by Brownell (1993), a recent study of African-American and European-American women who are hotel managers, found that several African-American women are concerned that their employers view African-American women who are single-parents as an impediment to career advancement (Farrar, 1996a). This concern is most prominent among African-American women who would like to advance their careers by gaining assignments in international hotels, while they feel their employers' racialized misgivings limit them to only those countries that would be "willing to accept an African-American woman as a manager" (ibid.).

PRIVATE DOMESTIC SERVICE WORK

Women who did domestic service work often received low wages and minimal benefits. Their salary could range from two to ten dollars a week, depending on where and what their jobs involved. They could work anywhere from 40 hours to more than 80 hours a week, with no social security, compensation, retirement, health care, or vacation time (Lerner, 1992).

> You might as well say that I'm on duty all the time–from sunrise to sunset, everyday of the week. I am the slave, body, and soul . . . And what do I get for this work . . . The pitiful sum of ten dollars a month! . . . . With this money I'm expected to pay my house rent . . . and . . . to feed and clothe myself and three children. ("More slavery," 1912)

As recently as 1990, the minimum wage for domestic workers was as low as three dollars an hour (Spaights & Whitaker, 1995).

Working these long hours for such low pay, not having time with their families, not being able to attend church services or participate in community activities, and being harassed by their employers (Katzman, 1978; Shaw, 1996) made many African-American women dislike working in domestic service, but it was the only work open to them (Greene & Woodson, 1930). African-American women viewed these jobs as "dirty, tedious, low-paying [because] service lacked the rewards of self-satisfaction and pride that supposedly accompanied such tasks when performed for one's own family" (ibid.). They also viewed this type of work as another form of servitude. Lerner (1992, p. 127) explains that the low wages and poor working conditions "reflect not only the general vulnerability of female labor and of workers in the service industries to exploitative practices, but are specific results of race prejudice."

One example of such racialized and gendered employment practices is that many African-American women who had been trained as typists or teachers could not find jobs for which they had been trained and were forced to take domestic service work (Dill, 1980). With this in mind, many parents did what was necessary to make sure their children, especially their daughters, obtained a good education. For it was the daughters who "would have to work all or most of their lives" and parents hoped they would "escape the unskilled, service job trap by getting a professional education" (Lerner, 1992, p. 220).

Out of the Frying Pan and into the Fryer: The Transition from Domestic Service to Hospitality Service

For these, among other reasons, the number of African-American women employed in domestic service work has consistently declined from approximately 1,010,336 in 1910 (U. S. Bureau of the Census, 1914) to an estimated 138,071 in 1990 (U. S. Bureau of the Census, 1992). Comparatively, the number of African-American women employed in hospitality service work–which for the purposes of this discussion includes bartenders, waitpersons, cooks, food counter, fountain and related occupations, maids, baggage porters and bellhops and their supervisors–increased from 7,451 to 542,477 during the same era (U. S. Bureau of the Census, 1914, 1992).

The work performed by African-American women in the hospitality industry parallels their traditional duties in domestic service. There is, however, one major difference: while domestic service is confined to private households, contemporary reproductive labor has been commodified and institutionalized in the hospitality industry (Braverman, 1974; Glenn, 1992). Similar work, different setting, different location, but the treatment of African-American women still parallels racial, gender, and class relationships of domination reminiscent of domestic work (Collins, 1990).

Some African-American women had to take jobs as domestics or in commercial service work, because they had limited education, because their husbands were working minimal hours or not at all or because of discriminatory employment practices:

> Both during and after the [second world] war, Black women entered the female urban labor force in large numbers only to occupy its lowest rungs. Women who did work in these industries and got married generally quit their live-in domestic jobs and sought day work or something part-time. Largely excluded from clerical and sales work, the growth sectors of the female labor force, Black women found work primarily in service jobs outside the household and in unskilled blue-collar categories. (Tucker, 1988, p. 274)

Even though the positions African-American women held were marginal, there were and continue to be proportionately more of them employed in hospitality service occupations than in any other.

Entrepreneurship was one avenue for moving from domestic service work to hospitality service work. As a way of supplementing their income and spending more time with their families, African-American women often took in other work–such as laundry or sewing–or they started their own part-time businesses. During the 1830s African-American feminist activist Maria Stewart, the first American-born woman to give public speeches, advised African-American women to resist both racist and sexist oppression through economic independence.

> Do you ask what we can do? Unite and build a store of your own. . . . Do you ask where is the money? We have spent more than enough for nonsense. . . . We have never had an opportunity of displaying our talents; therefore the world thinks we know nothing. . . . Possess the spirit of men, bold and enterprising, fearless and undaunted. Sue for your rights and privileges. Know the reason that you cannot obtain them. Weary them with your importunities. (Loewenberg & Bogin, 1976, p. 189)

Even before Stewart's call for entrepreneurship, African-American women were using hospitality-related business enterprises to maintain and in some cases to free both their families and their communities. For instance, J. E. Bruce, a former slave, describes her mother's work as first a cook, and then as an entrepreneur.

> My mother was a slave . . . owned by Mayor Harvey Griffin. . . . After my father was sold my master gave my mother permission to work for herself, provided she gave him one half she worked for which she agreed to do. She then obtained a situation as cook in the largest tavern in the village. . . . She did not stay there long because the mean brute threatened to whip her in one of his drunken sprees. . . .

My mother worked in the garrison [of Fort Washington, Maryland] a while and then she carried on a little business for herself by selling pies, hot coffee, etc. to the Marines and exchanging the same for their rations. Her business increased and it became necessary that she should buy a horse and wagon to convey her goods to the fort, which she did. . . . My mother then got along very comfortably for about three years. . . . (Lerner, 1992, p. 33)

Later, in the 1850s, Mary Ellen Pleasant, a compatriot of John Brown, owned boarding-houses and restaurants primarily in California that catered to European-Americans while doubling as safe havens for runaway slaves (Dauphin, 1994). In discussing African-American women's work during the same period, Mossell (1988) states "As managers of the finest grade of hotels, they have been a marked success" (p. 24). One such success was Millie Ringold, who ran the first hotel in Yasoo, Montana, and "established an enviable reputation as a prospector . . ." (ibid.). The number of African-American women entrepreneurs continued to increase during Reconstruction (1865-1877), as recently freed African-Americans established inns, restaurants, and catering services.

During the great migrations of the late nineteenth century from the South to the southwest and Northern cities, some African-American women hired themselves out as cooks. One such example is Eliza, an "Exoduster," who during the 1880 Southern migration to Kansas left her family and community to serve as army cook to Elizabeth Custer: "Miss Libbie, you's always got the ginnel, but I hain't got nobody, and there ain't no picnics nor church sociables nor no burying out here" (Custer, 1890). Others, especially those in large northern cities, took in lodgers and ran rooming houses (Marks, 1993). Henri (1975) estimates that among African-American rooming house owners in the north, up to eighty percent were women heads of households.

Between 1867 and 1917, the total number of African-American enterprises increased from four thousand to fifty thousand. In 1918-1919, 6,369 restaurants, cafes, and lunchrooms, more than any other type of business enterprise, were owned by African-Americans (gender not specified). In the same period, 973 African-Americans listed their occupation as hotel keeper and manager, while 652 owned saloons (Work, 1919). Between 1929-1932, African-Americans owned 7,918 restaurants and eating places, second only to the 10,755 food stores owned by African-Americans (Work, 1938). From the late 1930s until the Civil Rights Act of 1964, African-American hotels, restaurants, and institutions served African-Americans when Jim/Jane Crow laws made it illegal for European-American establishments to do so. More recently, among African-American women entrepreneurs, the number one business owned is eating and drinking places. As of 1992, African-American women owned approximately 6,321 eating and drinking places and 757 hotels and lodging places (calculated using data from U.S. Department of Commerce, 1996a, 1996b).

RACIALIZATION AND GENDERING IN HOSPITALITY WORK

The terms racialization (Omi & Winant, 1986) and gendering (Acker, 1992) refer to the ways in which work (or any social phenomenon) comes to be differentiated, segregated, and stratified along race and gender lines. Some historical examples, including those presented above, as well as more recent research findings suggest that hospitality service work is both racialized and gendered. African-American women, like all women, have experienced sexual discrimination in employment. As African-Americans, they also experience racial discrimination. For example, when in 1922 the minimum wage in hotels, restaurants, and similar establishments in Washington, DC increased to $16.50 for a forty-eight hour week, "practically all of the hotels and restaurants immediately discharged Negro [*sic*] workers and took on white ones" (Haynes, 1923, p. 385). This wage increase combined with the growing number of European-American women entering the labor force, to a very large extent displaced African-American women. In addition to the "fashion culture" that demanded waitresses meet a European-American standard of beauty, Cobble (1991) describes the social conventions of the day that contributed to the racialization and gendering of hospitality work.

> Because of their sex, [B]lack women had been excluded from the waiting jobs in which [B]lack men had found acceptance–those in elegant hotels, trains, and other situations that catered to travelers and businessmen, did not require a homelike, informal, or intimate atmosphere and hence were more amenable to [B]lack and male personnel. Yet because of their race, they were at a disadvantage in competing for the new jobs opening up to [European-American] women. (p. 23)

Yet, many tend to believe African-American women have a double advantage in the work place. African-American (and Latina) women continue to rank lowest on the economic and social ladder (Kemp, 1994; Lerner, 1992), and several research studies have described ways in which African-American and European-American women's career outcomes and experiences differ. For example, Glenn (1992) describes the racialization of nursing through stratification between predominantly European-American registered nurses, licensed practical nurses and predominantly African-American nurses' aides. Similarly, Grossman (1980) points out that while the typical African-American domestic service worker is most likely a middle-aged woman cleaner, the average European-American woman domestic is a young child-care worker.

Data from the 1990 census suggest that the "ghettoization" (Benjamin, 1991) of African-American women continues as they are disproportionately represented among staff positions such as human resource management and marketing to minority clients or in back-of-the-house food preparation and cleaning jobs, a phenomenon also described in Farrar's (1996a) study of African-American and European-American women's hotel management careers. That study proposes that hotel management careers are racialized and gendered through African-American women's and European-American women's relationships to European-American men. These differential relationships provide the two groups of women with different resources at each stage of their careers and influence the way their superiors, who were predominantly European-American men, apply human resource practices. The differences in the career experiences of the women who participated in this study were largely a result of the women's different positions in relation to European-American men. These relationships to European-American men were significant as the women described these men as "having an inborn advantage in this industry" and as "running things" (Farrar, 1996a, p. 127).

CONCLUSION

For the good of their families and despite employers' disregard for their families, African-American women have a long and neglected history first as domestic service workers and later as employees, entrepreneurs, and managers in hospitality service work. African-American women's sacrifices and efforts to balance their responsibilities to family and community while working as domestic service workers and later as hospitality service workers, are a sign of strength, power, and courage. While a small number of African-American women have progressed from housekeeper to executive despite organizationally-constructed barriers, the majority have remained in the lowest rungs of the hospitality career ladder. We hope this paper has raised some issues that will cause employers to recognize and challenge the ways hospitality-industry cultural norms, which were built on gendered and racialized assumptions, adversely impact African-American women and their families.

In gathering materials for this paper, we struggled through historical documents, census data, and writings from several disciplines to locate information on African-American women's hospitality service work. As is true in the wider literature on women's work, race and class differences are seldom acknowledged and investigated. Until our hospitality management theory and practice acknowledge the gendered and racialized nature of hospitality service work (and research) as well as the interactive role of work and family, our research will be, at best partial, or at worst all wrong. We cannot clearly understand the whole of hospitality service work until we understand the experiences of all hospitality service workers. Given African-American women's significant participation in the hospitality industry, such research is crucial in providing hospitality corporations and practitioners insight to more effectively manage increasingly diverse owner, employee and consumer populations.

REFERENCES

Acker, J. (1992). Gendering organizational theory. In A. J. Mills & P. Tancred (Eds.), *Gendering organizational analysis* (pp. 248-260). Newbury Park, CA: Sage.

Aldridge, D. P. (1989). African American women in the economic marketplace, a continuing struggle. *Journal of Black Studies, 20*(20), 129-154.

Anderson, K. T. (1982). Last hired, first fired: Black women workers during World War II. *Journal of American History, LXIX*, 87-112.

Benjamin, L. (1991). *The Black elite: Facing the color line in the twilight of the twentieth century.* Chicago: Nelson-Hall.

Betters-Reed, B. L. & Moore, L. L. (1992a). Managing diversity: Focusing on women and the whitewash dilemma. In U. Sekaran and F. T. L. Leong (Eds.), *Womanpower: Managing in times of demographic turbulence.* Newbury Park, CA: Sage Publications.

Betters-Reed, B. L. & Moore, L. L. (1992b). The technicolor workplace. *Ms. 3*(3), 84-85.

Brewer, R. (1993). Theorizing race, class, and gender: The new scholarship of Black feminist intellectuals and Black women's labor. In S. J. James and A. P. A. Busia, Eds. *Theorizing Black Feminism: The visionary pragmatism of Black women*, 13-30. New York: Routledge.

Brownell, J. (1993). Addressing career challenges faced by women in hospitality management. *Hospitality and Tourism Educator, 5*(4), 11-15.

Christensen, J. (1993). The diversity dynamic: Implications for organizations in 2005. *Hospitality Research Journal, 17*(1), 69-86.

Cobble, D. S. (1991). *Dishing it out: Waitresses and their unions in the twentieth century.* Urbana, IL: University of Illinois Press.

Collins, P. H. (1990). *Black Feminist Thought: Knowledge, consciousness and the politics of empowerment.* London: Harper Collins Academic.

Custer, E. P. (1890). *Following the Guidon.* New York: Harper and Brothers.

Dauphin, G. (1994, January). Book marks. *Essence*, p. 38.

Diaz, P. E. & Umbreit, W. T. (1995). Women leaders–A new beginning. *Hospitality Research Journal, 18*(3)/19(1), 47-60.

Dill, B. T. (1980). The means to put my children through: Child-rearing goals and strategies among Black female domestic servants. In L. Rodgers-Rose (Ed.), *The Black woman*, 107-123. Beverly Hills: Sage.

Dill, B. T. (1994). *Across the boundaries of race and class: An exploration of work and family among black female domestic servants.* New York: Garland.

Farrar, A. L. (1996a). *It's all about relationships: African-American and European-American women's hotel management careers.* Unpublished doctoral dissertation, Virginia Polytechnic Institute and State University, Blacksburg, VA.

Farrar, A. L. (1996b). [Transcript of interviews with African-American and European-American women hotel managers]. Unpublished raw data.

Fernsten, J. A., Lowry, L. L., Enghagen, L. K., & Hott, D. D. (1988). Female managers: Perspectives on sexual harassment and career development. *Hospitality Education and Research Journal, 12*(2), 185-196.

Fisher, W. P. & Bernstein, C. (1991). *Lessons in leadership: Perspectives for hospitality industry success.* New York: Van Nostrand.

Fraizer, E. F. (1966). *The Negro family in the United States.* Chicago: University of Chicago Press.

Franklin, J. H. (1988). A historical note on Black families. In Harriette P. McAdoo (Ed.), *Black families*, pp. 23-26. Newbury Park, CA: Sage.

Garey, J. G. (1995). Woman and other minorities in hospitality management. In R. A. Brymer, Ed., *Hospitality Management: An introduction to the industry*, pp. 191-203. Dubuque, IA: Kendall/Hunt.

Garey, J. G. (1996). An analysis of determinants of career success for elite female executive chefs. *Hospitality Education and Research Journal, 20*(2), 125-135.

Giddings, P. (1984). *When and where I enter: The impact of Black women on race and sex in America.* New York: William Morrow.

Glenn, E. N. (1992). From servitude to service work: Historical continuities in the racial division of paid reproductive labor. *Signs, 18*(1), 1-43.

Greene, L. J. & Woodson, C.G. (1930). *The Negro wage earner.* Washington, DC: The Association for the Study of Negro Life and History.

Gregg, J. B. & Johnson, P. M. (1990). Perceptions of discrimination among women as managers in hospitality organizations. *FIU Hospitality Review, 8*(1), 10-22.

Grossman, A. S. (1980, August). Women in domestic work: Yesterday and today. *Monthly Labor Review*, 17-21.

Gwaltney, J. L. (1980). *Drylongso: A self-portrait of Black America.* New York: Random House.

Hacker, A. (1992). *Two nations: Black and White, separate, hostile, unequal.* New York: Macmillan.

Harrison, A. O. (1989). Black working women: Introduction to a life span perspective. In R. L. Jones (Ed.), *Black adult development and aging.* Berkeley CA: Cobb and Henry.

Haynes, E. R. (1922). Two million Negro women at work. *The Southern Workman,* 51(2), 64-72.

Haynes, E. R. (1923). Negroes in domestic service in the U.S. *Journal of Negro History,* 8, 384-442.

Henri, F. (1975). *Black migration: Movement north 1900-1920.* New York: Doubleday.

Hill, R. (1972). *The strengths of Black families.* New York: Emerson-Hall.

Howe, L. K. (1977). *Pink collar workers.* New York: Putnam.

Hull, G. T., Scott, P. B. & Smith, B. (Eds.). (1982). *All the women are white, all the blacks are men, but some of us are brave.* Old Westbury, NY: Feminist Press.

Jones, J. (1985). *Labor of love, labor of sorrow: Black women, work, and the family from slavery to the present.* New York: Basic Books

Katzman, D. (1978). Domestic service: Woman's work. In A. H. Stromberg and S. Harkess (Eds.), *Women Working: Theories and facts in perspective,* 377-391. Palo Alto, CA: Mayfield Publishing.

Kemp, A. A. (1994). *Women's work: Degraded and devalued.* Englewood Cliffs, NJ: Prentice-Hall.

Laudadio, D. M. (1988). Sexual and gender harassment: Assessing the current climate. *Hospitality Education and Research Journal,* 12(2), 411-415.

Lerner, G. (1992). *Black women in White America.* New York: Vintage Books.

Lewis, E. A. (1989). Role strain in African American women: The efficacy of support networks. *Journal of Black Studies,* 20(2), 155-169.

Loewenberg, B. J. & Bogin, R. (Eds.) (1976). *Black women in nineteenth-century American life: Their words, their thoughts, their feelings.* University Park, PA: The Pennsylvania State University Press.

Malveaux, J. (1986). Section introduction: Employment issues. In M.C. Simms & J.M. Malveaux (Eds.), *Slipping through the cracks: The status of African-American women* (pp. 7-9). New Brunswick, NJ: Transaction Publishers.

Marks, C. C. (1993). The bone and sinew of the race: Black women, domestic service, and labor migration. *Marriage & Family Review,* 19(1/2), 149-173.

More slavery at the south (1912, 25 January). *Independent,* pp. 196-200.

Mossell, N. F. (1988). *The work of the Afro-American woman.* (The Schomburg library of nineteenth-century black women writers). New York: Oxford University Press.

National Research Council (1989). *A common destiny: Blacks and American society.* Washington, DC: National Academy of Sciences.

Nobles, W. (1974). Africanity: Its role in Black families. *The Black Scholar, 9,* 10-17.

Obleton, N. B. (1984). Career counseling Black women in a predominantly White coeducational university. *Personnel and Guidance Journal,* 365-368.

Omi, M. & Winant, H. (1986). *Racial formation in the United States: From the 1960s to the 1980s.* New York: Routledge and Kegan Paul.

Romero, M. (1992). *Maid in the U.S.A.* New York: Routledge.

Shaw, S. J. (1996). *What a woman ought to be and to do: Black professional women workers during the Jim Crow era.* Chicago: University of Chicago Press.

Spaights, E. & Whitaker, A. (1995). Black women in the workforce, a new look at an old problem. *Journal of Black Studies, 25*(30), 283-296.

Staples, R. (1973). *The Black woman in America.* Chicago, IL: Nelson-Hall.

Staples, R. (1978). The Black family revisited. In Robert Staples (Ed.), *The Black family: Essays and studies,* pp. 13-18. Chicago, IL: Nelson-Hall.

Staples, R. & Johnson, L.B. (1993). *Black families at the crossroads, challenges and prospects.* San Francisco, CA: Jossey-Bass.

Tucker, S. (1988). *Telling memories among southern women, domestic workers and their employers in the segregated South.* Baton Rouge, LA: State University Press.

U. S. Department of Commerce, Bureau of the Census (1914). *Thirteenth census of the United States, Vol. 4, Population: Occupation statistics.* Washington, DC.

U. S. Department of Commerce, Bureau of the Census (1992). *1990 Census of Population and Housing, Equal Employment Opportunity (EEO) File on CD-ROM* [machine-readable data files]. Washington, DC: The Bureau [producer and distributor].

U. S. Department of Commerce, Bureau of the Census (1992). *Census of population and housing: Alphabetical index of industries and occupations.* Washington, DC.

U. S. Department of Commerce, Bureau of the Census (1996). Minority-owned firms: Comparison of business ownership minority group and gender: 1992 and 1987. *1992 Economic census: Minority- and women-owned business United States* [On-line]. Available: http://www.census.goc/agfs/smobe/view/b_1.txt

U. S. Department of Commerce, Bureau of the Census (1996). Statistics for Black-owned firms by major industry group, 1992. *1992 Economic census: Minority- and women-owned business United States* [On-line]. Available: http://www.census.goc/agfs/smobe/view/s_pr2.txt

Woodson, C. G. (1930). The Negro washerwoman, a vanishing figure. *The Journal of Negro History, 15*(3), 269-277.

Work, Monroe N. (1919). *Negro Year Book, 1918-1919.* Tuskegee AL: Tuskegee Institute.

Work, Monroe N. (1938). *Negro Year Book, 1937-1938.* Tuskegee AL: Tuskegee Institute.

Zinn, M. B. & Dill, B. T. (Eds.). (1994). *Women of color in U. S. Society.* Philadelphia: Temple University Press.

Accounting for Changing Times: Aligning Human Resource Practices to Employees' Nonwork Lives

Beth G. Chung

SUMMARY. Many societal and demographic changes are occurring in the current workforce. These changes include a shortage of work age employees, changes in family structure, increased women in the labor pool, changes in societal values, and so on. As a result, hospitality organizations are faced with new challenges and can respond to these changes through effective human resource management. This article discusses the current trend toward increasing human resource management practices (benefits and services) that affect employees' nonwork lives. Specifically, this article provides some of the historical context of organizations that have influenced employees' off-the-job lives. It explores why employer involvement in employee nonwork lives has become an important issue, and presents current research on the study of employer influence through human resource management practices, in employee nonwork lives. It addresses the importance of this issue for hospitality, and recommends future research. *[Article copies available for a fee from The Haworth Document Delivery Service: 1-800-342-9678. E-mail address: getinfo@haworthpressinc. com]*

KEYWORDS. Employee nonwork lives, Work and family, Human resource practices, Off-the-job lives, Hospitality and family

Beth G. Chung is Assistant Professor at the Cornell University School of Hotel Administration.

[Haworth co-indexing entry note]: "Accounting for Changing Times: Aligning Human Resource Practices to Employees' Nonwork Lives." Chung, Beth G. Co-published simultaneously in *Marriage & Family Review* (The Haworth Press, Inc.) Vol. 28, No. 1/2, 1998, pp. 143-152; and: *The Role of the Hospitality Industry in the Lives of Individuals and Families* (ed: Pamela R. Cummings, Francis A. Kwansa, and Marvin B. Sussman) The Haworth Press, Inc., 1998, pp. 143-152. Single or multiple copies of this article are available for a fee from The Haworth Document Delivery Service [1-800-342-9678, 9:00 a.m. - 5:00 p.m. (EST). E-mail address: getinfo@haworthpressinc.com].

Dramatic societal and demographic changes are occurring that have great impact on the management of hospitality organizations. The baby boomers are nearing retirement while the baby boomlets have not yet come of age. The core of the workforce in the next ten years will consist of primarily the baby busters, those born between 1964-1981, whose numbers (approximately 44 million) are few and far below that of boomers and boomlets (approximately 76 million and 72 million respectively) (Greller & Nee, 1989). This means that there will be a severe shortage in the labor pool in the near future. In contrast to the annual growth rates of 2.0 percent from 1976 to 1988, the U.S. labor force is expected to grow an average of only 1.2 percent annually from 1988 to 2000 (Fullerton, 1989). Not only will there be a shortage overall but a distinct shortfall in front-line and supervisor level employees; workers which the hospitality industry employs in large numbers. The buster generation and the upcoming boomlet generation will want different things from an employer than their predecessors. They are becoming more concerned with their nonwork lives. A Roper Survey done in 1990 found that 41% of Americans rated leisure time as their highest priority, even higher than their jobs (Berger, Fulford, & Krazmien, 1993). This is just one example of current societal and demographic changes that require attention.

Another societal trend is the change in family structure. There are more women in the workforce than ever; there are also more single parents and two-career families (Hayes, 1993). Because of these and many other societal and demographic changes, many hospitality organizations are becoming increasingly concerned about providing for employee nonwork lives in an effort to attract and retain a viable workforce. Because of the importance of front-line employees to hospitality organizations, the industry has to take immediate action in researching and implementing human resource strategies to effectively cope with these changing societal trends.

This article discusses the current trend toward increasing benefits and services that affect employees' nonwork lives. It describes the historical context of organizations that have influenced employees' off-the-job lives. Also presented is current research on employer influence in employee nonwork lives. The importance of this issue for the hospitality industry is set forth and future research is recommended.

HISTORICAL CONTEXT

Corporations have historically influenced employees' nonwork lives. Mill and mining towns of the 1800s provided basic wages, housing, education, health services, and recreation for employees and families.

These organizations provided for employees' moral and religious concerns as well. Some firms went so far as to specify rules of conduct for employee public behavior and to inculcate certain political and social values in employees (Guzzo, Nelson, & Noonan, 1992). These employers had a pervasive and powerful influence on virtually every aspect of their employees' nonwork lives. Some of these organizations became involved in employees' nonwork lives because of the social idealism of the company or its founder. George Pullman, for example, sought to teach employees new values and beliefs which he felt would contribute to the betterment of society and believed that the best way to teach such values and beliefs was to influence all aspects of employees' lives on and off the job. Hence, Pullman built and ruled over a company town which, in combination with the manufacturing works, enabled him to have an almost omnipresent influence on employees.

Mill towns and Pullmans are not likely to reappear. However, today there is again a trend toward greater employer involvement in employees' nonwork lives through human resource practices in order to attract and retain quality employees. The next section explores reasons for doing so.

WHY ARE EMPLOYERS BECOMING MORE INVOLVED IN EMPLOYEES' NONWORK LIVES?

Search for a stable workforce. Aside from employers' pursuing social ideals, there are a variety of reasons why employing organizations might become involved in employees' nonwork lives. One overriding reason, mentioned previously, is the search for a stable and viable workforce. Because of the shortage of qualified workers available in the coming years, organizations will attempt to attract and retain employees by the range of benefits, services, and programs offered. Many of these expanded benefits and services carry the organization's influence into the nonwork sphere of life. Among the expanded benefits are day care vouchers for families with young children, family dental care, and opportunities for additional education and training. Many employers believe that increased involvement leads to distinct positive consequences such as greater employee commitment, a better company image, and lower absenteeism, turnover, and tardiness.

Change in societal values is one pressure that has led to the need for increased diligence in securing a stable workforce. A large portion of the future work force is greatly concerned with their nonwork lives and will seek out a company that provides benefits for their nonwork lives (Berger, Fulford, & Krazmien, 1993). This shift in values will necessitate alternatives to the standard 40-hour work week. Employees will be looking for options such as flextime, compressed work weeks, part-time work and job sharing. In compressed work weeks, employees will put in longer hours each day in exchange for time off on a weekly or biweekly basis. Flextime will allow employees to adjust the time they arrive at and leave work. That is, employees can choose their own start and stop times, usually within a specified framework (e.g., arrive between 6 and 9 a.m. and leave between 3 and 6 p.m.). Job sharing and part-time work, however, will allow employees to reduce their time at work. In the case of job sharing, employees coordinate their work with a partner. One employee may work 3 days a week while another works the other 2 days. In this way, the partners have the job responsibilities covered yet they are able to find time for their nonwork lives.

The changing context of work and family will also influence employees' needs. There are now more women than ever in the workforce. In fact, women will account for nearly half of the labor force by the year 2000. This means more two-career families. In addition, with the high rate of divorce and lifestyle alternatives, there will be more single parents as well. Similarly, changing values dictate that more men are also now becoming increasingly concerned with the balance of work and family. All of this translates to employees having greater needs for employer provisions. Quality employees are becoming attracted to organizations that offer a variety of benefits and services that are in tune with their nonwork life needs. Employees are looking for work-at-home arrangements (e.g., tele-commuting), child-care benefits (e.g., subsidies, on-site child care, education on parenting) and flexibility to accommodate elder care (as large numbers of boomers retire and the burden of care falls on their children) just to name a few.

Increased productivity. Another reason for increasing employer involvement in employee nonwork lives is in the possible benefit of increased productivity. Many hospitality organizations are already realizing this potential through unique child care benefits. Marriott International, for example, has a number of work/family programs in place for both professional staff and line-level staff as well. Marriott's Atlanta properties along with a nearby Omni Hotel have engaged in a 250-student, early learning center which will address the child-care needs of more than 1,800 hotel employees. In fact, this program is aimed at providing child care for its line-level employees–those employees who need this benefit the most. Marriott feels that the more stability they can give line employees, the better they can do their jobs (Wagner, 1994). In fact, their contention is well supported. The Hudson Institute's Opportunity 2000 study (1988) shows that firms with progressive work and family policies reported higher employee productivity overall.

Improved service quality. Improved service quality is another reason why employers are finding it necessary to provide more nonwork-life benefits. Research has shown that the way you treat your employees through human resource practices is evident to customers and affects customers' views of service quality (Schneider & Bowen, 1985; Ulrich, Halbrook, Meder, Stuchlik, & Thorpe, 1991; Wiley, 1991). Aside from this research base, there is anecdotal evidence to suggest similar trends. Many employees are reporting a greater sense of comfort and a reduced level of stress when they know their children are on site or well taken care of.

Decreased costs. Employers are also finding that costs associated with health insurance, absenteeism, and tardiness are decreased when the organization tries to take care of the whole person. Many organizations are offering extended employee assistance programs, health seminars and workshops, health and fitness facilities, and the like in an effort to reduce costs. One organization, Kimball Physics, has even instituted a strict "no smoking policy" as part of their attempt to protect employees' health. They have a 3-year-old policy in place which has a 2-hour rule. Anyone who smells like smoke, employees and visitors alike, or has smoked within the last 2 hours, is banned from entering the building. Kimball genuinely believes that people can be made ill by tobacco residue. They take the position that its "NOT OK to make people even mildly sick" (Webster, 1997). Whether this position will persist over time is still up to debate. What is of interest is that Kimball's employees like the policy and enforce it unanimously.

These and other reasons are why employers are becoming increasingly involved in employees' nonwork lives. Employers are finding it necessary to provide the benefits and services which best fit the changing needs of society while also finding that there are many positive organizational outcomes associated with providing these benefits as well. In the following section, I will discuss a study which explores the current trend toward increased employer influence.

EMPLOYER INFLUENCE IN THE 1990s

A recent study done by Guzzo and Noonan (1991) detailed employers' involvement in employee *nonwork* lives. They interviewed 35 executives of 25 organizations (e.g., Marriott Corporation, American Express, Johns Hopkins Health Systems, Bank of America, etc.). They gathered data on corporate philosophies guiding benefits and services offered; current benefits and services offered that influence off-the-job lives; and off-the-job issues not involving benefits and services. Additionally they collected information on future human resource management practices that were perceived to influence employees' nonwork lives; the consequences of employers' involvement in nonwork lives; and limits on employer influence. They used content analysis of responses to these issues and predicted the major themes. The top three reasons cited by study participants for offering benefits and services were to attract and retain employees, keep the company's hiring practices competitive, and keep up with changing demographics and changing needs.

Current practices that go beyond the usual line of benefits that employers were offering were financial benefits such as donating charitable contributions, adoption assistance, life insurance, and the like. This was followed by health and wellness programs. Health insurance was not included since all companies offered some type of health insurance, which included employee assistance programs, health and fitness screenings and checkups, and health seminars. The next most cited benefit was child and family assistance in the form of information and referral, subsidized child care, elder care referral or on-side facilities.

Employers said that they influenced employees' nonwork lives in a number of less traditional ways. Among the activities cited were: (1) indirect community involvement by giving employees time away from work to devote to their personal choice of community causes; (2) direct community involvement by making contributions or visible dedication of corporate resources; (3) lower expectations of taking work home; and (4) an organizational emphasis on moral character, citizenship, and conduct.

Employers were also asked about additional benefits and services their organizations might offer in the near future. By far, the most frequently-cited theme was expansion of dependent care initiatives. They also believed that these new or expanded programs would have the greatest impact on employee nonwork lives. Other expected future programs included more flexibility in both work arrangements and benefits for employee development.

Guzzo and Noonan (1991) also found both positive and negative consequences associated with employer involvement through human resource practices. Positive consequences included increased commitment, morale, positive attitudes, and greater motivation. Additionally they described more employee development and self-improvement, including an increase in productivity, higher rates of performance and greater employee retention. They also believed their organizations' reputations were enhanced.

Other positive consequences cited were community improvement and a sense of increased quality of life off the job.

Some negative consequences included the blurring of work and non-work lives. Additionally, there appeared to be some employee resentment, suspicion and concern regarding an invasion of privacy. The managers also believed there were increased employee expectations of the organizations. Thus, it seems that there should be limits on the amount of influence an employer has on employee nonwork lives. Some limits might include maintaining strict confidentiality and privacy and carefully protecting the right of employees to make their own choices in benefits selected. If care is given to the negative concerns as well as the positive benefits, organizations may better reach their goals of attracting and retaining employees while not interfering in their employees' lifestyles.

Overall, these results show that the employers sampled are presently already heavily involved in employees' nonwork lives and can be expected to add new programs. What's especially interesting to note is that employers of today, unlike the old mill towns and Pullmans, are focused on providing benefits and services that are attractive to their set of internal customers (employees). Organizations are no longer involved in employee nonwork lives in order to control or to instill moral values. Instead, companies are offering a variety of benefits and services that are valued by their employees.

Across organizations, there is a wide range of benefits and services offered by different employers. The key to successfully achieving the goals of these programs is to create a fit between the organization's specific set of employees and their needs and the types of benefits and services offered. Hospitality organizations need to look both within the industry to uncover needed human resource practices specific to the hospitality industry and within their particular organizations to examine the needs of their specific workforce.

IMPORTANCE FOR HOSPITALITY INDUSTRIES

Clearly, greater employer involvement in the form of human resource practices in employee nonwork lives is emerging as an area of research and concern across all organizations. In addition, there may be even greater concern and urgency for the hospitality industry. There are multiple reasons for this position. First, the hospitality industry is a labor intensive industry. It depends on having quality front line employees to deliver the service. There will clearly be a shortage in front line employees as indicated by the sheer lack of numbers of traditional hospitality employment aged persons. Hospitality organizations will have to find alternative avenues to attract and hire employees, and have policies and practices in place to retain quality employees.

Second, the hospitality industry is all consuming. That is, hospitality workers, perhaps more than employees in other industries, spend a large amount of their waking hours at work. This is especially true for operations workers. They are often at the hotel or restaurant 10-12 hours a day at various times of the day (including 4 a.m.). These workers spend a good part of their day/night at work. One way to attract and retain these employees is to offer benefits and services that ease the amount of stress they experience about their nonwork lives. Different employers have found unique ways to do this. For example, Whataburger allows workers to have flexible schedules. Workers are also allotted three days of emergency leave and may take sick leave for sick family members. They also are provided 24-hour child care which is crucial for the odd hours that hospitality employees might have to work.

Third, the hospitality industry is having trouble attracting and retaining quality employees due to burnout. Working for hospitality organizations is becoming less attractive to the new generation as they perceive a career in hospitality as over-demanding and consuming of their nonwork lives. As mentioned previously, the buster and boomlet generations have new values. They have different priorities and are interested in maintaining a balance between work and family. The hospitality industry has to find unique ways to attract this workforce using methods that specifically address the needs of this segment.

CONCLUSION

Overall, the hospitality industry has a unique set of challenges and has to find unique solutions to address these upcoming challenges. The following section addresses areas for future research and exploration.

Future Avenues of Research

Due to the current and impending changes in the societal and demographic makeup of the workforce, the hospitality industry must make strides in understanding and implementing action plans to adapt to these changes. As such, there are many research questions that need to be addressed:

1. What are the unique challenges of the hospitality industry in order to attract and maintain a stable workforce?

2. What are the human resource policies and practices most wanted and needed by current and incoming hospitality employees? Further, are there differing needs based on the demographic variables of age, race, gender, or marital status?
3. To what extent do hospitality employees want employers to influence their nonwork lives and what should be the limits set on employer involvement?
4. What are the short-term and long-term, positive and negative consequences of employer involvement for the hospitality industry?
5. What is the impact of employee dependence on the organization as a consequence of greater employer involvement in employee nonwork lives?
6. What can we learn from hospitality operations that already have in place benefits and services that influence employee nonwork lives? What benefits and services have they found to be successful?

These are just a few of the research questions that need to be addressed. The balance between family and hospitality is increasingly becoming an area of concern. Employees are no longer viewing their work lives in the same way; instead, they are looking for employers who view them as whole persons with needs off the job that also require attention.

AUTHOR NOTE

Beth G. Chung is Assistant Professor of Management and Human Resources at Cornell University's School of Hotel Administration. She received her PhD in Industrial/Organizational Psychology at the University of Maryland, College Park.

Dr. Chung has taught courses in industrial/Organizational Psychology, Human Resources Management, and Group Process and Leadership. Her primary interests are in services management (specifically the interface between customers and employees), strategic and market-focused human resources management, executive feedback and development, alternative selection systems, and diversity issues.

Dr. Chung has consulted for a number of Fortune 500 companies on organizational development and change, selection systems, coaching, executive assessment and training. She is also an active member of several professional associations, including the Academy of Management, Society for industrial and Organizational Psychology, American Psychological Association, Society for Human Resources Management, and Council on Hotel, Restaurant and Institutional Education.

REFERENCES

Berger, F., Fulford, M. D., & Krazmien, M. (1993). Human resources management in the 21st century: Predicting partnerships for profit. *The Council on Hotel, Restaurant, and Institutional Education, 17*(1), 87-102.

Fullerton, H. N., Jr. (1989). New labor force projections, spanning 1988 to 2000. *Monthly Labor Review, 112*(11), 3-12.

Greller, M. M., & Nee, D. M. (1989). *From baby boom to baby bust: How business can meet the demographic challenge.* Reading, MA: Addison-Wesley.

Guzzo, R. A., Nelson, G. L., & Noonan, K. A. (1992). Commitment and employer involvement in employees' nonwork lives. In S. Zedeck (Ed.), *Work, families, and organizations.* San Francisco: Jossey-Bass.

Guzzo, R.A., & Noonan, K.A. (1991). *HR Practices, Off-the-job Influences, and Employee Commitment.* Unpublished technical report, Department of Psychology, University of Maryland, College Park.

Hayes, L. O. (1993). The family is changing, and so must you. *Restaurant Hospitality, 77*(9), p. 66.

Hudson Institute (1988). *Opportunity 2000: Creative Affirmative Action Strategies for a Changing Workforce.* Washington, DC: U.S. Department of Labor.

Schneider, B., & Bowen, D. (1985). Employee and customer perceptions of service in banks: Replication and extension. *Journal of Applied Psychology, 70,* 423-433.

Ulrich, D., Halbrook, R., Meder, D., Stuchlik, M. & Thorpe, S. (1991). Employee and customer attachment: Synergies for competitive advantage. *Human Resource Planning, 14,* 89-104.

Wagner, G. (1994). For Atlanta hotels, family is bottom line. *Lodging Hospitality, 50*(6), p. 10.

Webster, K. (1997). They really mean NO SMOKING! *Ithaca Journal* (2/26/97).

Wiley, J. W. (1991). Customer satisfaction and employee opinions: A supportive work environment and its financial cost. *Human Resource Planning, 14,* 117-128.

Better Understanding
the Impact of Work Interferences
on Organizational Commitment

Debra Franklin Cannon

SUMMARY. Recent studies have shown that a large percentage of employees have considerable quality of life concerns, particularly in relation to combining work and family or personal responsibilities and activities. The hospitality industry, traditionally characterized by long and erratic work hours, has experienced numerous quality of work life challenges. This study analyzes the concept of organizational commitment as related to personal interferences that conflict with work in a sample of hotel employees. Organizational commitment, in past research, has been positively linked to reduced employee turnover and increased work productivity. Hotel employees were surveyed ranging from entry level hourly workers to managerial levels. An inverse relationship was found between organizational commitment and certain types of work interferences, specifically child care and medical problems. The implications of this research are numerous as hospitality organizations analyze ways to minimize work conflicts and maximize employee organizational commitment. *[Article copies available for a fee from The Haworth Document Delivery Service: 1-800-342-9678. E-mail address: getinfo@haworthpressinc.com]*

Debra Franklin Cannon is Assistant Professor in the Cecil B. Day School of Hospitality Administration, College of Business Administration, Georgia State University. Dr. Cannon has been teaching full-time since 1991 and was Adjunct Professor in the program from 1985 to 1991.

[Haworth co-indexing entry note]: "Better Understanding the Impact of Work Interferences on Organizational Commitment." Cannon, Debra Franklin. Co-published simultaneously in *Marriage & Family Review* (The Haworth Press, Inc.) Vol. 28, No. 1/2, 1998, pp. 153-166; and: *The Role of the Hospitality Industry in the Lives of Individuals and Families* (ed: Pamela R. Cummings, Francis A. Kwansa, and Marvin B. Sussman) The Haworth Press, Inc., 1998, pp. 153-166. Single or multiple copies of this article are available for a fee from The Haworth Document Delivery Service [1-800-342-9678, 9:00 a.m. - 5:00 p.m. (EST). E-mail address: getinfo@haworthpressinc.com].

KEYWORDS. Organizational commitment, Work interferences, Quality of work life, Hotel employees

The partnership between employer and employee has never been of greater importance than in today's organization. Downsized work forces, heightened competition and slimmer profit margins necessitate maximized employee performance.

Yet, in a study by the Families and Work Institute, 42% of the surveyed employees felt "used up" by the end of the work day. Sixty-six percent of the employees felt they did not spend sufficient time with their children. A sizeable proportion of the respondents indicated their willingness to make substantial trade-offs in order to receive flexible work schedules, work leave programs and dependent care assistance (Associated Press, *Atlanta Journal & Constitution*, September 3, 1993, p. A1).

The United States Department of Labor (1987) has listed among the six issues requiring revision by the year 2000 the need to reconcile the conflicting needs of work and families. Although not necessarily a gender issue, the changing demographics of the work force could heighten the conflicts between work needs and the personal needs of workers. By the year 2000, approximately 47% of the work force will be female and 61% of all females in the United States will work. In 1960, only 11 percent of women with children under the age of six worked. Today, approximately 52 percent of women with children in this age range work. Fifty-seven percent of dual-income families have children under the age of eighteen.

Hotel employees are particularly vulnerable to role conflicts with hotels open seven days a week, twenty-four hours per day. The hotel industry is known for challenging work schedules for both hourly and management personnel. This is an intense service-oriented industry with "front line" employees directly determining the level of guest satisfaction. It is an industry that historically has had high employee turnover often ranging in the triple digits. For some hospitality companies, the entire staff turns over two to three times per year (Woods, 1996).

This study analyzes the concept of organizational commitment as related to work interferences among hotel employees. Surveys were completed by a sample of hotel employees ranging from entry-level to managerial levels in ascertaining levels of conflict between specific work and personal roles. It was hypothesized that an inverse relationship would exist between organizational commitment and work interferences among the hotel employees.

PAST RESEARCH ON ORGANIZATIONAL COMMITMENT

Research on organizational commitment has primarily spanned the last two decades. Earlier studies found a negative relationship between commitment and costly behaviors such as absenteeism (Angle & Perry, 1981) and employee turnover (Arnold & Feldman, 1982; Decotiis & Summers, 1987; Hom & Hulin, 1981; Martin & O'Laughlin, 1984). Others have found positive relationships between organizational commitment and individual motivation, job involvement, and some aspects of job performance (DeCotiis & Summers, 1987; Farrell & Rusbult, 1981; Stumpf & Hartman, 1984). Organizational commitment was found to be positively related to customer satisfaction (Crosby, Grisaffe & Marra, 1994) and to employee job satisfaction (Smith, Gregory and Cannon, 1996).

Although the definitions of organizational commitment have varied in the literature, important distinctions have been maintained between the concepts of "job satisfaction" and "organizational commitment." Job satisfaction is an affective response to specific aspects of the job and, therefore, may be more transitory than commitment which is an affective response to the organization as a whole (Williams & Hazer, 1986). The concept of organizational commitment has been described as "the strength of an individual's identification with and involvement in a particular organization" (Porter, Steers, Mowday, & Boulian, 1974, p. 604). Sheldon (1971) referred to the concept as a linkage between the employee's identity and the organization which typically results in a positive evaluation of the organization. Hrebiniak and Alutto (1972) considered the variable to be evidenced by an unwillingness to leave the organization for incremental increases in pay, status, professional autonomy or increased social interactions. This study utilized the definition of organizational commitment from Mowday, Porter and Steers (1982, p. 27) which delineated three primary factors: "A strong belief in and acceptance of the organizational goals and values; a willingness to exert considerable effort on behalf of the organization; and a strong desire to maintain membership in the organization."

RESEARCH ON WORK-HOME ROLE CONFLICT

Role theory includes several components such as role expectations, role interpretations, role appraisal and role conflict (Bobbitt, Breinholt, Doktor & McNaul, 1978). Role conflict can be further delineated into several types including interrole conflict. Interrole conflict, the focus of this study, takes place when there are conflicting expectations among many simultaneous roles and a person "experiences pressures within one role that are incompatible with the pressures that arise within another role" (Kopelman, Greenhaus & Connolly, 1983, p. 201).

Good, Sisler and Gentry (1988), in a study of retail management personnel, found that work and family role conflicts led to lower organizational commitment leading to intentions to leave the organization. Welsch and LaVan (1981) also concluded that role conflict was detrimental to commitment in their study of upper and middle-level health care managers.

Pleck, Staines and Lang (1980) and Kopelman, Greenhaus and Connolly (1983) further stated that role conflict exerts a negative effect on life satisfaction. Coverman (1989) concluded that role conflict decreases job satisfaction and marital satisfaction of men and increases women's psychophysical symptoms. Voydanoff (1982) also reported positive relationships between job satisfaction and marital/family satisfaction and inverse relationships between job satisfaction and work/family conflicts.

Relevant factors to work-home role conflict have also been examined. Pleck (1977) stated that, for women, the demands of the family role are allowed to interfere with the work role more than the work role is allowed to interfere with the family role. For men, he stated, the opposite is true. Coverman (1989) has also noted the effect of role conflict on job satisfaction is greater for women than men. Younger, more recently married women have been found to experience higher levels of work-home role conflict when there are lower levels of marital happiness and life satisfaction.

Schuler (1977) has hypothesized that education is a key factor in effective coping approaches to role demands. He maintained that better educated, more experienced employees displayed more effective adaptation to role conflict and to role ambiguity.

Stoner, Hartman and Arora (1990) found that time pressures affect the degree of role conflict experiences. Work-home role conflict was positively related to the number of hours worked per week in their study with employees who worked longer hours showing higher levels of such conflicts.

Family size and children's ages have also been shown to determine role conflict levels. Keith and Schafer (1980) found higher levels of work-family role conflicts in larger families. Parents of younger children, in addition, experienced more work-home role conflict as compared to parents of older children (Greenhaus & Kopelman, 1981). The degree of family support, however, can be an important factor in affecting work-home role conflict. Holahan and Gilbert (1979) found a negative relationship between support from family members and the level of role conflict.

Cultural differences have been noted in several studies on role-related factors. Thomas and Neal (1978) found that Black males did not regard child care as predominantly a female responsibility to the extent White males did. Hays and Mindel (1973) also found that extended family members assisted with child care more often in Black families as compared to White families.

STUDY METHODOLOGY

Three hundred employees from hotels in an urban Southeastern city were randomly selected to participate in this study on organizational commitment. Subjects consisted of employees in the following job classifications with the participating hotels: housekeepers, kitchen stewards, front office clerks, reservation agents, concierges, and assistant managers/managers from these departments. These positions were selected because they represent traditionally high turnover areas (particularly housekeeping and stewarding) and high guest contact areas (front office, reservations and concierge).

Only subjects who had been employed in their positions for a minimum of three months were included in the study. This time period coincided with the typical probationary/try-out period required in most hotels. Subjects were randomly selected using a stratified sample from the participating hotels. Payroll registers for the involved departments were utilized with each name numerically coded and the sample selected using a table of random numbers (Minium, 1978, pp. 547-548).

Subjects were grouped into three levels: Level I–housekeepers and kitchen stewards (dishwashers, kitchen cleaning), N = 143, 47.7%; Level II–front office clerks, reservationists, N = 88, 29.3%; and Level III–departmental assistant managers and managers, N = 69, 23%. The demographic profile of the subjects including age, sex and race is displayed in Table 1.

Instruments utilized in this study included the Organizational Commitment Questionnaire developed by Porter and Smith (1970). An Interferences to Working Scale was also used which was a modification of the Barriers to Working section of the Vocational Opinion Index (Associates for Research in Behavior, Inc., 1974). The specific interferences that were measured included: child care; home maintenance and upkeep; family care; family and personal problems; personal medical problems; transportation problems; and personal activities (school, another job, hobbies, social and recreational activities collectively). Previous research has primarily involved global, unspecific role conflicts between one's work life

TABLE 1. Sample Demographics

Organizational Level	N	Average Age	Sex			Race	
			N	%		N	%
Level I –	143	33.41	F (101, 71)		Black	(129, 90)	
Housekeepers/ Stewards			M (42, 29)		White Asian Hispanic	(8, 5) (3, 2) (4, 3)	
Level II – Front Desk Clerks,	88	27.99	F (63, 72) M (25, 28)		Black White Asian	(50, 57) (34, 39) (3, 3)	
Reservationists, Concierges					Hispanic	(1, 1)	
Level III – Assistant Managers/Managers	69	31.19	F (38, 55) M (31, 45)		Black White Asian Hispanic	(28, 41) (39, 57) (1, 1) (1, 1)	
Total	300	31.3	F (202, 67.3) M (98, 32.7)		Black White Asian Hispanic	(207, 69.0) (81, 26.7) (6, 2.3) (6, 2.0)	

and personal life (Jackson, 1983; Klenke-Hamel & Mathieu, 1990; Voydanoff, 1982). This study differed in that specific interferences were included as variables.

ANALYSIS OF DATA

The relationship between organizational commitment and work interferences was analyzed along with predictor variables for each type of work interference. The predictor variables included job level, age, job tenure, education, income, and gender.

Specific interferences to working were analyzed in relation to organizational commitment by stepwise regression analysis. Child care responsibilities and medical problems were found to be significantly related to variance in the level of organizational commitment ($p < .001$). Both variables were negatively associated with the dependent variable combining to account for 7% ($R^2 = .07190$) of the variance in the organizational commitment level. With the additional interferences added (personal activities, transportation problems, home maintenance responsibilities, personal/family problems and family responsibilities), the variance accounted for in the dependent variable was approximately 8% ($R^2 = .0807$, $p < .001$).

Specific work interferences and overall job satisfaction were also analyzed by stepwise multiple regression. The significant variables among the types of work interferences included child care responsibilities, personal activities outside of work (such as hobbies, school, another job) and medical problems. All were negatively related to overall job satisfaction and combined to account for over 8% ($R^2 = .0866$, $p < .001$) of the variance in the dependent variable.

Certain factors were identified as predictors of personal interferences to work. Stepwise regression resulted in two variables being significant in predicting the degree of child care responsibilities interfering with work. The two predictors were level of responsibility for child care, as perceived by the subject, and the subject's educational level. A significant positive relationship existed between the extent of responsibility for the involved children and the degree of child care interferences to working ($p < .001$). A significant negative relationship existed between this type of work interference and educational level ($p < .001$). The combined variables of child care responsibility and educational level accounted for approximately 12.9% of the organizational commitment variance ($R^2 = .12866$).

Medical problems were the second significant type of work interference in negatively impacting organizational commitment. In analyzing all cases ($N = 300$), education was the significant independent variable ($p < .05$) in predicting that this type of interference would have a significant and negative impact on organizational commitment.

In analyzing the other work interference variables, certain patterns also were evident. Educational level and age were significant in predicting interferences based on home maintenance and upkeep responsibilities. Higher interference levels existed for younger and less educated employees ($p < .05$). Education and age were also significantly related to work interferences based on family responsibilities with negative relationships existing with both variables. Age was the significant predictor for interferences due to personal and family problems ($p < .01$), transportation difficulties ($p < .01$), and personal activities ($p < .001$) with negative relationships existing in these three areas. Older workers, therefore, tended to have fewer work interferences in these areas.

No significant differences were found between job levels regarding the degree of overall work interferences. When specific interference factors were analyzed, more similarities were found than differences. The most difficult interferences for entry-level employees (Level 1) were child care responsibilities and medical problems. Personal and family problems, medical problems and home upkeep responsibilities were the main interferences for Level 2 employees (front desk and reservations employees) and Level 3 workers (assistant managers and managers).

Differences in overall interferences to working did not exist among the racial/ethnic groups represented in the sample. In performing an analysis of variance, no significant differences were found between Blacks, Whites, Asians, and Hispanics (p = .576). Regarding gender differences, there were no significant differences between males and females in the overall level of conflict between work and personal roles (p = .07). This was particularly interesting in the area of child care (p = .8116) where it was hypothesized that females would experience this as a greater work interference.

CONCLUSIONS

The purpose of this study was to research the relationship between organizational commitment and work interferences. Two types of work interferences (child care and medical problems) were significant in negatively impacting organizational commitment. Age and education were predominant predictors of interferences to work with older employees, and more educated employees generally experienced lower levels of conflict between work and child care responsibilities and medical problems.

Age and educational levels have not been specified as variables in many of the studies reviewed on role conflict. Markham, Harlan and Hackett (1987) did note that age and educational level were most likely to be surrogate measures of employee aspirations and expectations regarding work roles. Wright and Hamilton (1979) discussed differences in work values according to educational achievement. Employees with higher educational levels were found to be strongly influenced by expectations for mobility and promotion which led to different perceptions and reactions to current employment situations.

There were certain preconceptions that were not supported in the findings of this study. For example, gender was not a significant predictor in determining any of the work interference types, including child care. Job level and race were also not significant predictors of the selected work interferences.

IMPLICATIONS

Knowledge of the relationship between organizational commitment and certain work interferences has potentially important practical implications for the management of human resources in the hotel industry. A large proportion of this industry's work force is comprised of individuals in lower-level positions who tend to have lower educational levels. As indicated in this study, there was an inverse relationship between education and certain work interferences. This study did not focus on specific coping techniques in handling work interferences so it can only be speculated that more educated employees have more effective resources or coping strategies in minimizing what interferes with their work or in preventing conflict between personal and work roles.

Hotels, as well as other hospitality companies, may benefit from helping employees learn ways to minimize working interferences. Managers must first be aware of individual employee needs. Such managerial awareness might be facilitated by training in active listening and empathy skills. Further organizational support could also include providing flexible work schedules and flexible benefit plans that adequately address varying employee needs.

In general, the hospitality industry has not been characterized by the hiring of large numbers of older workers. This study points out another positive dimension of the older worker in having fewer or lower levels of work interferences. With the overall American population becoming older (by the year 2000, the median age will reach 36, six years older than at any time in the history of this nation), an influx of older workers is inevitable in the hospitality industry with many resulting advantages to the employing companies (U.S. Department of Labor, 1987).

A report by the United States Merit Systems Protection Board (1991) described many programs that could be implemented by employers in addressing the changing work force and changing employee needs. The report collectively referred to such programs as "work and family" benefits while stressing that they potentially impact all employees–regardless of marital status or the presence of children. The main premise of this report was that it is in the best interest of major employers to assist employees in meeting their personal needs while still being productive members of the work force.

As this study showed, child care can present significant work-personal conflicts. There is the monetary impact of child care which usually is a family's fourth largest expense after housing, food and taxes. There are also the difficulties of availability, coordination with other school programs, location and flexibility in coordinating with work schedules. Possible benefits in the area of child care range from informal assistance (consisting of child care resource and referral services), to financial assistance (vouchers, flexible spending accounts), to direct care services (on-site, near-site day care, drop-in care when typical arrangements fall through, day care for mildly sick children, after-school and summer programs) to flexible personnel policies (using employee sick time to care for a sick child). While few employers provide all of these benefits, it is expected that a majority of employers will be offering at least one of the benefits by the year 2000 (U.S. Merit Systems Protection Board, 1991).

RECOMMENDATIONS

Organizational commitment is a multidimensional concept with many determining factors. The intent of this study was to study a specific set of variables, work interferences, in relation to this concept. It must be realized, however, that there are numerous other determinants influencing the level of commitment between employees and their companies of employment. Previous phases of this research (Cannon, 1991) analyzed other variables and found significant relationships between organizational commitment and pay, job satisfaction, and job autonomy. While work interferences were found to significantly impact organizational commitment, the results should not be interpreted as the sole determinants. Organizations, therefore, in wanting to maximize the commitment of their employees, are encouraged to consider multidimensional approaches.

The work force is rapidly changing and a large number of international employees work in the hospitality industry. Future studies should focus more on the multi-cultural dynamics of organizational commitment and specific work interferences.

Medical problems were significant in adversely affecting organizational commitment. Future research is warranted to better understand the types of problems affecting employees.

Since many companies, including hospitality organizations, are expanding benefits to address employee needs in the areas of child care and flexible scheduling, research of these companies would be advantageous. Studies involving pre-benefit implementation and post-implementation impact on organizational commitment would be helpful for companies to better understand ramifications of such programs.

Some organizations will maintain the old adage, "Employees should leave their personal problems at the employee entrance." In other words, do not bring your problems to work. More employee-oriented organizations realize that humans many times cannot do this. Certainly, workers should be encouraged to be responsible for personal situations and show professional work place behaviors. This study's results show that personal interferences do negatively impact organizational commitment which, based on prior research, can impact employee productivity and employee retention. Those organizations implementing supports to help minimize interferences to work are making wise investments for today's work force and for the workers of the future.

AUTHOR NOTE

Debra Franklin Cannon has over eleven years industry experience. She was Director of Human Resources for the Ritz-Carlton, Atlanta and the Ritz-Carlton, Buckhead and was Corporate Director of Professional Development for the Ritz-Carlton Hotel Company. She also worked with Hyatt Hotels in human resources. Dr. Cannon is the faculty coordinator for the Business Management Institute I sponsored by the Club Managers Association of America. She also teaches in the BMI I program as well as CMAA's Certification Review Course. She is a Certified Hospitality Educator and is one of only twelve instructors worldwide designated by the Educational Institute of the American Hotel and Motel Association to teach its Certified Hospitality Educator workshop. Dr. Cannon is on the editorial board of the journal *Hospitality and Tourism Educator.* Her research has focused on hospitality issues in human resources, employment law and quality service. Her doctorate degree, from Georgia State University, is in human resources development.

REFERENCES

Angle, H.L. & Perry, J.L. (1981). An empirical assessment of organizational commitment and organizational effectiveness. *Administrative Science Quarterly, 26,* 1-14.

Arnold, H. & Feldman, D.C. (1982). A multivariate analysis of the determination of job turnover. *Journal of Applied Psychology, 67,* 350-360.

Associated Press (1993) Wanted: jobs with freedom. *Atlanta Journal & Constitution,* September 3, A1.

Associates for Research in Behavior, Inc. (1974). *Transition to Work III: Development and Implementation of the VOI Transition System.* Philadelphia: Associates for Research in Behavior.

Beck, M. (1990). Trading places–More and more women are on the daughter track, working, raising kids, and helping aging parents. *Newsweek,* July 16, 49-50.

Bobbitt, H.R., Breinholt, R.H., Doktor, R.H. & McNaul, J.P. (1978). *Organizational Behavior–Understanding and Prediction.* Englewood Cliffs, N.J.: Prentice Hall, Inc.

Bohen, H.H. & Viveros-Long, A. (1981). Balancing jobs and family life–Do flexible schedules help? *Temple University Press*, Philadelphia, 147-148, 192.

Cannon, D.F. (1991). The relationship between job satisfaction, interferences to working and organizational commitment among hotel employees. Unpublished dissertation, Georgia State University.

Coverman, S. (1989). Role overload, role conflict and stress: Addressing consequences of multiple role demands. *Social Forces, 67*(4), 965-982.

Crosby, L., Grisaffe, D., & Marra, T. (1994). The impact of quality and customer satisfaction on employee organizational commitment. *Marketing and Research Today*, February, 23-24.

Crossen, C. (1990). Workplace–Where we'll be. *Wall Street Journal*, June 4, R6.

Decotiis, T.A. & Summers, T.P. (1987). A path analysis of a model of the antecedents and consequences of organizational commitment. *Human Relations, 40*(7), 445-470.

Farrell, D. & Rusbult, C.E. (1981). Exchange variables as predictors of job satisfaction, job commitment and turnover: The impact of rewards, costs, alternatives and investments. *Organizational Behavior and Human Performance, 27/28*, 78-95.

Good, L., Sisler, G.F., & Gentry, J.W. (1988). Antecedents of turnover intentions among retail management personnel. *Journal of Retailing, 64*(3), 295-314.

Greenhaus, J.H. & Kopelman, R.E. (1981). Conflict between work and non-work roles: Implications for the career planning process. *Human Resource Planning*, January, 1-10.

Hays, W.C. & Mindel, C.H. (1973). Extended kinship relations in black and white families. *Journal of Marriage and Family, 35*, 39-49.

Holahan, C.K. & Gilbert, L.A. (1979). Conflict between major life roles: Women and men in dual career couples. *Human Relations*, June, 451-467.

Hom, P.W. & Hulin, C.L. (1981). A competitive test of the prediction of reenlistment by several models. *Journal of Applied Psychology, 66*, 23-29.

Hrebiniak, L.G. & Alutto, J.A. (1972). Personal and role-related factors in the development of organizational commitment. *Administrative Science Quarterly, 17*, 555-572.

Jackson, S.E. (1983). Participation in decision-making as a strategy for reducing job-related strain. *Journal of Applied Psychology, 68*, 3-19.

Keith, P.M. & Schafer, R.B. (1980). Role strain and depression in two job families. *Family Relations*, July, 483-488.

Klenke-Hamel, K.E. & Mathieu, J.E. (1990). Role strains, tension, and job satisfaction influences on employees' propensity to leave: A multi-sample replication and extension. *Human Relations, 43*(8), 791-807.

Kopelman, R.E., Greenhaus, J.H., & Connolly, T.F. (1983). A model of work, family and interrole conflict: A construct validation study. *Organizational Behavior and Human Performance, 32*, 198-215.

Markham, W.T., Harlan, S.L. & Hackett, E.J. (1987). Promotion opportunity in organizations: Causes and consequences. *Research in Personnel and Human Resources Management*, 5, 223-287.

Martin, T.N. & O'Laughlin, M.S. (1984). Predictors of organizational commitment: The study of part-time Army reservists. *Journal of Vocational Behavior*, 25, 270-283.

Minium, E.W. (1978). *Statistical Reasoning in Psychology and Education.* New York: John Wiley & Sons.

Mowday, R.T., Porter, L.W., & Steers, R.M. (1982). *Employee–Organization Linkages.* New York: Academic Press.

Pleck, J.H. (1977). The work-family role system. *Social Problems*, April, 417-427.

Pleck, J.H., Staines, G.L., & Lang, L. (1980). Conflicts between work and family life. *Monthly Labor Review, 103*, 29-32.

Porter, L.W. & Smith, F.J. (1970). *The etiology of organizational commitment.* Unpublished paper, University of California, Irvine.

Porter, L.W., Steers, R.M., & Mowday, R.T., & Boulian, P.V. (1974). Organizational commitment, job satisfaction and turnover among psychiatric techniques. *Journal of Applied Psychology, 59*, 603-609.

Schuler, R.S. (1977). Role conflicts and ambiguity as a function of the task-structure technology interaction. *Organizational Behavior and Human Performance, 20*, 66-74.

Sheldon, M.E. (1971). Investments and involvements as mechanisms producing commitment in the organization. *Administrative Science Quarterly, 16*, 142-150.

Smith, K., Gregory, S.R., & Cannon, D.F. (1996). Becoming an employer of choice: Assessing commitment in the hospitality workplace. Unpublished manuscript.

Stoner, C.R., Hartman, R.I., & Arora, R. (1990). Work-home role conflict in female owners of small businesses: An exploratory study. *Journal of Small Business Management, 28*(1), 30-38.

Stumpf, S. & Hartman, K. (1984). Individual exploration to organizational commitment or withdrawal. *Academy of Management Journal, 27*, 308-329.

Tanke, M.L. (1990). *Human Resources Management.* Albany, N.Y.: Delmar Publishers, Inc.

The Partnership Group, Inc. (1990). Elder care: A clear misunderstanding in "Inform, The Dependent Care Reporter," Lansdale, PA, Fall Edition, 1.

Thomas, M.B. & Neal, P.A. (1978). Collaborating careers: The differential effects of race. *Journal of Vocational Behavior, 12*, 33-42.

United States Department of Labor (1987). *Workforce 2000–Work and Workers for the 21st Century.* Washington: U.S. Government Printing Office.

United States Merit Systems Protection Board (1991). *Balancing Work Responsibilities and Family Needs: The Federal Civil Service Response,* Washington: U.S. Government Printing Office.

Voydanoff, P. (1982). Work roles and quality of family life among professionals and managers. In B.M. Hirschlein & W.J. Braun (Eds.), *Families and Work* (pp. 118-124). Stillwater: Oklahoma State University Press.

Welsch, H.P. & LaVan, H. (1981). Interrelationships between organizational commitment and job characteristics, job satisfaction, professional behavior, and organizational climate. *Human Relations, 34,* 1079-1089.

Williams, L.J. & Hazer, J.T. (1986). Antecedents and consequences of satisfaction and commitment in turnover models: A reanalysis using latent variable structural equation methods. *Journal of Applied Psychology, 71*(2), 219-231.

Woods, Robert H. (1995). *Managing Hospitality Human Resources.* East Lansing, MI: Educational Institute of the American Hotel & Motel Association, 151.

Wright, J. & Hamilton, R. (1979). Education and job attitudes among blue-collar workers. *Sociology of Work and Occupations, 6,* 59-83.

The Relationship of Job Satisfaction and Family Life: Female Managers in Health Care Food Service

Howard R. Clayton
Vivian Odera
Daniel A. Emenheiser
Johnny Sue Reynolds

SUMMARY. This study assessed the impact work-related factors have on home and family life for female managers in health care food service. A random sample of 333 (33.0%) of the population, members of the American Dietetic Association's Management in Health Care Systems dietetic practice group, was surveyed. Work aspects with the most negative impact on quality of home life were number of hours worked per week, work schedule and job security. The employee attribute found to play a statistically significant role in predicting overall effect of job on home life was number of hours worked

Howard R. Clayton is Associate Professor, College of Business Administration, University of North Texas, Denton, Texas. Vivian Odera is Assistant Director of Food and Nutrition Services at Trinity Medical Center of Carollton, Carollton, Texas. Daniel A. Emenheiser is Assistant Professor and Johnny Sue Reynolds is Associate Professor at the School of Merchandising and Hospitality Management, University of North Texas, Denton, Texas.

Address correspondence to: Daniel A. Emenheiser, P.O. Box 311100, Denton, TX 76203-1100.

[Haworth co-indexing entry note]: "The Relationship of Job Satisfaction and Family Life: Female Managers in Health Care Food Service." Clayton et al. Co-published simultaneously in *Marriage & Family Review* (The Haworth Press, Inc.) Vol. 28, No. 1/2, 1998, pp. 167-185; and: *The Role of the Hospitality Industry in the Lives of Individuals and Families* (ed: Pamela R. Cummings, Francis A. Kwansa, and Marvin B. Sussman) The Haworth Press, Inc., 1998, pp. 167-185. Single or multiple copies of this article are available for a fee from The Haworth Document Delivery Service [1-800-342-9678, 9:00 a.m. - 5:00 p.m. (EST). E-mail address: getinfo@haworthpressinc.com].

per week. *[Article copies available for a fee from The Haworth Document Delivery Service: 1-800-342-9678. E-mail address: getinfo@haworthpressinc. com]*

KEYWORDS. Job satisfaction, Female managers, Home and family life, Health care food services

INTRODUCTION

As the number of women entering the work force increases, our society has become very concerned with problems of the family. It is predicted that by the year 2000, six out of seven working-age women will be employed. Approximately 75% of all working women are in their childbearing years (Jamieson & O'Mara, 1991). According to Burden and Googins (1987), less than nine percent of American families currently constitute the traditional model of two parents with children where the husband is the full-time employee in the labor force and the wife is the full-time homemaker. According to the United States Bureau of Census (1987), a related trend is seen on the rise in the number of dual earner families in which the husband and wife pursue work outside the home and maintain a family life together.

According to Marshall (1991), women will represent 64% of the new entrants in the work force over the next ten years. This group will also account for 50% of the college-level hospitality management graduates. Women will account for 47% of the work force by the year 2000 and it is expected that women will hold positions that were once occupied by white males (Thornburg, 1991). With this being the future trend, the hospitality industry and other industries must find ways to accommodate these new leaders.

Within the past decade the hospitality industry has experienced tremendous growth, which is expected to continue beyond the year 2000. If the hospitality industry is to successfully remain one of the fastest growing industries in the nation, Buergermeister (1983) urged the industry as a whole to find ways to attract and retain qualified minority groups. To meet this challenge, the hospitality industry must identify the needs and wants of its diversified work force and also eliminate prejudicial attitudes against different minority groups. In addition, the hospitality industry must develop programs that will attract and retain its future work force.

Health care food service, a segment of the hospitality industry, has been very successful in attracting and retaining female managers. Bryke and

Kornblum (1991) conducted a study which revealed that women accounted for 90% of management staff. However, women in these positions still experience considerable discrimination.

Women will continue to enter the work force in large numbers. However, there are certain barriers and prejudices that still exist in today's society which prevent women from attaining their maximum potential in their jobs and also continue to play the roles society has set for them in their homes. Brownell (1994) stated that:

As more women move into hospitality management, it becomes ever more critical to understand the variables that affect their career development and to identify the kinds of initiatives that can be taken to facilitate women's career progress. (p. 101)

PURPOSE AND OBJECTIVES OF THE STUDY

The primary purpose of this study was to evaluate demographic information and assess the impact work-related factors have on home and family life for female managers in the health care food service industry. Variables examined in this study included work schedule, job security, advancement opportunities, and benefits.

The research objectives for the study were the following:

1. To determine if the workplace of managers in health care food service has a positive impact on the home and family lives of female managers.
2. To determine if female managers in health care food service experience a high degree of home and family life satisfaction due to job security, flexible work schedules, excellent benefits, career advancement, and other factors.
3. To determine if female managers in health care food service experience discrimination because of age, sex, educational level, race, or seniority.

TERMINOLOGY

The hospitality industry includes many and varied businesses catering to guests; four major industry segments are food service, lodging, travel, and recreation (Brymer, 1991). Health care food service includes hospital and nursing home dietary services, as well as residential retirement centers, other extended care facilities, and community food service programs (Walsh, 1991). The American Dietetic Association (A.D.A.) members with management responsibilities in health care delivery systems include food and nutrition care managers generally employed in institutions, e.g., directors of departments or facilities and administrative dietitians and technicians (American Dietetic Association, 1993).

Job satisfaction is the positive mental attitude experienced by the worker in response to the presently occupied work role (Ivancevich & Donnelly, 1968). Family life satisfaction is the pleasurable or positive emotional state resulting from various aspects of one's family or family experiences (McIntyre, 1989).

MOTIVATIONAL THEORY ASSOCIATED WITH THE WORK ENVIRONMENT

A component of the research study presented in this paper focuses on job satisfaction for female managers in the health care food service industry. Therefore, it is significant to review the findings of Herzberg (1966) relating to job satisfaction. The two-factors theory of motivation developed by Herzberg (1966) stated that motivational factors contributed to job satisfaction and included: (a) achievement, (b) recognition, (c) responsibility, and (d) intrinsic qualities of the job itself. Herzberg identified satisfiers and dissatisfiers within the workplace. Satisfiers are factors whose presence increases job satisfaction, and may or may not cause dissatisfaction when missing. Dissatisfiers are factors that decrease job satisfaction. Dissatisfiers may contribute to job satisfaction when absent. Herzberg identified factors which enhanced job satisfaction by eliminating dissatisfiers. These factors included: (a) salary and benefits, (b) supervision, (c) physical working conditions, (d) company administrative policies, and (e) job security. Herzberg discussed motivation in the context of bureaucratic and decentralized organizations. Employees were bound by predetermined rules in bureaucracies and rewards often ceased to be reflective of success. This led to a decrease in available motivation as bureaucratic complexity intensified (Herzberg, 1966).

ISSUES RELATED TO WOMEN IN THE HEALTH CARE FOOD SERVICE SECTOR

There still exist a high degree of discrimination and barriers for women in health care food service management. According to Blank and Slipp (1994) in *Voice of Diversity:*

Despite the Equal Pay Act of 1963, in 1990 women earned only seventy-four cents for every dollar earned by a man. Even taking into account differences in education and experience in the work world, the pay gap is real. At every age, within every work category, men still take home more pay than women. And the more education a woman has, the wider the gap. (p. 151)

The United States Department of Labor's prediction for the year 2000, is that women will comprise approximately 47% of the work force and will earn wages equal to 74% of men's. In addition, for females, level of education is not always a critical factor in the salary earned (Johnson, 1987). According to research documented by Lorenzini and McDowell (1995), the annual salary of the average food service manager is $41,744. The salaries of female managers are $10,000 less than the salaries of their male counterparts. The salary gap increases in higher salaried positions.

To show this is an ongoing trend that is not likely to discontinue/ change, Barrett, Nagy, and Maize (1992) conducted a study on salary discrepancies between male and female food service directors. The findings from this study revealed that men in food service management positions earned a mean of $10,000 more per year than did women, an increase of $3,700 (37%) from 1980. According to the United States Bureau of Census (1987), incomes of males in health care exceeded those of females by at least 30%. Barrett et al. (1992) indicated this is an issue that should be of concern to the American Dietetic Association because its membership is 98% women.

Other studies have been undertaken in the area of health care food service to measure job satisfaction of both men and women. McNeil, A. G. Vaden and R. E. Vaden (1981) discovered interesting demographics of males in health care food service management in comparison to women in the same field. McNeil, A. G. Vaden and R. E. Vaden (1981) found that male food service administrators tended to be younger than women in the positions. Sixty percent of the men were under 40 years of age while 40.3% of the women administrators were over 50 years of age. This study also revealed the majority of the females' bachelor's degrees were in dietetics or nutrition while the males' bachelor's degrees were primarily in restaurant management, institutional management, or business.

EFFECT OF WORK ON FAMILY LIFE
RELATED TO THE BROAD WORKFORCE

Work can have a variety of effects on family life and similarly, family matters may have a direct effect on females' work lives. Wilensky (1960) pointed out variables such as work schedules, job training, and career patterns are sometimes better predictors of behavior than both special class and previous job experience. Blank and Slipp (1994) reported "that women earn less, have less prestigious job titles, and are promoted less often. Many women face the reality of problematic child care, which can have a detrimental effect on job opportunities" (p. 151).

Previous research discussed several aspects of the structure and organization of work life as important in shaping and influencing family systems. The first aspect is the relative absorptiveness of an occupation, referring to the extent to which the job affects other family members. The second aspect is timing concerned with the effect of work hours and schedules. Another aspect involves the rewards and resources provided by the occupation. The last dimension is the emotional climate of work, whereby this aspect of the job relates to how workers feel about themselves. The set of feelings caused by the experiences on the job are brought home and affect the family (Aldous, 1982; Kanter, 1983).

Conflict occurs when the time devoted to the requirements of one role make it difficult to fulfill the requirements of the other role. Studies (Boyd & Butler, 1982; Lawhon, 1984) have reported time-based conflicts in areas related to work/family demands. These factors may produce pressures to participate extensively in the work role or the family role. Conflict is experienced when time pressures were incompatible with the demands of the other role.

Voydanoff (1978) identified demands associated with time shortage such as being a female working parent, the presence of pre-school and school-age children, experiencing three or more important family changes, and work hours and scheduling. Factors for coping with time demands included high income, job satisfaction, not marrying early, and an ability to arrange time for family activities.

In the broad workforce, job aspects which often have a negative impact on home and family life include work hours and work schedule. Factors relating to job security such as job training, promotion and emotional climate of work are also significant considerations.

METHODS

The subjects for the final study were members of the American Dietetic Association and A.D.A.'s Management in Health Care Systems dietetic practice group. A random sample of 333 (33.0%) of the population was surveyed for the final study.

A questionnaire was used to identify demographic information and to determine the impact work-related factors have on home and family lives of food service managers in health care delivery systems. The first segment of the questionnaire was designed to identify demographic information of managers in health care food service. Twenty-two questions were included in this section. The questions were adapted from the American Dietetic Association's annual survey and the "Work, Home, and Family Questionnaire" used by McIntyre (1989). Permission from appropriate persons was received by the researchers to use questions from these instruments.

The second segment of the instrument focused on the impact of work on home and family life. This section included nineteen work-related variables. In regard to sixteen variables, the respondent was asked "How satisfied are you with your work?" The possible responses ranged from "very satisfied" to "very dissatisfied." The respondent was then asked "What effect do you believe each work variable has on the quality of your home life?" The responses for the second set of questions in this section ranged from "very positive" to "very negative." The format of this segment of the instrument was adapted from the "Work, Home, and Family Questionnaire" developed by Felstehausen, Glosson, and Couch (1987). In modifying their survey, the researchers used a seven-point Likert scale and labeled each possible answer included as part of the Likert scale.

In an effort to establish content validity and clarity, a preliminary draft of the questionnaire, consisting of items modified from existing instruments, was reviewed by professors of the School of Merchandising and Hospitality Management at the University of North Texas, a class of hospitality management graduate students and female managers working in hospital food service. Based upon their recommendations, several items were rewritten, eliminated, or added, prior to the pre-test and approval by the University of North Texas Institutional Review Board for the Protection of Human Subjects.

The sample for the pre-test included members of the American Dietetic Association's Management in Health Care Systems dietetic practice group. All 70 members of this practice group located in Texas were surveyed. A 74% response rate, 52 completed questionnaires, was achieved for the pre-test and reliability of the research instrument was established. Results from the pre-test were not included in the final study.

The subjects for the final study were members of the American Dietetic Association and A.D.A.'s Management in Health Care Systems dietetic practice group. All subjects were employed at locations throughout the United States. A mailing list was obtained from the American Dietetic Association representing the population surveyed.

A random sample of 333 (33.0%) of the population was surveyed for the final study. The participants were asked to complete the questionnaire and were assured individual responses would be kept confidential.

One hundred and thirty-six questionnaires, 40.8%, were returned. During the course of the statistical analysis, eight of the questionnaires were eliminated due to insufficient data. Of the 128 participants remaining, 122 were female managers and the remaining 6 were males. Because male managers comprised only about 5% of the participants, these questionnaires were also eliminated. Comparison between males and females would not have been reliable; moreover, leaving out male responses made analysis among female responses easier.

The Statistical Analysis Software (SAS) program was used to evaluate the multiple-item additive scales for both the family life satisfaction and job satisfaction measures. Internal consistency of the questionnaire was checked by a factor analysis. For the question pertaining to overall satisfaction, four distinct factors emerged among the various job aspects. Four separate factors also emerged for the question pertaining to the overall effect on home life. The reliability coefficient scores measured by Cronbach's alphas were high for all the factors: scores ranged from .84 to .69 for the satisfaction factors and from .91 to .84 for the job impact factors.

Data were examined using a variety of procedures including frequency distributions and cross-tabulations, comparison of mean scores, and analyses of variance. Frequency counts and percentages were tabulated for the demographic characteristics. Mean scores were calculated for responses to questions relating to: (a) satisfaction with various work aspects, and (b) effect of these work aspects on quality of family life. Seniority on the job and income were used as covariates as much of the research on job satisfaction point to a significant increase in satisfaction as seniority and income increase.

RESULTS

Interesting demographic information resulted. Sixty-five percent of the participants were married, 92% of them were over 40 years of age, 84% were white, and just 8% were black.

In reference to the participants' educational level and work responsibility, 40% of the respondents held a Master's Degree and all had at least an Associate Degree. Ninety percent of the respondents had a degree in food and nutrition and over 80% practiced in food and nutrition management. Ninety-seven percent of the participants held jobs in managerial positions yet as many as 77% of them (90 out of 117) did not specifically major in management while a student. Sixty-one percent of the respondents earned over $45,000 annually.

The study also revealed that 79% of the participants worked more than forty hours per week. More than 50% of the respondents have worked in their current position for over seven years and nearly 75% had been with their current employer for more than seven years. Thirty-six percent of the participants work for a government agency (local, state, or federal) and 51% control an annual budget of over a million dollars. More than half (52%) supervise forty or more employees.

Results from this study indicated that 29% of the participants had children under 18 years of age. Eleven percent of the respondents had children or adults requiring special care.

Examination of Research Objectives

Objective 1

To determine if the workplace of managers in health care food service has a positive impact on the home and family lives of female managers.

Data collected from this study revealed that 55% of the participants felt that work had some positive impact on the quality of their family lives, as illustrated in Figure 1. Although the majority of the respondents felt their work positively impacted their home lives it should be noted this was only a slight majority. The study also revealed that 36% of the managers believed the workplace has a negative impact on their home lives. Nine percent expressed neither negative or positive impacts.

Persons most satisfied with their work expressed positive impacts on their family life. The components of satisfaction were: (a) opportunity to work independently, (b) benefits, and (c) amount of control over how they do their work. This information is shown in Figure 2.

Work aspects with highest satisfaction levels are provided in Table 1. Results from this study indicate that 91% of the respondents were at least somewhat satisfied with the tasks of their jobs. Eighty-nine percent of the respondents were somewhat satisfied because they were able to work independently. Eighty-eight percent of the participants were somewhat satisfied with the amount of control over their work. Eighty-seven percent were somewhat satisfied with the challenge of their jobs. Eighty-three percent of the respondents exhibited a degree of satisfaction regarding benefits. Respondents ranked at the highest level of satisfaction, the opportunity to work independently (41% of respondents); and the amount of control over their work (36% of respondents).

FIGURE 1. Overall Impact of Work on Family Life

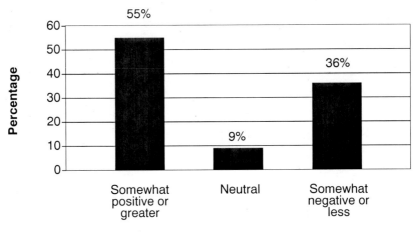

FIGURE 2. Work Aspects with Most Positive Impact on Family Life

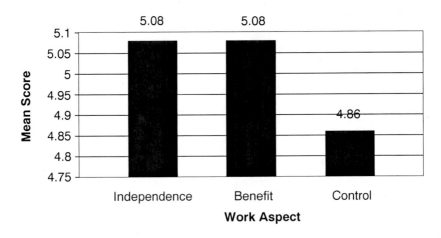

There was a 0.6 correlation (p-value .0001) between the overall level of satisfaction with their work and the impact it had on the quality of their family life.

The job aspects that exhibited the three highest correlations with overall effect on family life were "opportunity to work independently" (0.52,

TABLE 1. Work Aspects with Highest Satisfaction Levels

	Variety of work tasks		Opportunity to work independently		Control over work		Challenge of the job		Benefits	
	%	Cum. %	%	Cum. %	%	Cum. %	%	Cum. %	%	Cum. %
Very satisfied	31.4	31.4	41.3	41.3	35.5	35.5	29.7	29.7	22.5	22.5
Satisfied	46.3	77.7	37.1	78.5	36.3	71.9	45.4	75.2	39.1	61.6
Somewhat satisfied	13.2	90.9	10.7	89.2	16.5	88.4	11.5	86.7	20.8	82.5
Neutral	4.9	95.8	3.3	92.5	2.4	90.9	6.6	93.3	10.0	92.5
Somewhat dissatisfied	2.5	98.3	6.6	99.1	7.4	98.3	4.1	97.5	3.3	95.8
Dissatisfied	1.7	100	.8	100	.8	99.1	2.4	100	1.6	97.5
Very dissatisfied					.8	100			2.5	100

p-value .0001), "salary" (0.51, p-value .0001), and "job security" (0.50, p-value .0001).

Objective 2

> To determine if female managers in health care food service experience a high degree of home and family life satisfaction due to job security, flexible work schedules, excellent benefits, career advancement, and other factors.

Information from Table 2 shows that among the 82% of the female managers who were satisfied with their jobs, the distribution of the effect of job on family life was fairly well dispersed among the positive (64%), neutral (10%) and negative (26%) categories. In contrast, the distribution is more focused among the 16% that were dissatisfied with their jobs. Here, nearly 90% of the female managers believed the job had a negative impact on their home life. This contrast is supported by the values of the correlation coefficients between job satisfaction and impact of job on family life. Overall, this value was 0.58, with just 0.29 for satisfied managers and as high as 0.70 for dissatisfied managers.

Results from this study showed which work aspects were the least satisfying and had the highest level of dissatisfaction. The number of hours worked per week and the opportunity for advancement showed the greatest level of dissatisfaction. Twenty-nine percent of the participants were dissatisfied with the opportunity for advancement, while 31% were dissatisfied with the number of hours they worked per week.

As shown in Figure 3, data revealed the work aspects which had the most negative impact on the quality of home life for female managers. Fifty-nine percent of the managers stated that the number of hours they worked per week had, at best, a somewhat negative impact on their family lives. Thirty-three percent and 25%, respectively, stated their work schedules and job security impacted their home lives negatively.

The results further indicated that there was generally a high correlation between the respondents' level of satisfaction about various work aspects and the respective effect each of these aspects had on the quality of their home lives. Correlations ranged from .79 (p-value .0001) for "support from management" to .55 (p-value .0001) for "challenge of the job." Other aspects among the top six were "job status," correlation .76 (p-value .0001); "opportunity for advancement," correlation .74 (p-value .0001); "job security," correlation .70 (p-value .0001); "salary," correlation .66 (p-value .0001); and "work schedule," correlation .64 (p-value .0001).

TABLE 2. Job Satisfaction and Effect on Family Life

	Somewhat positive or better	Neutral	Somewhat negative or worse	All
Somewhat satisfied or better	64.00% [a]95.52%	10.00% 90.91%	26.00% 59.09%	100.00% 81.97%
Neutral	66.67% 2.99%	– –	33.33% 2.27%	100.00% 2.46%
Somewhat dissatisfied or worse	5.26% 1.49%	5.26% 9.09%	89.47% 38.64%	100.00% 15.57%
All	54.92% 100.00%	9.02% 100.00%	36.07% 100.00%	100.00% 100.00%

Note: [a]Percentage of column

FIGURE 3. Work Aspects with Most Negative Impact on Family Life

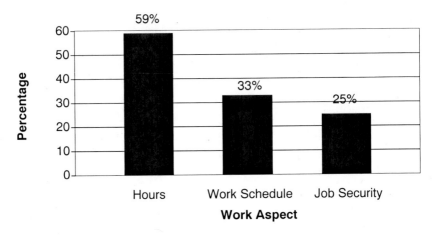

The job aspects that exhibited the three highest correlations with overall satisfaction level were "job status" (0.70, p-value .0001), "amount of control over how you do your work" (0.62, p-value .0001), and "support from management" (0.61, p-value .0001).

Objective 3

> To determine if female managers in health care food service experience a high degree of discrimination because of age, sex, educational level, race, or seniority.

Results show that 40% of the participants believe they had experienced some sort of discrimination during their employment in the health care industry. Distribution among types of discrimination is shown in Figure 4. Of the 49 participants who said they had been discriminated against, 78% indicated they were discriminated against because of their sex. Eighteen percent of the respondents said they were discriminated against due to their race, while 16% indicated age was the reason for discrimination.

DISCUSSION AND CONCLUSION

The main purpose of the study was to investigate the relationship between work and family life satisfaction for female managers in the

FIGURE 4. Distribution Among Types of Discrimination-Overlap Among Categories Results in >100% (N = 49)

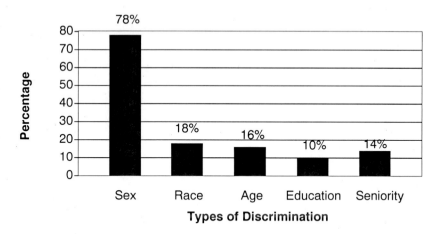

health care food service industry. Achieving and maintaining family life satisfaction is an important issue as the majority of women are in the workforce today and the tendency is likely to continue in the future. The tradition of family management and "bread-winning" responsibilities being assigned primarily by gender have all but disappeared. Work satisfaction has been studied as an entity in itself with strict boundaries between it and the home leading to a theory of separate worlds of work and family. The complicated relationship between work, family and home life can be examined through studies such as this one.

The main findings of this study include the following:

1. In the health care food service industry, a majority (55%) of female managers believe their work place positively affects their family life.
2. Job aspects with the most positive impact on family life are fringe benefits, independence, and control over how work is done.
3. Job aspects with the most negative impact on family life are work hours, work schedule, and lack of job security. This information is consistent with the researchers' expectations and is also similar to results identified in the literature.
4. There is a moderately high correlation between job satisfaction and its impact on family life. However, the correlation tends to be higher among dissatisfied managers and lower among satisfied managers.

5. The perception of sex discrimination far exceeds that of any other type of discrimination.

In the ensuing general discussion it is assumed that what impacts family life could have a profound impact on society as a whole. A more harmonious home life could lead to a decrease in domestic violence, decrease in drug abuse, worker absenteeism, and other social ills. These factors in turn could result in greater productivity and less medical and welfare expenses in our society.

Fifty-five percent of the respondents felt their jobs had a positive impact on family life. Thirty-six percent of the managers felt their jobs had a negative effect on their family life, while 9% indicated no effect. This finding does not bode well for health care organizations, society as a whole, as well as individual families. It is important for health care administrators to communicate with managers and employees to understand what is most important to achieve a motivated and satisfied workforce. With the demands placed on today's female managers, it is very important for managers to achieve personal satisfaction and success both at work and home.

The second major finding implies that if female managers in the health care industry are empowered with more benefits, more independence, and greater control at the workplace, their particular work institution could benefit directly as would their home environment.

The third finding supports the argument that if the health care industry does not give their female managers more flexible work hours and schedules, thus giving them a greater sense of job security, the particular institution and society as a whole will be faced with insurmountable problems. Health care organizations should listen to the unique needs of their employees, and allow flexible scheduling so that female managers can meet their responsibilities on the job and at home. Managers are encouraged to communicate to administrators specific strategies for this end.

The implication of the fourth finding is that among dissatisfied female health care food service managers the negative impact on home life and society is tremendous. The fifth major finding is that while race discrimination has been far more publicized and evokes greater emotional response, sex discrimination is a larger problem in the health care food service industry. This finding is consistent with the literature describing the larger workforce. Today's work environment is not always free of gender discrimination. This concern must be addressed by administrators to achieve fairness within the growing female workforce characterized as becoming more vocal in communicating needs and expectations. The persistence of this hiatus may result in professionalization of the workers in this field with imminent unionization.

Results of this study are consistent with the researchers' expectations and are similar to the literature describing both the broader workforce and health care food service. Job aspects which have a negative impact on family life are work hours, schedule and job security factors. Excellent benefits and independence in the workplace serve as satisfiers for today's female managers and have a positive impact on family life.

A recommendation for future research is to undertake comparable studies with female and minority managers in other hospitality industries as well as industries within the broader workforce. Similarly, male managers could be studied and the results compared.

AUTHOR NOTE

Howard R. Clayton has been Associate Professor of Management Science at the University of North Texas for the past six years. During this time, he has taught undergraduate and graduate courses in Statistics and Computer Simulation. Prior to his position at UNT, Dr. Clayton attended the University of Georgia, where he received a PhD in management sciences. He has published a number of articles in a variety of journals including *Communications in Statistics, Journal of Business and Economic Statistics,* and *Journal of Statistical Computation and Simulation.* As an active member of the Decision Sciences Institute and the American Statistical Association, Dr. Clayton has presented several papers at national and regional meetings as well as published in the respective conference proceedings. Prior to his studies at the University of Georgia, Dr. Clayton was a high school teacher of Mathematics and Science for a number of years in his native Jamaica and the Bahamas.

Vivian Odera earned the Bachelor of Science Degree in Biology at Mercer University and completed the Master of Science Degree in Hotel and Restaurant Management at the University of North Texas. Vivian has 17 years of professional work experience in the hospitality industry, including 9 years in quick service managerial positions. Vivian was employed for six years as a Nutrition Technician at Children's Medical Center, Dallas, Texas. Since 1995 Vivian has been employed for six years as a Nutrition Technician at Children's Medical Center, Dallas, Texas. Vivian is currently Assistant Director of Food and Nutrition Services at the Trinity Medical Center of Carrollton, Carrollton, Texas. Daniel A. Emenheiser earned the Bachelor of Science Degree in Food Service and Housing Administration at the Pennsylvania State University, completed the Master of Science Degree in Restaurant, Hotel and Institutional Management at Purdue University, and earned the Doctor of Education Degree in Occupational and Adult Education with a minor in Marketing Management at Oklahoma State University. His professional work experiences include regional entertainment manger with Stuart Anderson Black Angus/Cattle Company restaurants and Manager of Food and Nutrition Services at Christ Hospital and Medical Center, Oak Lawn, Illinois. Dr. Emenheiser has taught in the Hotel and Restaurant Management programs at Oklahoma State University, University of Hawaii, Purdue University–Calumet and the University of North Texas. At the University of North Texas, he is Assistant Professor in the School of Merchandising and Hospitality Management and has served as Graduate Coordinator in the school and presently is Associate Dean. His research interests include management and marketing of visitor, leisure and entertainment attractions; nutrition; and course content and teaching methods of hospitality curriculum.

Johnny Sue Reynolds earned the Bachelor of Science Degree at the University of Mary Hardin-Baylor, completed the Master of Science Degree at the University of North Texas, and earned the Doctor of Philosophy Degree from Texas Woman's University. Her professional work experiences include 17 years of teaching in public schools including kindergarten, secondary and adult education. Dr. Reynolds has taught for the past seven years at the University of North Texas, six of which she served as General Manger of The Club at College Inn, the Hotel and Restaurant Management program's student-operated restaurant. Currently, she is Associate Professor and Chair of the Division of Hotel and Restaurant Management. Her research interests include consumer aspects of the hospitality industry, bed and breakfast operations, and the fast food industry.

REFERENCES

Aldous, J. (1982). From dual-earners to dual-career families and back again. In J. Aldous (Ed.) *Two paychecks: Life in dual-earner families* (pp. 11-26). Beverly Hills, CA: Sage Publications.

American Dietetic Association. (1993). *Dietetic Practice Group of the American Dietetic Association* [Brochure]. Chicago, IL: Author.

Barrett, E. B., Nagy, C. M., & Maize, R. S. (1992). Salary discrepancies between male and female food service directors in JCAHO-accredited hospitals. *Journal of the American Dietetic Association 92*(9), 1078-1082.

Blank, R. & Slipp, S. (1994). *Voices of diversity.* New York: AMACOM.

Boyd, L., & Butler, S. (1982). Families and work: Another perspective. *Illinois Teacher, 25,* 179-181.

Brownell, J. (1994). Women in hospitality management: General managers' perceptions of factors related to career development. *International Journal of Hospitality Management, 13*(2), 101-117.

Bryke, J. & Kornblum, M. (1991). Report on the 1991 membership data base on the American Dietetic Association. *Journal of American Dietetic Association, 93,* 211-215.

Brymer, R. A. (1991). *Hospitality management: An introduction to the industry* (6th ed.). Dubuque, IA: Kendall/Hunt Publishing Company.

Buergermeister, J. (1983). Assessment of the education skills and competencies needed by beginning hospitality managers. *Hospitality Education & Research Journal, 8,* 38-53.

Burden, D. S., & Googins, B. (1987). *Balancing jobs and home life study: Managing work and family stress in corporations.* Boston University, School of Social Work, Boston.

Felstehausen, G., Glosson, L. R., & Couch, A. S. (1987). *A study to determine the relationship between the workplace and the home* (Document No. 66420060). Lubbock: Texas Tech University.

Herzberg, F. (1966). *Work and the nature of man.* Cleveland: World.

Ivancevich, J. M., & Donnelly, J. H. (1968). Job satisfaction research: A manageable guide for practitioners. *Personnel Journal, 47,* 172-177.

Jamieson, D. & O'Mara, J. (1991). *Managing workforce 2000.* San Francisco, CA: Jossey-Bass Inc., Publishers.

Johnson, W. B. (1987). *Work Force 2000: Work and workers for the 21 Century.* Indianapolis, IN: Hudson Institute.

Kanter, R. M. (1983). Productivity and the quality of life. *Forum, 5,* 14-16.

Lawhon, T. M. (1984). Work and stress in the home: How do you help in the family? *Journal of Home Economics, 76,* 2-5.

Lorenzini, B. & McDowell, B. (1995). Jobs$: Think your salary's too low? Compare your career status with peers' in R&I 27th annual survey. *Restaurants & Institutions, 105,*(30). 41,44,46,48,50,52,56,57.

Marshall, A. (1991). Is hospitality industry hospitable to Women? *Hotel & Motel Management, 206*(14), 25.

McIntyre, E. H. (1989). *Family life satisfaction and job satisfaction for women in dual-earner marriages and traditional and non-traditional occupations.* Unpublished dissertation. Texas Woman's University, Denton, Texas.

McNeil, G. F., Vaden, A. G., & Vaden, R. E. (1981). Job satisfaction is still high for hospital food service directors. *Hospitals,* 106-111.

Thornburg, L. (1991). What's wrong with work force 2000? *HR Magazine, 36,* 38-32.

U.S. Bureau of the Census. (1987). *Current population reports.* U.S. Government Printing Office, Washington, DC.

Voydanoff, P. (1978). The relationship between perceived job characteristics and job satisfaction among occupational status groups. *Sociology of Work and Occupation, 5,* 179-192.

Walsh, T. E. (1991). Foodservice in institutions. In Brymer, R. A. (Ed.) *Hospitality management: An introduction to the industry* (6th ed.) (p. 508). Dubuque, IA: Kendall/Hunt Publishing Company.

Wilensky, H. L. (1960). Work, career, and social integration. *International Social Science Journal, 12*(1), 543-556.

An Occupational Hazard:
Alcohol Consumption
Among Hospitality Managers

David L. Corsun
Cheri A. Young

SUMMARY. One hundred eighty-three alumni of a hospitality program at a Northeastern university were surveyed to examine the relationships between work stressors, strains, social support, and several demographic variables and alcohol consumption among hospitality managers. The data provide compelling support for the presence of an occupational subculture whose norms promote drinking. No support was found for the work stress perspective of alcohol consumption; however, significant negative correlations between each of three measures of strain and alcohol consumption indicate that alcohol may serve as a buffer between work stressors and strains. Implications and future research needs are discussed. *[Article copies available for a fee from The Haworth Document Delivery Service: 1-800-342-9678. E-mail address: getinfo@haworthpressinc.com]*

David L. Corsun and Cheri A. Young are completing doctoral degrees at Cornell University. They will be faculty members at Washington State University in the fall of 1998.

Address correspondence to: David L. Corsun, School of Hotel Administration, Ithaca, NY 14853 (E-mail: dlc7@cornell.edu).

The authors wish to thank Leo Renaghan and the *Center for Hospitality Research* for funding this research; Leo Gruenfeld and Tim Judge for their guidance in the early stages; and Craig Lundberg, Kirsti Lindberg, Reed Fisher, Jeff Shay, two anonymous reviewers, and the editors of this volume for their comments on an earlier draft of this chapter.

[Haworth co-indexing entry note]: "An Occupational Hazard: Alcohol Consumption Among Hospitality Managers." Corsun, David L., and Cheri A. Young. Co-published simultaneously in *Marriage & Family Review* (The Haworth Press, Inc.) Vol. 28, No. 1/2, 1998, pp. 187-211; and: *The Role of the Hospitality Industry in the Lives of Individuals and Families* (ed: Pamela R. Cummings, Francis A. Kwansa, and Marvin B. Sussman) The Haworth Press, Inc., 1998, pp. 187-211. Single or multiple copies of this article are available for a fee from The Haworth Document Delivery Service [1-800-342-9678, 9:00 a.m. - 5:00 p.m. (EST). E-mail address: getinfo@haworthpressinc.com].

KEYWORDS. Alcohol consumption, Hospitality managers, Work stress, Workplace culture

The cost of alcohol abuse to individuals, their organizations, and the government is in the billions of dollars (Frank, McGuire, Regier, Manderscheid, & Woodward, 1994; Pallarito, 1995; Savitz, 1995). Three-quarters of the work force drinks and ten percent experience difficulties at work due to alcohol (McKibben, 1990). It is estimated that approximately one-third of hospital admissions are related to alcohol (Savitz, 1995). Hospitality organizations are certainly not immune to these costs. On the contrary, hospitality workers have been identified as one of several at-risk occupational populations with regard to alcohol abuse (Hitz, 1973; Plant, 1977, 1978; Whitehead & Simpkins, 1983).

Most of the data peculiar to hospitality workers omits management from the population of interest (Hitz, 1973; Plant, 1977, 1978; Whitehead & Simpkins, 1983). However, tales of alcohol-abusing hotel, restaurant, and club managers are legion. The fast pace of the industry, constantly increasing competition, and the long hours (often including nights and weekends) that severely limit personal and/or family time, all exert pressure on managers. It is important to examine the alcohol consumption patterns of this group to help us understand what about the work and the workplace is associated with hospitality managers' propensity to drink.

Trice and Sonnenstuhl (1988) inductively identified four perspectives from which social scientists examine risk factors related to the workplace that promote alcohol consumption: the work stress, workplace culture, alienation, and social control perspectives. In this chapter, we examine alcohol consumption among hospitality managers from the work stress perspective and the workplace culture perspective. In addition, we investigate the relationships between drinking and social support and several demographic variables.

THE STRAIN OF HOSPITALITY WORK

The hospitality industry is driven by societal, occupational, and organizational norms or expectations regarding expression of emotion or feelings and ways of handling customers. These "feeling rules" (Hochschild, 1983) or "display rules" (Rafaeli & Sutton, 1989) "are norms that specify the range, intensity, duration, and object of emotions that should be experienced" or expressed (Ashforth & Humphrey, 1993: 89). When purchasing a hospitality service, from the customers' perspective, the employees "are" the product, and as such, their expressions of feeling have a strong impact on organizational effectiveness and the quality of service perceived by the customers (Ashforth & Humphrey, 1993). Regardless of their own emotional state during a stress-inducing customer encounter, hospitality employees are expected to be friendly, cheerful, and helpful.

Personal-contact service work, such as that characterized by the hospitality industry, produces "emotional strains" (Schneider & Bowen, 1995). Such demands or "strains" result from displaying appropriate emotion behaviors while under pressure, such as being personable, warm, and cheerful, the characteristics expected by the customers. Employees, especially those in guest-contact positions, must carefully monitor the manner in which they display feelings. Because expression of emotions is dictated and controlled by the organization, it has been termed "emotional labor" (Hochschild, 1983). According to Hochschild (1983: 7) "emotional labor is the management of feeling to create a publicly observable facial and bodily display, in exchange for a wage in the public sphere."

Many researchers argue that the manipulation and control of emotional expression threatens the employee's emotional well-being, creates stress, and can cause social and psychological damage, in that the employee becomes dissonant with him/herself. Ashforth and Humphrey (1993: 106) indicate that "one's sense of authentic self may also be impaired by performing emotional labor." As the hospitality industry continues to grow, filling jobs requiring emotion management with greater and greater numbers of workers, it becomes important to understand the nature and consequences of this type of work, particularly the conditions under which it may be psychologically damaging (Wharton & Erickson, 1993).

> In particular, little attention has been devoted to systematic study of issues Hochschild and others raise concerning the social-psychological and affective effects of emotional labor on incumbents of these frontline service jobs. To the extent that these issues have been addressed, studies highlight its negative social-psychological consequences, implicitly or explicitly sustaining the view that frontline service work has affective costs for workers. (Wharton, 1993: 207)

The notion of emotional labor highlights the stressful nature of hospitality work and may help explain alcohol consumption among hospitality managers from the work stress perspective identified by Trice and Sonnenstuhl (1988).

The alcohol literature in which stress is associated with drinking suffers from the same muddled terminology as the stress literature. In order to avoid contributing to this confusion, we define our terms below.

CLARIFYING THE TERMINOLOGY

Researchers' use of the term *stress* has obfuscated, rather than clarified, its meaning (Jex, Beehr, & Roberts, 1992; Matheny, Aycock, Pugh, Curlette, & Cannella, 1986). Stress has alternately been referred to as the antecedent to and outcome of the interaction of person and environment as well as the person-environment interaction itself. For the purposes of this research, the clarifications provided by Matheny and his colleagues (1986) and Jex and his colleagues (1992) are employed. Specifically, work stress is defined as an interaction between the person and the work environment. The antecedent to this interaction, the psycho-social demands (internal or external to the individual) in the work environment necessitating adaptive responses, are considered *stressors*. The individual's physiological responses to the presence of stressors in the work environment we refer to as *strains* (Bhagat, Allie & Ford, Jr., 1991; Jex et al., 1992; Matheny et al., 1986).

Related to the problem of definitional dissensus among researchers is the ambiguity inherent in any pen and paper measure of stress that includes the word stress (Jex et al., 1992). Just as researchers do, survey respondents may interpret stress in any of the three ways mentioned above. Some measures of stressors and strains rely on respondents to interpret the word stress as the researcher intends. To the degree that respondent interpretations are consonant with researchers' construct definitions, the findings of studies employing ambiguously phrased items are valid. However, there is no way to determine the degree of consonance or discord between these researchers and their survey respondents. The findings of any such research must, therefore, be interpreted with and inferred from with great caution. This research avoids such interpretational complications by eschewing measures of stressors and strains that include the word *stress*.

THE WORK STRESS PERSPECTIVE

Trice and Sonnenstuhl's (1988) work stress perspective identifies work stressors and strains as the risk factors promoting alcohol consumption. Although Fennell, Rodin, and Kantor (1981) do not explicitly test stress/strain-consumption relationships, they point to data trends indicating a strong likelihood that such hypotheses would be supported. Fennell and colleagues examined the relationship between a set of stressors and reasons why people drink (rated on a Likert-type scale of importance). They provide evidence that the presence of stressors in the work environment significantly increases the likelihood of citing a specific reason for drinking as important (Fennel et al., 1981). Margolis, Kroes, and Quinn (1974: 660) found a statistically significant, though practically modest relationship between "escapist drinking" and role ambiguity, workload, and job insecurity. Parker and Brody (1982: 120) reported that work strains such as "frequency of feeling tense, worried or upset about job circumstances" explained variation in dependency on alcohol. Hingson, Mangione, and Barrett (1981) examined the relationship between boredom, work stressors, and other job-related variables (e.g., amount of supervision, whether one's work was respected by others) and alcohol consumption. Only work stressors and boredom were significantly related to drinking.

Stressors in the Work Environment

Although there are a multitude of stressors in work environments, a handful of them appear repeatedly in the stress literature. Our review of this literature and knowledge of the interpersonal demands of hospitality work led us to investigate the role of the following stressors in alcohol consumption: role conflict, role ambiguity, interpersonal conflict, workload, lack of opportunities to deal with others, lack of friendship opportunities, and boredom.

Role conflict refers to the presence of coexistent antagonistic job pressures (Kahn, Wolfe, Quinn, Snoek, & Rosenthal, 1964), such that responding to one set of pressures hinders one's ability to comply with the other(s). Role conflict has been identified as a significant source of stress by several researchers across a variety of occupations (Kahn et al., 1964) including child care workers (Manlove, 1994), emergency medical residents (Revicki, Whitley, Gallery & Allison, 1993), and teachers (Burke & Greenglass, 1993). It is noteworthy that all of these occupations involve emotional labor.

Role ambiguity is simply an incumbent's doubt regarding some aspect of her job. One might be uncertain about such things as basic as the tasks and responsibilities one's job entails, who the members of one's work group are, or how one's work helps the organization accomplish its desired ends (Katz & Kahn, 1978). Role ambiguity has been identified as a source of stress, particularly for those who are organizational newcomers (Ruben, 1986), have an external locus of control (Arney, 1988), are risk averse (Siegall & Cummings, 1995), change-phobic (Callan, 1993), or are coronary-prone Type A's (Howard, Cunningham, & Rechnitzer, 1986a, 1986b).

Work in the areas of leader-member exchange and team-member exchange indicate that concordant relationships are related to positive organizational and individual outcomes: organizational commitment, reduced intent to turnover, and job satisfaction (Major, Kozlowski, Chao & Gardner, 1995). Harmonic relations with one's supervisor and work group members had the further effect of reducing the impact of newcomers' unmet role expectations (Major et al., 1995). It is hardly surprising, then, that *interpersonal conflict* is among the most frequently mentioned causes of work stress (Keenan & Newton, 1985). Spector (1987) examined the relationship between stressors and strains and found interpersonal conflict correlated significantly with three commonly reported stress outcomes: anxiety, frustration, and somatic symptoms.

Workload refers to an individual's perception that the demands of her job are excessive. These excessive demands may manifest themselves as a particularly burdensome quantity of work, the requirement that one work especially diligently or quickly, or as the absence of discretionary time on the job (Spector, 1987). The more frequently one experiences any or all of these work demands, the greater is one's workload. Workload has been significantly related to strain in women office workers (Piotrkowski, Cohen, & Coray, 1992), middle and pre-retirement age adults (Remondet & Hansson, 1991), computer users (Yang & Carayon, 1995), and Type A individuals (Kushnir & Melamed, 1991).

As the economy moves increasingly toward being service driven, it is virtually certain that more and more jobs will involve substantial interpersonal contact. Service workers cannot just pick and choose when, or with whom, their interactions will occur. Even among manufacturing workers, the movement toward team-based organizations has made the isolated assembly line job an anachronism. Whether one's client base is internal or external to the organization, dealing with others will continue to assume greater importance. People whose work does not provide such opportunities may feel increasingly like social isolates and may perceive the *lack of opportunities to deal with others* as a stressor.

Social support has been shown to moderate the relationship between some stressors and strains (Fisher, 1985). Such support can come from co-workers, one's supervisor, and/or from friends and relatives outside the workplace. Each of these three potential sources of social support is important–the absence of one may not be mitigated by the presence of the others. Individuals, frustrated in their attempts to forge friendships and develop social support networks in the workplace due to organizational or structural impediments, may therefore experience the *lack of friendship opportunities* as a stressor.

Fisher (1993: 396) defines *boredom* as "an unpleasant, transient affective state in which the individual feels a pervasive lack of interest in and difficulty concentrating on the current activity." The likelihood of a task inducing boredom should decrease as skill variety, task identity, task significance, autonomy, and feedback increase (Hackman & Oldham, 1980). The potential outcomes resulting from boredom include affective irritation and strain (O'Hanlon, 1981), and increased alcohol consumption (Ames, 1987; Hingson et al., 1981). Although Trice and Sonnenstuhl (1988) include boredom in the alienation perspective in their classification of alcohol studies, the evidence presented above from the stress literature indicates that boredom can justifiably be included in the work stress perspective.

Psychological and Physiological Strains

Stress-related research typically treats strain and work performance variables as outcome measures. Of these outcomes, only strains are relevant to this study. The three strain measures that are particularly relied upon in the stress literature are work frustration, anxiety, and somatic symptoms (Spector, 1987; Spector and O'Connell, 1994; Spector et al., 1988).

Work frustration assesses the degree to which one experiences disappointment or defeat on the job as a result of barriers between one's behaviors and goals (Peters, O'Connor, & Rudolf, 1980). *Anxiety* is a measure of the feelings of psychological distress individuals experience (Spector & O'Connor, 1984). Finally, *somatic symptoms* are health complaints commonly associated with stress (Spector, 1988).

From the work stress perspective on alcohol consumption we derive the following hypotheses:

H1: Individuals who perceive a greater magnitude of work stressors in the environment will consume more alcohol than those who perceive a lesser magnitude of work stressors.

H2: The more strains an individual reports, the more alcohol she or he will consume.

THE WORKPLACE CULTURE PERSPECTIVE

Researchers operating within the workplace culture perspective focus on the drinking norms associated with a given workplace or occupation as risk factors that promote alcohol consumption (Trice & Sonnenstuhl,

1988). Studies conducted in this vein examine these organizational and/or occupational subcultures for signs that they somehow encourage heavy drinking. Many such studies include hospitality workers, particularly those whose work somehow involves the sale of alcohol, among the at-risk population because of their occupations (Hitz, 1973; Plant, 1977, 1978; Whitehead & Simpkins, 1983).

Hitz (1973) and Plant (1978) postulate that heavy drinkers may be attracted to these occupations. In contrast, Cosper (1979) points out that with the data gathered thus far, we are unable to determine whether these occupations attract heavy drinkers. Perhaps more likely is the influence of norms and customs regarding workgroup socialization, both on and off-duty. Even Hitz (1973: 504) allows for this possibility, offering that "drinking together may well form a large part of the social and even work life of these groups." Cosper's (1979) thesis is that individuals conform to the local drinking custom, be it heavy or light consumption.

In addition to an occupational subculture whose norms promote alcohol consumption, the workplace culture perspective suggests that an administrative subculture may also encourage drinking among managers. Tales of the two-martini business lunch, office parties and conferences at which heavy consumption is the standard, and even management retreats at which drinking and drunkenness are supposed to bond individuals (Trice & Sonnenstuhl, 1988), are testimony to such administrative subcultural norms. Given the hospitality industry's occupational subculture, it is likely that such an administrative culture is endemic to hospitality organizations. Thus, even hospitality managers in non-operational positions may be subject to cultural norms that encourage drinking. While this group may be slightly removed from the occupational subculture, they are members of the administrative culture.

In keeping with the workplace culture perspective, the following hypotheses are offered:

H3: Those employed in the hospitality industry will drink more frequently and will engage in heavy drinking[1] more frequently than those employed in other industries.

H4: Individuals employed in hospitality operations will drink with the same frequency and will drink heavily with the same frequency as hospitality executives in non-operational positions.

DEMOGRAPHIC FACTORS

Several demographic variables are also associated with drinking. The literature provides evidence that men drink more frequently than women

(Fennell et al., 1981; O'Hare, 1995), consume more alcohol than women (Fillmore, Golding, Leino, & Motoyoshi,1993; Hingson et al., 1981), and have a higher incidence of alcohol problems than women (O'Hare, 1995; Parker & Brody, 1982). Studies also reveal that white collar workers drink more than blue collar workers (Fennell et al., 1981) and those with higher incomes consume more than lower income individuals (Barnes, Welte, & Dintcheff, 1991; Dight, 1976; Young & French, 1994). Although there is evidence they consume more, we do not expect that those with higher incomes drink heavily with greater frequency than lower income individuals. Last, drinking varies inversely with age (Fennell et al., 1981; Fillmore et al., 1993; Hingson et al., 1981). However, we believe that the strong occupational and administrative norms that encourage drinking among hospitality employees will eliminate the relationship between age and alcohol consumption. This expectation is supported by research findings across several studies that among older persons, those with higher incomes drink more than their lower income peers (Liberto, Oslin, & Ruskin, 1992). Thus, we hypothesize that:

H5:   Men will drink more frequently and engage in heavy drinking more frequently than women.

H6a: Individuals with higher incomes will drink more frequently than those with lower incomes.

H6b: There will be no association between the frequency of heavy drinking and income.

H7:   Among those employed in hospitality, there will be no relationship between age and alcohol consumption.

SOCIAL SUPPORT

There are a multitude of studies providing evidence that social support has positive outcomes with regard to individuals' perceptions of stressors and the reporting of strains (Fisher, 1985). For example, Daniels and Guppy (1994) provide evidence that social support acts as a buffer between stressors and strains. Data collected by Lin, Simeone, Ensel, and Kuo (1979) and Turner (1981) reveal that social support has a negative main effect on strains. In addition, Burke and Greenglass (1995) found that a lack of social support was directly related to psychological burnout.

In the alcohol-related literature, Fennell and colleagues (1981) state that social support is inversely related to the probability of characterizing seven or more different reasons for drinking as important. They, too, offer that social support from other organizational members "can buffer stress or tension on the job" (Fennell et al., 1981: 126). These findings lead us to hypothesize that:

H8: The more social support one has, the less frequently one will drink and drink heavily.

In summary, the hypotheses articulated here argue that the occupational culture associated with the hospitality industry, perceived work stressors, reported strains, sex, and income are all positively related to alcohol consumption. Because of the strong occupational cultural encouragement of drinking in hospitality, age will not be related to drinking for those employed in the industry. Last, support from one's boss, peers, and friends and family will be inversely related to consumption. To test these hypotheses a mail survey was conducted.

METHOD

Sample

A random sample of 600 U.S. resident alumni of a hospitality program in a Northeastern university were selected for participation in the study. A survey instrument was mailed to each of the selected alumni. The survey consisted of questions designed to assess the presence of work stressors, strains, social support, frequency of alcohol consumption, and demographic information. Participants returned their surveys via business reply mail.

The effective sample size was 565. Two surveys were returned undelivered due to incorrect mailing information. In addition, thirty-three members of the sample indicated that they were not employed and, therefore, did not qualify for the study. These people were either retired, not working outside the home, or between jobs. A first mailing yielded ninety usable responses. A second, follow-up mailing produced another ninety-three responses (total n = 183) resulting in an overall response rate of 32.4%. Therefore, inference to the larger alumni population should be made with caution.

One hundred thirty respondents were male (71%) and fifty-three were female (29%). Although recent alumni classes are approximately half male and half female, the sex distribution of the sample is reflective of the alumni population. It should be noted that we cannot be certain whether the sample is representative of the broader population of hospitality managers. However, approximately six thousand of these alumni work in hospitality management, many at the corporate level. It may well be that their responses accurately reflect the occupational and administrative subcultures of the industry.

Respondents ranged in age from twenty-three to seventy-four with a mean age of forty-one. The vast majority of them received bachelor of science degrees (90.2%), with the remainder having received graduate degrees (8.8%). These alumni graduated between 1943 and 1994, with a median graduation year of 1979. Fifty-nine percent of the respondents reside in the Eastern U.S. (North and South combined) with the remainder split almost equally between the Midwest (21%, including the Southern Central states) and the West (20%). Sixty-four percent of the respondents (n = 117) are employed in the hospitality industry and thirty-six percent (n = 66) are not. Of those employed in hospitality, sixty percent (n = 70) are employed at the unit level.

Measurement

Work Stressors: We relied on the stress literature to select the most appropriate measures to operationalize the relevant work stressors. Specifically, we referred to the work of Spector (1987), Spector, Dwyer, and Jex, (1988), and Spector and O'Connell (1994) in designing an instrument measuring workload, unenriched work/boredom, interpersonal conflict, lack of friendship opportunities, lack of opportunities to deal with others, and role conflict and role ambiguity.

Role conflict and ambiguity were measured using the scales developed by Rizzo, House and Lirtzman (1970). The role conflict subscale consisted of eight items measured on a Likert type scale from one, *very false,* to seven, *very true.* The measure focuses on receiving assignments without the manpower to complete them, having to do things that should be done differently, and working with two or more groups that operate quite differently. The reliability coefficient (Cronbach's alpha) was .85 for this study. *Role ambiguity,* a subscale consisting of six items, was measured on the scale mentioned above and had a reliability coefficient of .86. This measure focuses on the certainty one has about his/her authority, knowing what his/her responsibilities are, and receiving clear explanations of what has to be done.

The intrinsic job characteristic subscale, taken from the Idaszak and Drasgow (1987) revision of the Job Diagnostic Survey (Hackman & Oldham, 1974, 1975) was used as a proxy measure for *boredom.* Cronbach's alpha for this scale was .76. This subscale measures the core dimensions of task identity, task significance, skill variety, autonomy and feedback, with items focused on the number of complex or high-level skills required, the opportunity to completely finish a piece of work, and the significance and importance of the job itself. The thinking is that boring or unenriched work is related to boredom.

Spector's (1987) five-item *workload* scale, measured on a five-point Likert-type scale (from *never* to *very often*), had a reliability coefficient of .83 in this study. The items focus on how often the job required the respondent to work fast or hard, quantity of work, and amount of time to complete the work.

Four items were used to measure *interpersonal conflict* (Spector, 1987). This measure focuses on the degree to which the respondent argued with others at work and how often the respondent was yelled at or treated rudely by others at work. The subscale was measured on a 5-point Likert-type scale from *never* to *extremely often* and had a reliability coefficient of .74.

Lack of friendship opportunities was assessed with Sims, Szilagyi, and Keller's (1976) six-item "friendship opportunities" subscale from the Job Characteristics Inventory. Items were reverse scored on a Likert-type scale from one, *very much,* to five, *a minimum amount.* Once reversed, this scale measures the degree to which one's job fails to provide the opportunity for personal, rather than just work-related, interaction. A reliability coefficient of .86 was found for this scale.

Opportunities for interaction were measured with the "dealing with others" subscale of the Job Characteristics Inventory (Sims et al., 1976). This scale consists of four items focusing on the extent to which one's work requires working with others and provides opportunities to meet and interact with other people. The items are measured on a five-point Likert-type scale ranging from *very little* to *very much,* and reverse scored to reflect the *lack of opportunities to deal with others.* The Cronbach's alpha for this measure was .72.

Strains: Participants completed three strain-related subscales; one measuring anxiety, a second for frustration, and the third assessed somatic symptoms.

Spector's ten item *anxiety* scale (1994) which was adapted from the State-Trait Personality Inventory (Speilberger, 1979) was used to measure anxiety. Respondents reported how they have felt at work during the thirty day period prior to completing the survey. Using a four point Likert-type scale, ranging from *not at all* to *very much so,* participants indicated whether they experienced feelings such as calmness, tension, nervousness, and fright. An alpha reliability of .89 was found for this scale.

Three items designed by Peters and colleagues (1980), measured on a six point Likert-type scale, were used to assess *frustration.* Respondents indicated their agreement with three statements regarding the degree to which they experience frustration on the job. Cronbach's alpha was .73 for this measure.

Spector's (1988) measure of health complaints was used to assess *somatic symptoms.* Respondents indicated whether, during the previous thirty days, they experienced each of eighteen health complaints associated with stress. Three response options were provided: (1) No, I didn't, (2) Yes, I did, but did not see a doctor, and (3) Yes, I did, and I saw a doctor. As the health complaints themselves are not necessarily associated, computation of a reliability coefficient for this scale is inappropriate.

Social Support: To measure this construct we used Caplan, Cobb, French, Harrison, and Pinneau's (1975) four-item scale. Respondents use a four point Likert-type scale from one, *not at all,* to four, *very much,* to describe the degree to which their immediate supervisor, others at work, and significant other, friends, and relatives provide *social support.* A response option (zero) corresponding to *don't have any such person* was also available. The alpha reliability for this measure was .80 for this study.

Alcohol Consumption: The two items taken from Cahalan, Cisin, and Crossley (1969), when combined, form a frequency-quantity measure of *alcohol consumption.* These authors combine responses to two questions: (1) how often do you usually have a drink of beer, wine, or liquor? and (2) if you drink more than once a month, when you drink, how often do you have as many as three or four drinks? to generate categorical responses from one, "abstains," to eight, "drinks on two or more occasions daily." However, collapsing the continuous data these questions yield into the categories proscribed in previous use of this instrument results in the loss of information. Additionally, the statistical analyses available for hypothesis testing are more limited with categorical data. For these reasons, the two items were treated as individual measures of consumption. The first item measures frequency and the second measures frequency of heavy drinking.

It should be noted that the consumption measures used in this study rely on self-reports and may, therefore, result in biased data. Typically, the concern with self-report measures is centered on social desirability and this is particularly so with regard to alcohol-related items (Martin, Blum, & Roman, 1992). The belief is that respondents will under-report their drinking (Polich, 1982). However, there is evidence that the validity and reliability of self-reported alcohol measures are acceptable (Cherpitel, 1992; O'Farrell & Maisto, 1987; Polich, 1982; Stacy, Widaman, Hays, & Di Matteo, 1985). Further, Polich (1982: 123) offers that "broadly based outcome measures are not likely to be significantly biased by under-reporting errors."

ANALYSIS

The data were examined using SPSS for Windows (Release 6.1.2). Prior to computing descriptive statistics and correlations, and testing hypotheses, the data were examined to determine whether the assumptions of normal distribution and equal variance (where applicable) were met. For all variables except the two measures of alcohol consumption, the assumptions were met. In order to normalize the consumption variables, we performed a log transformation. This is the procedure recommended by Mosteller and Tukey (1977) when working with count data. The transformed variables were distributed approximately normally and enabled us to proceed with our analysis.

In order to control for overall error rate in our tests for difference of means, we computed a critical p-value based on an overall alpha of .05 for six pre-planned tests (Ott, 1993). Solving for alpha in the equation $1 - (1-\alpha)^6 = .05$ resulted in a critical alpha of 0.009 for the six pre-planned difference of means tests.

RESULTS

Means, standard deviations, and correlations for all of the measured variables are provided in Table 1. The correlations among the stressors indicate that those who perceive the presence of stressors in the environment tend to perceive more than one at a time.

The significant, positive correlations among the strain variables indicate that one is likely to report more than one type of strain when one reports feeling strain. Other than *dealing with others,* which is only associated with *somatic symptoms,* all the stressors are significantly related to at least two of the strain variables. These relationships are expected–one who perceives stressors in the environment should be more likely to report strains.

TABLE 1. Variable Means, Standard Deviations, and Correlations

variable	mean	st dev	1	2	3	4	5	6	7	8	9	10	11	12	13	14	15
role conflict (1)	28.75	10.71															
role ambiguity (2)	16.74	7.06	.52***														
interpersonal conflict (3)	6.89	2.22	.40***	.29***													
workload (4)	19.09	3.54	.36***	.17*	.21**												
lack of dealing (5)	8.49	3.36	-.08	.21**	.00	-.21**											
lack of friendship (6)	15.54	5.88	.09	.24***	.19**	-.05	-.75***										
boredom (7)	23.70	8.21	.24***	.46***	.17*	.00	.23**	.24***									
anxiety (8)	22.16	6.38	.26***	.23**	.34***	.32***	.09	.22**	.15*								
frustration (9)	12.28	3.50	.35***	.29***	.22**	.37***	.00	.07	.18*	.46***							
somatic symptoms (10)	22.81	3.24	.05	.17*	.13	.08	.16*	.19**	.11	.40***	.19**						
social support (11)	34.04	7.75	.01	-.18*	-.20*	.09	-.41***	-.40***	-.21*	-.06	-.05	-.21**					
age (12)	40.99	12.20	-.19**	-.29***	-.23***	-.30***	-.12	-.13	-.23**	-.30***	-.30***	-.21**	-.16*				
income (13)[1]	7.87	3.48	-.10	-.19**	-.12	.12	.19**	-.23**	-.24***	-.09	-.03	-.07	.00	.32***			
drinking frequency (14)[2]	11.82	12.80	-.06	-.03	-.07	-.06	.22**	-.22**	.01	-.19*	-.21**	-.30***	.02	.30***	.30***		
heavy frequency (15)[2]	1.82	3.43	.08	.08	-.21*	-.14	-.06	-.09	-.25*	-.02	-.04	.03	.05	.16	.06	.57***	

*   p ≤ 0.05
**   p ≤ 0.01
***   p ≤ 0.001

1   Multiply income (mean and s.d.) by $10,000.

2   The means and standard deviations presented were computed prior to transformation. The Pearson correlation coefficients presented for these variables were computed after a log transformation was performed on the frequency data.

Hypotheses

The correlations presented in Table 1 indicate no support for Hypothesis 1 regarding the relationship between perceptions of stressors in the environment and frequency of alcohol consumption. Three of the stressor variables, *role conflict, role ambiguity,* and *workload* are unrelated to alcohol consumption. The remaining significant results of Hypothesis 1 are counter-intuitive. *Interpersonal conflict* was significantly, negatively related to heavy drinking ($r = -.21, p \leq .05$). That is, the more interpersonal conflict one experiences at work, the *less* frequently one engages in heavy drinking. There was no relationship between interpersonal conflict and drinking frequency. The relationships between the *lack of friendship opportunities* and *lack of opportunities to deal with others* and drinking frequency were not in the hypothesized direction ($r = -.22, p \leq .01$ for both associations). The less friendship opportunities one perceives in the work environment and the less opportunity one has to deal with others at work, the *less* frequently one drinks. No relationship exists between lack of friendship opportunities and lack of opportunities to deal with others and frequency of heavy drinking. Last, *boredom* was inversely related to heavy drinking. The more boring one's work is, the lower one's frequency of heavy drinking ($r = -.25, p \leq .02$). No association was found between boredom and drinking frequency.

Hypothesis 2 was not supported. Although the relationship between each strain variable and drinking frequency is significant, none is in the hypothesized direction. *Anxiety* ($r = -.19, p \leq .02$), *frustration* ($r = -.21, p \leq .01$), and *somatic symptoms* ($r = -.30, p \leq .001$) are all negatively related to drinking frequency. The less strains one reports the more frequently one drinks. The strain variables and heavy drinking are not associated.

Using the critical alpha controlling for overall error rate left Hypothesis 3 unsupported. The difference in mean drinking frequency between hospitality and non-hospitality workers was in the hypothesized direction but was not significant [$t(157) = 1.63, p > .05$ (2-tailed)]. There was no difference in the reported instances of heavy drinking between the two groups [$t(88) = 0.55, p > .05$ (2-tailed)].

Hypothesis 4 received unqualified support. Among hospitality employees, those working in operations (e.g., food and beverage, rooms division) drink and drink heavily with the same frequency [$t(157) = 0.53, p = .60$ and $t(88) = 0.75, p = .46$ (2-tailed)] as those in non-operational positions (e.g., sales and marketing, accounting, corporate positions).

Men drink more frequently [$t(157) = 4.42, p \leq .001$ (2-tailed)] and engage in heavy drinking more often [$t(88) = 2.45$, $p = .007$ (2-tailed)] than women. These results provide unmitigated support for Hypothesis 5.

Hypotheses 6a and 6b, regarding the relationship between income and alcohol consumption, were fully supported. Income is significantly correlated with drinking frequency ($r = .30$, $p \leq .001$). This result indicates that the higher one's income, the more frequently one drinks. Further, there is no relationship between income and heavy drinking ($r = .06$, $p = .60$).

It was hypothesized there would be no relationship between age and alcohol consumption among those employed in hospitality. This hypothesis received partial support. Heavy drinking is unrelated to age among this sub-sample ($r = .22$, $p = .11$). However, the data indicate that for hospitality employees, the older one is, the more frequently one drinks ($r = .35$, $p \leq .001$).

Hypothesis 8, in which we examined the relationship between social support and alcohol consumption, was not supported. Neither drinking frequency nor instances of heavy drinking were associated with the degree to which one received support from one's supervisor, peers, or friends and family ($r = .02$, $p = .79$ and $r = .05$, $p = .63$, respectively).

DISCUSSION

This study contributes to the goal of knowledge about the relationship between hospitality work and alcohol consumption in several important ways. First, rather than being singular in its perspective, this study takes a two-perspective approach to examining this relationship. The measured variables relate drinking to both the work stress and workplace culture perspectives (Trice & Sonnenstuhl, 1988). Second, we clarify the stress terminology required to examine alcohol consumption from the work stress perspective. Last, we extend the examination of drinking among hospitality employees to the population of managers and executives.

The results do not provide support for the work stress perspective. None of the seven measured stressors are positively related to drinking. Rather, the counter-intuitive evidence presented in the results of Hypothesis 1 seem to support the workplace culture perspective. The more one deals with others and has friendship opportunities, the less interpersonal conflict one has with others in the workplace, and the less bored one is (possibly as a result of lots of interpersonal contact), the more one drinks. The evidence indicates that the workplace culture of hospitality encourages social drinking, not drinking in isolation. This finding may also explain why there is no relationship between social support and alcohol consumption. The social support one derives from one's supervisor and peers may actually be associated with increased consumption while friends and family may provide the type of support that would mitigate one's drinking.

Further evidence for the workplace culture perspective is found in the support for Hypothesis 4. Drinking frequency is unrelated to the type of management position one holds (operational versus non-operational). It appears drinking is more related to the occupation than to the individual's position. Some qualified support for occupational culture as an important risk factor in alcohol consumption among hospitality managers is found in the near-significant finding regarding consumption differences between this focal group and the sub-sample of those not employed in hospitality. Ninety-three percent of non-hospitality respondents worked in the industry after completing their undergraduate degrees. If alcohol consumption was unrelated to occupation and was strictly a person-centered phenomenon, one would expect these hospitality "alumni" to drink with the same frequency as those currently employed in the industry. This seems not to be the case. Given the near-significant directional trend in these data, it would be reasonable to expect that hospitality managers and executives drink more frequently than their peers from other industries *without* experience in the hospitality industry. This is an area requiring further study.

This type of cultural interpretation is intuitively appealing when explaining the prevalence of heavy drinking among hospitality workers. The availability of alcohol in hotels and restaurants makes on-the-job drinking a possibility for management and line employees alike. In some operations, management sponsors wine/beverage tastings for all staff members as part of ongoing product-related training. Management personnel often participate in tastings underwritten by wineries and/or distributors, and may be permitted to consume alcohol during their meals and, in some cases, when interacting with customers. Further, it is not unusual to hear of restaurants offering a "shift drink" to each employee upon the completion of each day's work. Many operations permit employees to continue to drink as paying customers after their shifts, with some operations even offering their employees two-for-one discounts. It may also be that the constant presence of alcohol in the work environment de-sensitizes workers to the social undesirability of heavy drinking in the larger population. In any case, something about hospitality work appears to be related to alcohol consumption.

The results regarding reported strains and alcohol hint at a possible refinement or correction to the work stress perspective which might improve its accuracy and usefulness. The negative associations between the strains and drinking frequency indicate that drinking may moderate the relationship between work stressors and anxiety, frustration, and somatic symptoms. That is, drinking acts as a buffer between stressors and strains. The recent clinical evidence that moderate alcohol consumption reduces the risk of heart disease (Goldberg, Hahn, & Parkes, 1995; Kannel & Wilson, 1995) seems to point in this direction as well. Further, the absence of significant associations between the frequency of heavy drinking and strains indicates that while regular, light to moderate alcohol consumption may serve as a buffer, heavy drinking does not.

The relationships found between demographic variables and alcohol consumption are generally supportive of the literature. The finding that men drink and drink heavily more frequently than women is not surprising. The consequences of drinking are more hazardous for women than men. When drinking, women are at greater risk of being abuse victims (Gleason, 1994). Pregnant women who drink increase the likelihood of birth defects through fetal alcohol syndrome. Mothers who are nursing are also discouraged from drinking because of the effect the alcohol has on their milk. It may be that women are conditioned not to drink as frequently as men by the negative reinforcements their bodies and society provide.

As anticipated, income and drinking frequency covary. There are several logical explanations for this relationship. First, it may be that positions higher in the organizational hierarchy provide more on-the-job drinking opportunities. At the very least, one could reasonably expect more organizationally sanctioned opportunities to present themselves. Second, disposable income tends to rise with gross income. Those earning higher wages may engage in more social drinking off the job simply because they can afford to. We did not expect the frequency of heavy drinking to covary with income and it does not. It may be that the social undesirability of drunkenness increases as one goes up the socioeconomic ladder. It would be useful for researchers to explore this relationship further in the future.

The results regarding the relationship between age and alcohol among hospitality managers run counter to those from other studies (Fennell et al., 1981; Hingson et al., 1981). While we expected occupational culture to exert a significant enough influence to mitigate the inverse relationship found in other populations, we did not expect a complete reversal of this association. It may be that higher income plays a role in the age-alcohol relationship (age and income covary: $r = .32$, $p \le .001$). Another possibility is that occupational drinking norms in hospitality were even stronger years ago than they are today. Bar and restaurant operators are more likely to be involved in liquor liability cases than in the past, and are more sensitive to the dangers of serving those who are drunk or are driving. Less than twenty years ago one could purchase alcohol at eighteen years of age in some states. The legal drinking age is now twenty-one. Whether sincere or not, alcoholic beverage producers now pay for advertisements promoting temperance and encouraging the practice of designated driving. Last, it may be that baby boomers, who sowed their wild oats in the 1960s and '70s with illegal drugs, have made alcohol their drug of choice. Further research is required to better understand what makes the relationship between age and alcohol different for the population of hospitality managers than for other groups.

CONCLUSIONS AND LIMITATIONS

This study has explored some of the risk factors associated with alcohol consumption among hospitality employees, specifically those in managerial positions. We find compelling statistical evidence that workplace and occupational cultures are important to understanding why hospitality managers drink. While anecdotal evidence to this effect has always been available, this study helps legitimate the drinking-related stories many hospitality workers, including managers, share.

Specifically, the data revealed that the association between interpersonal conflict and heavy drinking is significant and negative. Both the lack of friendship opportunities and lack of opportunities to deal with others were negatively related to drinking frequency. As evidenced by the significant negative relationships between anxiety, frustration, and somatic symptoms and drinking frequency, alcohol appears to act as a buffer between stressors and strains.

It was further determined that there is no difference in alcohol consumption across functional areas among hospitality managers. Not surprisingly, men are more frequent and heavier consumers of alcohol than women. Counter to expectations, age and frequency of consumption are significantly associated. Finally, it was determined that income and instances of drinking are significantly, positively related.

Prior to making inference to the population of hospitality managers one should consider that these data come from a sample of alumni from one university. Replication of the results included herein with a broader sample would enable one to make such inference with greater external validity.

The second limitation of this study is its reliance on self-report data and the single source bias associated with the survey methodology employed. As discussed earlier, self-reports of alcohol consumption are reliable and valid (Cherpitel, 1992; O'Farrell & Maisto, 1987; Polich, 1982; Stacy, Widaman, Hays, & Di Matteo, 1985). With regard to the stressor and strain measures, our interest is in the individual's perception of stressors in the environment and whether or not s/he felt strain. The focal individual is the appropriate source for such perceptual data. Additionally, this study is exploratory in nature and simply assesses the presence of relationships. Future research in this area would be strengthened by a multimethod approach with multiple data sources.

Future studies would also benefit by engaging in longitudinal research. Panel data would enable us to learn more about how occupational culture and the stressors present in the work environment affect alcohol consumption. It would be particularly useful to follow organizational and industry newcomers over time to explore the socialization process as it relates to drinking. In the future, researchers might also endeavor to gather data from non-hospitality executives who have never worked in the industry. This second comparison group would allow us to learn more about the impact of occupational culture on drinking. It is clear, given the cost of alcohol abuse and the at-risk status of hospitality workers, that these issues merit serious attention in the future.

NOTE

1. For the purposes of this study heavy drinking is defined as the consumption of three or more drinks on a given occasion.

REFERENCES

Ames, G.M. (1987). Environmental factors can create a drinking culture at the worksite. *Business and Health, 5,* 44-45.

Arney, L.K. (1988). Effects of personality-environment fit on job stress. *Educational and Psychological Research, 8,* 1-18.

Ashforth, B. E., & Humphrey, R. H. (1993). Emotional labor in service roles: the influence of identity. *Academy of Management Review, 18,* 88-115.

Barnes, G.M., Welte, J.W., & Dintcheff, B. (1991). Drinking among subgroups in the adult population of New York State: A classification analysis using CART. *Journal of Studies on Alcohol, 52,* 338-344.

Bhagat, R.S., Allie, S.M., & Ford, D.L., Jr. (1991). Organizational stress, personal life stress and symptoms of life strains: an inquiry into the moderating role of styles of coping. *Journal of Social Behavior and Personality, 6,* 163-184.

Burke, R.J. & Greenglass, E.R. (1993). Work stress, role conflict, social support, and psychological burnout among teachers. *Psychological Reports, 73,* 371-380.

Burke, R.J. & Greenglass, E.R. (1995). A longitudinal examination of the Cherniss model of psychological burnout. *Social Science and Medicine, 40,* 1357-1363.

Cahalan, D., Cisin, I.H., & Crossley, H.M. (1969). *American Drinking Practices, a National Study of Drinking Behavior and Attitudes*. Rutgers Center of Alcohol Studies: New Brunswick, NJ.

Callan, V.J., (1993). Individual and organizational strategies for coping with organizational change. *Work & Stress, 7*, 63-75.

Caplan, R.D., Cobb, S., French, J.R.P., Jr., Harrison, R.D., & Pinneau, S.R., Jr. (1975). *Job Demands and Worker Health: Main Effects and Occupational Differences*. Washington, DC: U.S. Government Printing Office.

Cosper, R. (1979). Drinking as conformity: A critique of sociological literature on occupational differences in drinking. *Journal of Studies on Alcohol, 40,* 868-891.

Daniels, K. & Guppy, A. (1994). Occupational stress, social support, job control, and psychological well-being. *Human Relations, 47*, 1523-1544.

Dight, S. (1976). *Scottish Drinking Habits*. London: Office of Population Censuses and Surveys, Social Survey Division, HMSO.

Fennell, M.L., Rodin, M.B., & Kantor, G.K. (1981). Problems in the work setting, drinking, and reasons for drinking. *Social Forces, 60,* 114-132.

Fillmore, K.M., Golding, J.M., Leino, E.V., & Motoyoshi, M. (1993). Cross-national comparisons of drinking behavior as determined from the Collaborative Alcohol-Related Longitudinal Project. *Alcohol Health and Research World, 17,* 198-204.

Fisher, C.D. (1985). Social support and adjustment to work: A longitudinal study. *Journal of Management, 11*, 39-53.

Fisher, C.D. (1993). Boredom at work: A neglected concept. *Human Relations, 46,* 395-417.

Frank, R.G., McGuire, T.G., Regier, D.A., Manderscheid, R., & Woodward, A. (1994). Paying for mental health and substance abuse care. *Health Affairs, 13,* 337-342.

Gleason, N.A. (1994). College women and alcohol: A relational perspective. *Journal of American College Health, 42*, 279-289.

Goldberg, D.M., Hahn, S.E., & Parkes, J.G. (1995). Beyond alcohol: Beverage consumption and cardiovascular mortality. *Clinica Chimica Acta, 237,* 155-187.

Hackman, J.R. & Oldham, G.R. (1974). *The Job Diagnostic Survey: An instrument for the diagnosis of jobs and the evaluation of job redesign projects* (Report No. 4). New Haven, CT: Yale University, Department of Administration Science.

Hackman, J.R. & Oldham, G.R. (1975). Development of the job diagnostic survey. *Journal of Applied Psychology, 60*, 159-170.

Hackman, J.R. & Oldham, G.R. (1980). *Work Redesign*. Reading, MA: Addison-Wesley.

Hingson, R., Mangione, T., & Barrett, J. (1981). Job characteristics and drinking practices in the Boston metropolitan area. *Journal of Studies on Alcohol, 42*, 725-738.

Hitz, D. (1973). Drunken sailors and others: Drinking problems in specific occupations. *Quarterly Journal of Studies on Alcohol, 34*, 496-505.

Hochschild, A.R. (1983). *The Managed Heart: Commercialization of Human Feeling*. Berkeley: University of California Press.

Howard, J.H., Cunningham, D.A., & Rechnitzer, P.A. (1986a). Role ambiguity, Type A behavior, and job satisfaction: Moderating effects on cardiovascular and biochemical responses associated with coronary risk. *Journal of Applied Psychology, 71*, 95-101.

Howard, J.H., Cunningham, D.A., & Rechnitzer, P.A. (1986b). Personality (hardiness) as a moderator of job stress and coronary risk in Type A individuals: A longitudinal study. *Journal of Behavioral Medicine, 9*, 229-244.

Idaszak, J.R. & Drasgow, F. (1987). A revision of the job diagnostic survey: Elimination of a measurement artifact. *Journal of Applied Psychology, 72*, 69-74.

Jex, S.M., Beehr, T.A. & Roberts, C.K. (1992). The meaning of occupational stress items to survey respondents. *Journal of Applied Psychology, 77*, 623-628.

Kahn, R.L., Wolfe, D.M., Quinn, R.P., Snoek, J.D., & Rosenthal, R.A. (1964). *Organizational Stress: Studies in Role Conflict and Ambiguity*. New York: Wiley.

Kannel, W.B. & Wilson, P.W. (1995). An update on coronary risk factors. *Medical Clinics of North-America, 79*, 951-971.

Katz, D. & Kahn, R.L. (1978). *The Social Psychology of Organizations* (2nd edition). New York: Wiley.

Keenan, A. & Newton, T.J. (1985). Stressful events, stressors, and psychological strains in young professional engineers. *Journal of Occupational Behaviour, 6*, 151-156.

Kushnir, T. & Melamed, S. (1991). Work-load, perceived control and psychological distress in Type A/B industrial workers. *Journal of Organizational Behavior, 12*(2), 155-168.

Liberto, J.G., Oslin, D.W., & Ruskin, P.E. (1992). Alcoholism in older persons: A review of the literature. *Hospital and Community Psychiatry, 43*, 975-984.

Lin, N., Simeone, R.S., Ensel, W.M., & Kuo, W. (1979). Social support, stressful life events, and illness: A model and an empirical test. *Journal of Health and Social Behavior, 20*, 108-119.

Major, D.A., Kozlowski, S.W.J., Chao, G.T., & Gardner, P.D. (1995). A longitudinal investigation of newcomer expectations, early socialization outcomes, and the moderating effects of role development factors. *Journal of Applied Psychology, 80*, 418-431.

Manlove, E.E. (1994). Conflict and ambiguity over work roles: The impact on child care worker burnout. *Early Education and Development, 5*, 41-55.

Margolis, G.L., Kroes, W.H., & Quinn, R.P. (1974). Job stress: An unlisted occupational hazard. *Journal of Occupational Medicine, 16*, 659-661.

Martin, J.K., Blum, T.C., & Roman, P.M. (1992). Drinking to cope and self-medication: Characteristics of jobs in relation to workers' drinking behavior. *Journal of Organizational Behavior, 13*, 55-71.

Matheny, K.B., Aycock, D.W., Pugh, J.L., Curlette, W.L., & Silva Cannella,

K.A. (1986). Stress coping: A qualitative and quantitative synthesis with implications for treatment. *The Counseling Psychologist, 14*, 499-549.

McKibben, J. (1990). Work and drink–A dangerous cocktail. *Industrial Society*, March, 22-24.

Mosteller, F. & Tukey, J.W. (1977). *Data Analysis and Regression*. Reading, MA: Addison-Wesley Publishing Company.

O'Hanlon, J.F. (1981). Boredom: Practical consequences and a theory. *Acta Psychologica, 49*, 53-82.

O'Hare, T. (1995). Mental health problems and alcohol abuse: Co-occurrence and gender differences. *Health and Social Work, 20*, 207-214.

Ott, R.L. (1993). *An Introduction to Statistical Methods and Data Analysis* (4th edition). Belmont, CA: Duxbury Press.

Pallarito, K. (1995). Financial toll of substance abuse studied. *Modern Healthcare, 25*, 18.

Parker, D.A. & Brody, J.A. (1982). Risk factors for alcoholism and alcohol problems among employed women and men. In *Occupational Alcoholism: A Review of Research Issues*. Rockville, MD: U.S. Department of Health and Human Services.

Peters, L.H., O'Connor, E.J. & Rudolf, C.J. (1980). The behavioral and affective consequences of performance-relevant situational variables. *Organizational Behavior and Human Performance, 25*, 79-96.

Piotrkowski, C.S., Cohen, B.G., & Coray, K.E. (1992). Working conditions and well-being among women office workers. *International Journal of Human-Computer Interaction, 4*, 263-281.

Plant, M.A. (1977). Alcoholism and occupation: A review. *British Journal of Addiction, 72*, 309-316.

Plant, M.A. (1978). *Drinking careers: Occupations, drinking habits, and drinking problems*. London: Tavistock.

Polich, M. (1982). The validity of self-reports in alcoholism research. *Addictive Behaviors, 7*, 123-132.

Rafaeli, A. & Sutton, R.I. (1989). The expression of emotion in organizational life. In L.L. Cummings & B.M. Staw (Eds.), *Research in Organizational Behavior* (vol. 11, pp. 1-42). Greenwich, CT: JAI Press.

Remondet, J.H. & Hansson, R.O. (1991). Job-related threats to control among older employees. *Journal of Social Issues, 47*, 129-141.

Revicki, D.A., Whitley, T.W., Gallery, M.E., & Allison, E.J. (1993). Impact of work environment characteristics on work-related stress and depression in emergency medicine residents: A longitudinal study. *Journal of Community and Applied Social Psychology, 3*, 273-284.

Rizzo, J.R., House, R.J. & Lirtzman, S.I. (1970). Role conflict and role ambiguity in complex organizations. *Administrative Science Quarterly, 15*, 150-163.

Ruben, D.H. (1986). The management of role ambiguity in organizations. *Journal of Employment Counseling, 23*, 120-130.

Savitz, S.A. (1995). Mental health plans help employees, reduce costs. *Best's Review, 96*, 60-62.

Schneider, B. & Bowen, D.E. (1995). *Winning the Service Game.* Cambridge, MA: Harvard Business School Press.

Siegall, M. & Cummings, L.L. (1995). Stress and organizational role conflict. *Genetic, Social, and General Psychology Monographs, 121,* 65-95.

Sims, H.P., Szilagyi, A.D. & Keller, R.T. (1976). The measurement of job characteristics. *Academy of Management Journal, 19,* 195-212.

Spector, P.E. (1987). Interactive effects of perceived control and job stressors on affective reactions and health outcomes for clerical workers. *Work and Stress, 1,* 155-162.

Spector, P.E. (1988). Development of the work locus of control scale. *Journal of Occupational Psychology, 61,* 335-340.

Spector, P.E., Dwyer, D.J., & Jex, S.M. (1988). The relationship of job stressors to affective, health and performance outcomes: A comparison of multiple data sources. *Journal of Applied Psychology, 73,* 11-19.

Spector, P.E. & O'Connell, B.J. (1994). The contribution of personality traits, negative affectivity, locus of control and Type A to the subsequent reports of job stressors and strains. *Journal of Occupational and Organizational Psychology, 67,* 1-11.

Speilberger, C.D. (1979). *Preliminary Manual for the State-Trait Personality Inventory (STPI).* Unpublished Manuscript, University of South Florida, Tampa.

Stacy, A., Widaman, K., Hays, R., & Di Matteo, M. (1985). Validity of self-reports of alcohol and other drug use: A multitrait-multimethod assessment. *Journal of Personality and Social Psychology, 49,* 219-232.

Trice, H.M. & Sonnenstuhl, W.J. (1988). Drinking behavior and risk factors related to the work place: Implications for research and prevention. *Journal of Applied Behavioral Science, 24,* 327-346.

Turner, R.J. (1981). Social support as a contingency in psychological well-being. *Journal of Health and Social Behavior, 22,* 357-367.

Wharton, A.S. & Erickson, R.J. (1993). Managing emotions on the job and at home: Understanding the consequences of multiple emotional roles. *Academy of Management Review, 18,* 457-486.

Wharton, A.S. (1993). The affective consequences of service work. *Work and Occupations, 20,* 205-232.

Whitehead, P.C. & Simpkins, J. (1983). Occupational factors in alcoholism. In B. Kissin & H. Begleiter (Eds.), *The Biology of Alcoholism,* Vol. 6: The Pathogenesis of Alcoholism: Psychological Factors, ch. 11. New York: Plenum.

Yang, C.L. & Carayon, P. (1995). Effect of job demands and social support on worker stress: A study of VDT users. *Behaviour and Information Technology, 14,* 32-40.

Young, T.J., & French, L.A. (1994). Taxable wealth and alcoholic beverage consumption in the United States. *Psychological Reports, 74,* 813-814.

PART III:
INDIVIDUAL
AND FAMILY TARGET MARKETS
FOR THE HOSPITALITY INDUSTRY

From the Golden Arches
to the Golden Pond:
Fast Food and Older Adults

Johnny Sue Reynolds
Lisa R. Kennon
Nancy L. Kniatt

SUMMARY. This research addresses the issues of older adults and the frequency of fast food patronage, fast food meals purchased most

Johnny Sue Reynolds is Associate Professor, Lisa R. Kennon is Assistant Professor, and Nancy L. Kniatt is Lecturer at the School of Merchandising and Hospitality Management, Division of Hotel and Restaurant Management.

Address correspondence to: Johnny Sue Reynolds, University of North Texas School of Merchandising and Hospitality Management, P.O. Box 311100, Denton, TX 76203-1100 (E-mail: Reynolds@scs.unt.edu).

[Haworth co-indexing entry note]: "From the Golden Arches to the Golden Pond: Fast Food and Older Adults." Reynolds, Johnny Sue, Lisa R. Kennon, and Nancy L. Kniatt. Co-published simultaneously in *Marriage & Family Review* (The Haworth Press, Inc.) Vol. 28, No. 1/2, 1998, pp. 213-224; and: *The Role of the Hospitality Industry in the Lives of Individuals and Families* (ed: Pamela R. Cummings, Francis A. Kwansa, and Marvin B. Sussman) The Haworth Press, Inc., 1998, pp. 213-224. Single or multiple copies of this article are available for a fee from The Haworth Document Delivery Service [1-800-342-9678, 9:00 a.m. - 5:00 p.m. (EST). E-mail address: getinfo@haworthpressinc.com].

213

often, and reasons for fast food patronage. A randomly selected sample of 500 mature adults (50 years of age and older) was surveyed. The response rate was 36 percent (n = 175). Results of this study indicate that older males are more likely to patronize fast food restaurants than their female counterparts. Mature adults who were in the 60-64 age group were significantly more likely to frequent fast food restaurants than other mature age segments. *[Article copies available for a fee from The Haworth Document Delivery Service: 1-800-342-9678. E-mail address: getinfo@haworthpressinc.com]*

KEYWORDS. Older adults, Fast food, Eating out, Elderly, Senior citizens, Restaurants, Quick-serve restaurants

The fast food industry has infiltrated all aspects of our lives, encompassing all ages and stages of the life cycle. The impact of fast food on children has been recognized and investigated in recent years. However, the impact of the fast food industry on another segment of the American population, those adults who are over the age of 50, has not been adequately addressed. Many of today's older adults spent their younger years frequenting fast food restaurants, either individually or with friends or family. As they approach retirement and the pace of their lives begins to slow, will fast food restaurants continue to meet the needs of their changing lifestyles?

In contrast to earlier years, when high fertility and mortality rates were the driving demographic forces keeping the nation's population young, increasing life expectancy is now contributing to the graying of America. Life expectancy at birth in 1989 reached a record high of 75.3 years, according to the United States Census Bureau. This is up from a life expectancy of 47.3 years at the turn of the century, when most people did not survive to old age, and therefore did not have to worry about financing their retirement, or maintaining long-term healthy eating habits (Iwamuro, 1993a). The "size of the elderly population will continue to skyrocket at rates never before seen in human history" (Lago & Poffley, 1993, p. 30).

The purpose of this study was to determine frequency of fast food patronage by older adults and to ascertain which meal was purchased most often by these consumers. Also, the researchers wanted to identify factors that influence older adults to eat at fast food restaurants.

ECONOMIC CENTER OF GRAVITY

The need for information related to the older adult market has been gradually increasing due to the imminent arrival of the 76 million baby boomers who will soon enter the ranks of this market (Moschis, Mathur & Smith, 1993). Lago and Poffley (1993) described the aging baby boomers as the "U.S. population's economic center of gravity" (p. 44). The over-50 population owns 77 percent of all American financial assets. This age segment spends more money on travel and recreation than any other segment, as well as purchasing 80 percent of all luxury travel and eating out an average of three times weekly (Knutson and Patton, 1993).

As older consumers increase in number and in proportion to the population, certain economic benefits will affect the hospitality industry. These benefits will be due to the fact that mature consumers spend more money per capita on travel than any other age segment. This occurs in part because of increases in their discretionary income–the luxury of a recently emptied nest (Iwamuro, 1993b).

Baby boomers' expenditures on food eaten away from home should rise as older boomers approach age 50 and enter their peak earning years. Households headed by persons age 45 to 54 posted the highest household income ($48,413) as well as the highest per capita spending on food away from home ($679) in 1991 (Iwamuro, 1993b).

REASONS THAT OLDER ADULTS EAT OUT

According to Knutson and Patton (1993), the two strongest motivators for older adults to eat out are convenience and companionship. At this stage in their lives, these consumers do not want to spend a large portion of their time in the kitchen. This market segment, especially females, indicates that an important reason for eating out is the escape from the hassle of creating a meal, from grocery shopping to cooking to cleanup. Older diners also perceive going out to eat in a restaurant as an opportunity to socialize in a welcoming, comfortable atmosphere, and report that being with friends and family is another important factor in choosing to eat out (Knutson & Patton, 1993).

Older consumers are often seen as having firmly entrenched dining-out patterns. The truth is that they have very distinctive preferences for both service and food (NPD Group, 1992). For example, it would appear that acquired tastes and dining habit patterns are carried forward as the customer ages. Some older restaurant patrons are continuing to use quick-service restaurants (QSR's). Between 1983 and 1988, consumers in the 65 to 69 age bracket increased their use of QSR's from 41% to 45%. Those in the 70 plus age bracket showed an increase from 46% to 50%. NPD Research also reported that older adults are much more likely to patronize QSR's for pizza, burgers, and fries than their earlier cohorts (NPD CREST,

1988). Logically, how else could it be? "Baby boomers raised on a particular range of foods cannot be expected to suddenly abandon those items for porridge and meat loaf" (Lago and Poffley, 1993, p. 42).

Several national organizations have recognized the impact of the older market on the restaurant industry. According to a spokesman for the Washington-based American Association of Retired Persons (AARP), "older people tend to dine with other people and not alone. So when seniors dine out, that usually means larger parties" (Carlino, 1994, p. 53). Mike Hurst, past-president of the National Restaurant Association, attributes the growing popularity of casual, lower priced dining establishments to economic recession and the aging of the baby boomers (1991).

MARKETING TO THE MATURE SEGMENT

In a survey of older Americans, over half (about 41 million of the approximately 65 million adults older than age 50) have eaten out at least once in the previous month (Carlino, 1994). Industry has not always recognized the significance of this market segment. In one recent survey, three-fourths of respondents aged 65 and older were dissatisfied with the techniques companies use in marketing to older adults (Tibbett, 1993). To attract the mature market, businesses must find ways to demonstrate how their products or services meet the goals of the older consumer. Lago and Poffley (1993) identify some of those goals as "a perceived high quality of life, continued personal control and a sense of independence, good economic value, and supporting social closeness with family and friends" (p. 43). Appropriate offerings could be in the form of new products aimed at enhancing the independence of older people (Baker et al., 1992); product lines tailored to their changing biophysical needs such as declining ability to see, taste, and hear, and altered dietary requirements; special promotions (e.g., senior discount programs); and advertising information aimed at helping older adults in decision making (Schewe, 1988).

Lago and Poffley (1993) discussed several important components of marketing to seniors:

1. They predict that a larger proportion of tomorrow's older adults will patronize fast food restaurants.
2. Speed and quality of service will be important features of successful restaurants.
3. Nutrition and healthy cooking methods will be increasingly important to these older consumers.
4. Provision of nutrition information will increase brand loyalty from this age group. "In a size-static market, when consumers are 'aging

in place,' brand loyalty will become as valuable to a restaurant as new customers" (p. 44).

Population changes are easy enough to describe, but fast food restaurateurs must make changes in their programs and products based on the needs of that changing population. This research addresses the issues of mature adults and the frequency of fast food patronage, fast food meals purchased most often, and reasons for fast food patronage.

Objectives

Specific objectives of this study were:

a. to develop a measurement tool to determine the frequency of fast food patronage by older adults,
b. to determine the significance of the demographic variables of gender, age, ethnicity, income, education, marital status, and level of activity on the frequency of fast food patronage,
c. to ascertain the meal purchased most often at fast food restaurants by older adults, and
d. to identify factors that influence older adults to patronize fast food restaurants.

METHODOLOGY

Instrument

In keeping with the objectives of the study, a questionnaire was developed which would provide information regarding the respondents' demographic characteristics, including gender, ethnicity, age, marital status, highest level of education, total family income, lifestyle, and employment status. In another section of the questionnaire, respondents were asked to provide details about their consumption patterns in terms of meals eaten away from home. This included frequency and type of restaurant selected and amount of money spent weekly on eating out. Respondents were also asked to indicate which meal they purchased most often in a fast food restaurant and their reasons for patronizing this type of establishment. The instrument was then reviewed and approved by the University of North Texas Human Subjects Review Committee prior to data collection. Human

Subjects Review is a pre-research requirement to insure protection of all human subjects. All studies requiring the use of human subjects must pass this stringent review process.

Pretesting and Validation

For pretest purposes, the survey was administered to a convenience sample consisting of a combination of 10 hospitality educators and older adults who were asked to complete the instrument and to suggest additions, corrections, or other changes they felt could improve the survey. The pretest respondents also evaluated the instrument for clarity of instruction, format of the questions, and ambiguity and provided input for additional questions. Minor changes were made based on the pretest results.

Sample

Lago and Poffley (1993) stated that aging is a complex, essentially continuous process, with no discrete definitions that are very satisfactory. For this research, the authors adopted the practice of defining the older population as those persons aged 50 or older, as defined by AARP. The population for this study, therefore, consisted of mature adults who were 50 years of age and older. A randomly selected sample of subscribers 50 years of age and older was purchased from *S R Texas,* a magazine for mature adults. The sample consisted of 500 mature adults, drawn from a mailing list of 61,300 subscribers. The NEA Small Sample Formula was used to determine the appropriate size for the sample. The response rate was 36 percent (n = 175), after deletion of five cases where respondents reported being under 50 years of age. Unusable responses were also due to incorrect addresses, incomplete questionnaires, and deceased subscribers.

Results

Fifty-four percent of the respondents were female and 46 percent were male (see Table 1). A typical participant was Caucasian (90%), between 65 and 74 years of age (50%), and married (62%). Fifty-nine percent of the respondents were retired, and 73% reported having either an active lifestyle (go out 3-4 times per week with some travel) or very active lifestyle (go out 5+ times per week and travel). The respondents were well educated with 33 percent having a graduate degree and another 15 percent having completed college. Thirty-nine percent of the respondents reported an income of between $25,001 to $50,000 per year, while 19 percent

TABLE 1. Demographic Attributes of Respondents

Value	#	%
Gender		
Female	94	53.7
Male	80	45.7
Missing	1	.6
Ethnicity		
American Indian	1	.6
Asian/Pacific Islander	1	.6
African American	4	2.3
Caucasian	157	89.7
Hispanic	7	4.0
Other	2	1.1
Missing	3	1.7
Age		
50-54 years	9	5.1
55-59 years	11	6.3
60-64 years	33	18.9
65-69 years	39	22.3
70-74 years	49	28.0
75-79 years	18	10.3
80-84 years	11	6.3
85 years and older	4	2.3
Missing	1	.6
Marital Status		
Never married	5	2.9
Married	109	62.3
Divorced	18	10.3
Widowed	43	24.6
Highest level of education		
Some high school	4	2.3
Completed high school	23	13.1
Some college	64	36.6
Completed college	27	15.4
Graduate degree	57	32.6
Total family income		
Under $25,000	33	18.9
$25,001-$50,000	68	38.9
$50,001-$75,000	26	14.9
$75,001-$100,000	19	10.9
Over $100,000	15	8.6
Missing	14	8.0

TABLE 1 (continued)

Value	#	%
Lifestyle		
Not active	8	4.6
Somewhat active	35	20.0
Active	64	36.6
Very active	64	36.6
Missing	4	2.3
Employment status		
Retired	104	59.4
Semi-retired	31	17.7
Employed full-time	35	20.7
Missing	4	2.3

n = 175

reported an income of less than $25,000 per year. Thirty-four percent of the participants indicated having an income of $50,000 or more. The remaining eight percent did not respond to the question regarding income.

One-way analysis of variance (ANOVA) was used to determine the significance of the difference between the means for the categories of each independent variable (age, ethnicity, gender, etc.) in response to the question regarding the frequency of eating out. After analyzing responses based on gender, males were found to patronize fast food restaurants significantly more often than females: $F(1,168) = 5.70$, $p < .0181$ (see Table 2). Age was also a significant demographic characteristic: $F(7,161) = 3.34$, $p < .004$. Joint univariate analysis showed that persons in the 60-64 age group were significantly more likely to patronize fast food restaurants than their older or younger counterparts ($p < .0001$).

Over one-half of respondents (52%) indicated a preference for lunch as the primary meal purchased in a fast food restaurant. Thirty-seven percent selected dinner in response to this question, while seven percent selected breakfast and only four percent selected the response 'drink or snack.'

The respondents were also asked why they patronized fast food restaurants. Through a review of literature, the authors identified ten factors which were found to be factors in customers frequenting fast food restaurants: speed of service, reduced price promotions and coupons, drive through access, keep the kitchen from getting dirty, lack of time to prepare meals, lack of time to shop for food, quality of food, visit with friends or family members, convenience, and inexpensive. The respondents were given a list of these ten factors and asked to select five factors which most

TABLE 2. Meal Purchased Most Often in Fast Food Restaurants by Mature Adults

Meal	#	%
Breakfast	11	6.9
Lunch	83	52.2
Dinner	59	37.1
Drink or Snack	6	3.8

n = 159 (*n* varies due to missing responses)

influenced them to patronize fast food restaurants. Rank order of factors selected by respondents were: (1) convenience (77%), (2) speed of service (54%), (3) inexpensive (45%), (4) reduced price promotions and coupons (38%), (5) lack of time to prepare meals (31%), and (6) visit with friends or family members (31%) (see Table 3).

DISCUSSION

Results of this study indicate that older males are more likely to patronize fast food restaurants than their female counterparts. This may be due to the older consumer's adherence to traditional concepts of male and female roles in meal preparation. It remains to be seen whether this situation will continue as baby boomers, with their less conventional attitudes toward traditional roles, enter this market segment.

It is interesting to note that persons in the 60-64 age group were significantly more likely to frequent fast food restaurants than other mature age segments. This may be due to the fact that many members of this group have retired, and thus have more time to eat out, but are not yet slowing down their lifestyles. They are also the segment which is most likely to be finally enjoying the freedom–in terms of money and time–that is a result of an "empty nest."

Factors that influence seniors in choosing to patronize fast food restaurants should be given careful consideration by the management of these establishments. It is no surprise that this investigation verifies earlier studies in finding that convenience is a primary factor in the older consumer's restaurant choice. After long years of shouldering responsibility, mature adults are ready to let someone else do it for them! Speed of service and the relative inexpensiveness of fast food are also important, because like all Americans, older consumers have learned to value their time, to expect promptness from all service industries, and to demand full value for their dollar.

Respondents were invited to make comments at the end of the questionnaire. Several indicated that their patronage of fast food restaurants was, at least in part, directly influenced by their grandchildrens' preferences. Comments included "Their choice–not ours" and "Sometimes they win."

An increased awareness of the nutritional aspects of fast food menus is evident in many of the comments included by respondents. Several indicated their unhappiness with the perceived lack of nutritious and healthy choices. Remarks ranged from "I feel it is completely unhealthy," "Food is too fat and unhealthy," to the thoroughly honest "I don't believe fast food is particularly healthy, but it is soooo good!"

IMPLICATIONS

Since fast food is virtually accessible to anyone, will this industry adapt to reach the older market, as it once did to reach young children? Will we

TABLE 3. Factors Influencing Mature Adults in Choosing Fast Food Restaurants

Factor	#	%
Convenience	135	77.1
Speed of service	95	54.3
Inexpensive	79	45.1
Reduced price promotions and coupons	66	37.7
Lack of time to prepare meals	54	30.9
Visit with friends or family members	54	30.9
Drive-thru access	47	26.9
Quality of food	28	16.0
Keep the kitchen from getting dirty	17	9.7
Lack of time to shop for food	13	7.4

(Multiple responses possible)

see special meal packages for older adults only, games and specific menu merchandising promotions and gimmicks, or perhaps a special section in the restaurant designated for the older patron? Will fast food eventually be found in long-term care and retirement facilities, just as we have seen fast food invade elementary and secondary schools?

Innovative concepts combining branded or unbranded fast food outlets with social interaction sites such as senior centers, recreation centers, coffee bars, bookstores/libraries could be developed. Food service operators must be inventive regarding generational dining.

A similar study should be conducted to include a large sample which is more representative of the national population. Future research could also be conducted to determine if older adults desire more nutritious menu choices, and how much more, if any, they would be willing to pay for this improvement.

AUTHOR NOTE

Johnny Sue Reynolds earned the Bachelor of Science Degree at the University of Mary Hardin-Baylor, the Master of Science Degree at the University of North Texas and the Doctor of philosophy from Texas Woman's University. Her professional work experiences include 17 years of teaching in public schools including kindergarten, secondary and adult education. Dr. Reynolds has taught for the past seven years at the University of North Texas, six of which she served as General Manager of The Club at College Inn, the Hotel and Restaurant Management program's student-operated restaurant. Currently, she is Associate Professor and Chair of the Hotel and Restaurant Management Program. Her research interests include consumer aspects of the hospitality industry, bed and breakfast operations, and the fast food industry.

Lisa R. Kennon earned the Bachelor and Master of Science Degree at the University of North Texas and the Doctor of Philosophy from Texas Woman's University, with a major in Nutrition with emphasis in Institutional Administration. She has taught at the University of North Texas for the past nine years. She is currently teaching food preparation and food sanitation classes. Her research interests include food safety for children and the elderly, mature travelers, and the fast food industry.

Nancy L. Kniatt earned the Bachelor of Arts degree at the University of Oklahoma and the Master of Science Degree at the University of North Texas. She has worked in industry for over 20 years. She is currently Lecturer in the Hotel and Restaurant Management Program at the University of North Texas, where she serves as General Manager of the Club at College Inn, the program's student-operated restaurant. Her research interests include service quality in the hospitality industry; training methods and standards; mature travelers, guests and consumers; and female travelers, guests and consumers.

REFERENCES

Baker, G., Griffith, B., Carmone, F., & Krauser, C. (1992). *Report on Products to Enhance the Independence of Elderly.* Gerontology Center, University of Maryland.

Carlino, B. (1994). Operators strike gold with seniors. *Nation's Restaurant News, 28* (40), 53, 56.

Hurst, M. (1991, June 15). Editorial. *Cooking for Profit,* p. 4.

Hysen, P., Boehrer, J., Greenburg, A., Noseworthy, E., Prentkowaki, D., Wilson, T., & Boss, D. (1993, January). Anticipating paradigm shifts in foodservice. *Food Management,* (1), 101-108.

Iwamuro, R. (1993a). Seniors: Who they are and how they spend. *Restaurants USA, 13* (8), 37-41.

Iwamuro, R. (1993b). The Baby-Boomers: Who they are and how they spend. *Restaurants USA, 13*(9), 44-47.

Knutson, B. & Patton, M. (1993). Restaurants can find gold among silver hair: Opportunities in the 55+ market. *Journal of Hospitality and Leisure Marketing, 1*(3), 79-89.

Lago, D., & Poffley, J. (1993). The aging population and the hospitality industry in 2010: Important trends and probable services. *Hospitality Research Journal, 17*(1), 29-47.

Moschis, G., Mathur, A., & Smith, R. (1993). Older consumers' orientations toward age-based marketing stimuli. *Journal of the Academy of Marketing Science, 21*(3), 195-205.

NPD CREST. (1988). Marketing to seniors. (In a Consumer Reports on Eating Share Trends {CREST} report), p. 92-96. Park Ridge, IL: Author.

NPD Group. (1992). *Eating patterns of older Americans.* Park Ridge, IL: Author.

Shewe, C. (1988). Marketing to our aging population: Responding to Physiological Changes. *Journal of Consumer Marketing, 5*(Summer), 61-73.

Tibbett, L. (1993). Older consumers follow different rules. *American Demographics, 15*(2), 21-23.

The Importance of Hotel/Motel Products and Services as Perceived by Older Consumers

Beth E. S. Wuest
Daniel A. Emenheiser
Richard F. Tas

SUMMARY. Consumer satisfaction, an important concept in consumer behavior theory, is directly influenced by the availability of quality service which has become an increasingly important objective of hotel/motel managers. The purpose of this study was to investigate hotel/motel products and services valued most by older consumers–a substantial and growing market segment with special concerns. The sample for this study consisted of consumers age 55 and older in the state of Texas. Results indicate value and security were considered highly important, and suggest lodging operators

Beth E. S. Wuest is Program Coordinator, Fashion Merchandising Department, Department of Family and Consumer Sciences, Southwest Texas State University, San Marcos, Texas. Daniel A. Emenheiser and Richard F. Tas are both associated with School of Merchandising and Hospitality Management, University of North Texas, Denton, Texas.

Address correspondence to: Beth E. S. Wuest, Department of Family and Consumer Sciences, Southwest Texas State University, 601 University Drive, San Marcos, TX 78666-4602.

Funding for this research was provided by a grant from the Texas Institute for Research and Education on Aging of the Texas College of Osteopathic Medicine and the University of North Texas.

[Haworth co-indexing entry note]: "The Importance of Hotel/Motel Products and Services as Perceived by Older Consumers." Wuest, Beth E. S., Daniel A. Emenheiser, and Richard F. Tas. Co-published simultaneously in *Marriage & Family Review* (The Haworth Press, Inc.) Vol. 28, No. 1/2, 1998, pp. 225-238; and: *The Role of the Hospitality Industry in the Lives of Individuals and Families* (ed: Pamela R. Cummings, Francis A. Kwansa, and Marvin B. Sussman) The Haworth Press, Inc., 1998, pp. 225-238. Single or multiple copies of this article are available for a fee from The Haworth Document Delivery Service [1-800-342-9678, 9:00 a.m. - 5:00 p.m. (EST). E-mail address: getinfo@haworthpressinc. com].

225

should concentrate their efforts on providing and marketing value and security features in order to attract and satisfy older consumers. *[Article copies available for a fee from The Haworth Document Delivery Service: 1-800-342-9678. E-mail address: getinfo@haworthpressinc.com]*

KEYWORDS. Older consumers, Customer service, Lodging services, Hospitality services

The older population has been cited as the fastest growing consumer segment (Owen, 1989). Although the older population may be defined as those persons 55 and older and at other times defined as persons 65 and older, the older population is still marked as a strong and growing segment of the market. For example, between the years 1990 and 2025 the number of persons aged 65 and older is expected to grow by 101% (U.S. Bureau of Census, 1992). By the year 2025, it has been projected that those age 55 and older will comprise approximately 30.4 percent of the national population (U.S. Bureau of Census, 1995). The U.S. Census Bureau (1991) reports approximately 32 million households with older consumers equaling just over one-third of all U.S. households. As consumers, the older population wields significant buying power (Doka, 1992) with a combined annual personal income in excess of $800 billion (Pollock, 1989).

The effect of the older market segment on the marketplace cannot be ignored. Businesses are generally operating with a lack of understanding of the true characteristics and concerns of older consumers. Conaway's (1991) study reports that the majority of older consumers like to travel, are concerned about food, comfort and accessibility to conveniences, and value economy; however, many businesses have not effectively responded to this segment. Therefore, it has been suggested that success will belong to businesses who take the initiative to reach the special needs of all facets of the older population (Legler, 1990; Rager, 1991; "America's Aging Consumers," 1993).

CONSUMER BEHAVIOR THEORY

The selection of hospitality facilities and services, like other consumer decisions, is influenced by a variety of factors. Consumer behavior theory, as discussed by Engel, Blackwell, and Miniard (1990) and Williams (1982) indicates that consumers' purchasing decisions and level of satisfaction are influenced by consumer characteristics and outside stimuli.

Consumer characteristics such as age and background, as well as outside stimuli such as products and services offered by hotels/motels, most likely influence consumer behavior and level of satisfaction of travelers. Because consumer satisfaction is directly influenced by the availability of customer services, the provision of quality customer service has become an increasingly important concern of businesses (Berry, 1988; Berry & Parasuraman, 1991).

TRAVELERS' DESIRES FOR HOSPITALITY SERVICES

Research currently exists which describes the perceptions of the importance of hotel product offerings to a variety of travel market segments, such as businessmen, businesswomen, and families with children. Business travelers, both male and female, note communication services including telephone, fax and computer hookup are important hotel amenities. Business travelers also prefer adequate desk space and lighting (Cooper, 1996). Offering business travelers timely and efficient service in an accurate and consistent manner is important (Koss, 1992). A high level of service must be provided to anticipate, meet and exceed the needs of business travelers (Rigby, 1990). Businesswomen consider security, in-room services and amenities such as a hair dryer, and low price to be more important selection criteria than do businessmen. Male business travelers are more likely to value suites (McCleary, Weaver & Lan, 1994).

In 1994 approximately 43.4 million, or 15% of all business trips taken in the U.S., included a child. The trend of bringing children along on business trips is becoming an important factor to consider for hotel operators, meeting planners, and day-care specialists (Dunkin & Chandler, 1996). In the same vein, approximately 50 million adults vacationed with their children during the summer of 1994. Nearly 50% of the 1,500 adults surveyed noted they would take advantage of special children's meals or menus, video games and arcades, or hotel discounts (Fisher, 1994).

In the competitive marketplace of today, there is an increasing number of specific travel market segments with special needs when staying at hotels. As an example, within the U.S., there are 43 million "ecotourists" who are willing to pay 8.5% more for environmentally friendly travel supplies (Rushmore, 1993).

Unfortunately, research has focused on the service needs of only a few market segments in the hospitality industry. Whereas much of the existing research concentrates on business travelers and travelers with families, these studies generally exclude the older traveler who may be retired and/or no longer travels with their family.

OLDER CONSUMERS AND THE HOSPITALITY INDUSTRY

The over-50 group is an economically lucrative market for the travel industry (Anderson & Langmeyer, 1982; Mann, 1994). Older consumers, characterized as having time and disposable income, represent a discretionary spending market segment. The older consumers of today are better educated and more experienced consumers of hospitality products and services, and they are healthier and more active than their predecessors ("Seniors: Who They Are," 1993; Lago & Poffley, 1993). Older travelers are further characterized as discerning consumers who often utilize hotel and restaurant services at non-peak periods, and when provided good quality and value often become repeat customers (Carlino, 1994; Weiss, 1995). It is important to provide efficient, friendly service in a sanitary and pleasant environment to best meet the needs of this market (Withiam, 1994).

Older travelers are demographically and psychographically diverse (Mann, 1994). Market segmentation is paramount to successfully promote products and services to older consumers (Spiller & Hamilton, 1993). Family members and friends of older consumers often play an important role in introducing older persons to new products and services (Moschis, Mathur, & Smith, 1993).

Brand loyalty and design features are assumed to be important to older travelers. Koss (1994) suggests that older travelers want hotel packages and promotions that are value-oriented, and that they are often interested in local attractions and sporting events. Likewise, several hotel corporations have attempted to meet the needs of the older market by offering specific products and services intended for their older travelers. These corporations include Holiday Inn Worldwide, Hilton Hotels Corporation, and Choice Hotels International, Inc.'s Rodeway Inns (Mann, 1994). The Rodeway Choice room specifically attempts to cater to seniors by offering lever handles on doors; brighter light with 12,750 lumens; large, easy-to-read TV channel directories; large buttons on TV remote controls; larger digital numbers on alarm clocks; and oversized push-button telephones ("Rodeway Seniors get Choice Room," 1993). Classic Residence by Hyatt and Marriott's Brighton Gardens are additional examples of lodging corporations exhibiting market segmentation strategies by attempting to respond to the diverse needs of older consumers. Classic Residence by Hyatt offers condominium-like living arrangements while Marriott's rapidly expanding Brighton Gardens provide assisted living accommodations. Both corporations focus on the provision of quality products and services designed to meet and exceed the expectations of the older consumer and their family members and, at the same time, to provide tremendous value.

Although corporations have identified the need to provide services for their older guests and have made attempts to meet the needs of the older market, little information is available on the service needs of the older population. Currently, corporations must base their strategies on speculation of the needs of their older guests or knowledge obtained from indirectly related or limited market studies. More direct information pertaining to the importance placed on various hotel/motel products and services by older travelers would be valuable as corporations develop service strategies for their older guests.

PURPOSE

The purpose of this exploratory study was to investigate older consumers' perceptions of the importance of hotel/motel products and services. Specifically, the intent of this study was to examine the perceived importance of hotel/motel services by consumers ages 55 and older in the state of Texas using a modified version of an existing research instrument. This study was designed to address the following research objectives:

1. To identify specific hotel/motel products and services valued by older travelers,
2. To classify hotel/motel products and services into categories of similar products and services,
3. To identify and rank hotel/motel products and services categories valued by older travelers.

METHODS

Operational definitions were identified for the purpose of this study. Older travelers were operationally defined as individuals who reported themselves to be 55 years of age or older and who also reported that they had stayed a minimum of one night in a hotel/motel in the past calendar year. Perceptions of hotel/motel customer services were operationally defined as the degree to which older consumers place importance on various customer services and hospitality products in promoting their level of satisfaction when staying in a hotel/motel.

The research design for this study included a descriptive survey investigating the importance of hotel/motel products and services as perceived by older consumers. A self-administered questionnaire was developed and pretested according to guidelines suggested by Babbie (1989, 1990), Dillman (1978), Fink and Kosecoff (1985), and Kerlinger (1986). Consumer perceptions of the importance of products and services were measured with a 58-item, modified version of Ananth, DeMicco, Moreo, and Howey's (1992) Likert scale. Because the scale was already shown to be valid and reliable, only minor changes in the instrument were made. Modifications were intended only for the ease of reading and responding to questions, and were not substantive in nature. Questions regarding the socioeconomic characteristics and traveling patterns of the respondents and their households were incorporated into the questionnaire.

The questionnaire was pretested in a two-phase process in order to determine validity and reliability for application in this study. In the first stage, the questionnaire was critiqued by a select group of hospitality management professionals. Next, the questionnaire was completed by a group of older travelers. Results of the second stage were statistically analyzed for reliability.

The final version of the questionnaire was mailed to a randomly selected sample of the population of older consumers in Texas. A mailing list of 500 consumers, 55 years of age or older and with Texas zip codes, was acquired from a listing service that secures names, addresses, and basic demographic data of consumers. The list included a computer-generated random sample with proportionate representation of zip code areas within the state.

The initial mailing of the questionnaire was followed with two subsequent mailings. After the cessation of data collection, reliability measures, descriptive statistics, analysis of variance, and factor analysis results were obtained to address the purpose of this study.

RESULTS

Of the 500 consumers in the initial sample, 11 were removed due to inaccurate addresses or lack of compliance with sample criteria. A total of 187 questionnaires out of 489 were returned and deemed usable, yielding a response rate of 38.2%.

Reliability of the Instrument

The modified version of Ananth, DeMicco, Moreo, and Howey's (1992) Likert scale was determined to be useful for measuring the importance of hotel/motel products and services for a different sample. With an alpha of 0.96, the 58-item scale was considered reliable for measuring the importance of hotel/motel products and services as perceived by older consumers.

Importance of Hotel/Motel Products and Services

Respondents' ratings showed a moderate-to-high level of importance for the majority of items included in the scale. Means for the 58 items in the scale varied from 2.05 to 4.84 out of a possible range of 1.0 to 5.0, with 1.0 indicating not important and 5.0 indicating important. Rank order, means and standard deviations for items with a mean greater than 3.50 are illustrated in Table 1. Of the specific items, eight had a mean value greater than 4.50. Those that were rated most important included: well-lit public areas, restaurants and garages (4.84); 24-hour security (4.80); good value for money spent (4.79); in-room temperature-control mechanism (4.74); free parking services (4.71); sound proof rooms (4.68); price of accommodation (4.62); and loud fire alarms (4.62).

Factors of Hotel/Motel Products and Services

Principal components factor analysis with VARIMAX rotation of the scale items produced six basic groups. Each group had a factor loading equal to or greater than 0.55 and an Eigenvalue greater than 1.5. The results of the factor analysis are shown in Table 2. Those groups are described as: specialty services, recreational/leisure services, safety features, value, security, and convenience. Value included three items: good value for money spent, in-room temperature-control mechanisms, and price of accommodations. Security consisted of three items: well-lit public areas, restaurants and garages; security personnel on floors; and loud fire alarms.

Importance of Factors of Hotel/Motel Products and Services

Of the six factors, four were considered moderately to highly important; two were considered less than moderately important. Rank order, means and standard deviations of each factor are noted in Table 3. Value and security were rated most important. The average mean values for the items in each of the six factors, in order of descending importance, were as follows: value, 4.71; security, 4.48; convenience, 3.78; safety features, 3.68; recreational/leisure services, 2.69; and specialty services, 2.55.

TABLE 1. Rank Order of Important Hotel/Motel Products and Services

Rank	Hotel/Motel Products and Services	Means*	Standard Deviation
1	Well-lit public areas, restaurants and garages	4.84	0.42
2	24-hour security	4.80	0.47
3	Good value for money	4.79	0.49
4	In-room temperature-control mechanism	4.74	0.51
5	Free parking services	4.71	0.55
6	Sound proof rooms	4.68	0.58
7	Price of accommodation	4.62	0.65
8	Loud fire alarms	4.62	0.75
9	Convenient location of hotel	4.46	0.70
10	Firmness of mattress	4.44	0.76
11	Legible, visible signs in public areas, hallways, restaurants	4.41	0.81
12	Non-smoking rooms	4.38	1.07
13	Central "800" reservation number	4.33	0.96
14	Easily maneuvered door handles	4.26	0.93
15	Information services and general assistance	4.22	0.93
16	Special discounts available	4.19	0.87
17	Large-size beds	4.17	0.96
18	Remote control for TV	4.05	1.09
19	Express check-out	4.01	1.04
20	Security personnel on floors	3.99	1.02
21	Full-service restaurant	3.95	1.06
22	Night light in bathroom	3.92	1.15
23	Grab-bars, supports in bathroom	3.92	1.21
24	Airport transportation	3.89	1.10
25	Early dining hours	3.87	1.11
26	Bathroom amenitites such as: shampoo, soap, shower cap	3.73	1.18
27	Extra blankets	3.73	1.17
28	24-hour coffee shop	3.66	1.16
29	Legible, large printing on schedules, information, menus	3.66	1.20
30	Wide doorways to accommodate wheelchairs and walkers	3.57	1.40

*Minimum is 1; maximum is 5.

TABLE 2. Factor Analysis of Hotel/Motel Products and Services

Rank	Hotel/Motel Products and Services	Factor 1 Specialty Services	Factor 2 Recreational Services	Factor 3 Safety Features	Factor 4 Value	Factor 5 Security	Factor 6 Convenience
1	Well-lit public areas, restaurants and garages	.1010	.1099	.1509	.2783	.7059*	.0674
2	24-hour security	.0803	.0227	.2311	.4176	.4556	.1990
3	Good value for money	−.0187	.1094	.0828	.8370*	.0795	−.0421
4	In-room temperature-control mechanism	−.0333	.0580	.0744*	.7822*	.0023	.2017
7	Price of accommodation	.0894	.0246	.1031*	.6851*	.3303	−.0116
8	Loud fire alarms	.0019	.2063	.3169	.1070	.6083*	.0060
23	Grab-bars, supports in bathroom	−.0078	.0401	.7681*	.0359	.1425	.0914
24	Airport transportation	.1708	.2904	.1517	.0256	.1803	.7001*
28	24-hour coffee shop	.1712	.1401	.0536	.1065	.0991	.6786*
30	Wide doorways to accommodate wheelchairs and walkers	.1409	.2089	.7340*	−.0313	.2192	.0059
40	Car rental and airline reservations	.1720	.5704*	.2854	.0830	.1573	.2881
41	Automated check out	.5760*	.0594	−.0906	.0510	.2829	.4196
42	Laundry service	.5693*	.2035	.2436	.0628	.0549	.1031
44	Health facilities	.1919	.7558*	.1569	.1160	.0686	.1246
45	Swimming pool	.2609	.5576*	.0507	.0097	.0891	.1736
46	Larger than normal bath	.5843*	.1268	.0210	−.0199	−.1965	−.0064
47	Quiet lounge/bar	.2644	.6524*	.0708	.0709	.1016	.0169
48	Tie-in with airline frequent-flyer programs	.3303	.6466*	.1887	.0335	.1177	.2669
49	Business-related small meeting rooms	.5623*	.4669	.2309	.0490	.1045	.1475
50	Recreation facilities	.4092	.6001*	.1789	.0562	.1015	.0837
51	Valet parking, services	.6280*	.1966	.2597	.1929	−.1171	.2928
52	VCR and video tape rental available	.7034*	.1557	.0194	.0234	.2799	.1418
53	Specialty restaurants	.7506*	.3214	.0913	−.0234	−.0207	−.0235
54	All-suite rooms	.7767*	.3279	.0462	.0238	.0085	.0544
55	Sauna	.4311	.6924*	.0990	.0112	.0778	.0688
56	Entertainment in lounge/bar	.2920	.7576*	.0751	.0239	.0400	.0943
57	Secretarial services	.7446*	.3208	.1859	−.0406	.0440	.1187
58	In-house library	.7016*	.2653	.1451	−.0835	.1304	.1301

* Factor loading greater than or equal to 0.55

TABLE 3. Rank Order of Importance of Factors of Hotel/Motel Products and Services

Rank	Factors of Hotel/Motel Products and Services		Means*	Standard Deviation
1	Factor 4	Value	4.71	0.43
2	Factor 5	Security	4.48	0.60
3	Factor 6	Convenience	3.78	0.98
4	Factor 3	Safety Features	3.68	1.02
5	Factor 2	Recreational Services	2.69	0.98
6	Factor 1	Specialty Services	2.55	0.91

*Minimum is 1.00; maximum is 5.00.

CONCLUSIONS

Older travelers perceive value and security to be most important, including the following features: good value for money spent, in-room temperature-control mechanism, price of accommodation, well-lit public areas, restaurants and garages, security personnel walking floors, and loud fire alarms. Older travelers are less concerned with specialty and recreational services. They may actually perceive these services to be related to the lack of other, more important features.

IMPLICATIONS

Research findings suggest several measures that could benefit lodging managers. Commercial lodging managers representing both chain and independent properties should recognize the importance older travelers place on lodging products and services. With this knowledge, managers should make every effort to provide products and services deemed important by the older segment of the market (Calver, Vierich, and Phillips, 1993). Fortunately, many of the highly valued products and services are already being offered by properties catering to a variety of market segments. Further, it is assumed that many, if not most, of the products and services valued by older guests may also be valued to some degree by younger guests.

Older travelers want value for dollars spent. Therefore, offering accommodations at a reasonable price, and possibly with senior discounts, will provide older guests with a sense of good value for the money spent. Also, providing in-room temperature controls whenever possible is also a means of offering perceived value to the older traveler.

Because services related to security are also very important to older travelers, offering convenient restaurant service within the hotel/motel allows guests to dine in a secure environment. It is important to offer well-lighted and security monitored parking garages, parking lots, walkways, building entrances, exits, hallways, lobbies, elevator areas, and guestrooms. It would behoove hotel operators to provide security officers and security monitors to canvass the inside and outside of the hotel, particularly during late evening and early morning hours. As the possibility of fire exists in hotels, noticeable fire detection devices and alarms are also needed in all public areas and guestrooms.

In making these accommodations, managers will be more apt to develop the strong reputation that is also very important to the older market. If additional specialty and recreational/leisure services are offered, managers must be able to provide these services while maintaining a competitive pricing policy in order to satisfy the value-related needs of the older market.

To attract older travelers, hotel/motel operators should inform seniors that the desired products and services are being offered. By placing appropriate advertisements in senior publications and sharing information with senior associations, older travelers will become better aware of the value hotels/motels are offering. This aggressive and specific marketing strategy is particularly important in today's competitive marketplace. It is the hospitality business that understands the importance of products and services as perceived by the older market, and takes effective operational and training measures to provide these services that may be rewarded with a loyal and highly profitable following both at present and in the future (Mann, 1994).

Fortunately, it can be noted that although there are many different travel market segments, even among older travelers, the perceived importance of various hotel/motel products and services is often quite similar. Although the importance of specific services may vary, most market segments have at least a moderate level of preference for virtually all services. This premise enables hotel operators and marketers not only to attract specific market segments, but also to attract families, seniors and business travelers who often travel to the same destination.

Older consumer characteristics found to be important in this study might have implications for other service industries. For example, retail businesses that cater to an older clientele should provide adequate lighting;

wider aisles for wheel chair access; adequate security measures throughout the store and parking lots; and merchandise being sold with the perception of providing value for the dollars spent. It might behoove other service related businesses to pay more attention to consumer service aspects deemed important to the older market segment so that they might ensure future growth and success.

FUTURE RESEARCH

Because this study is limited by its small and localized sample, as well as its narrow scope, caution must be taken when applying the findings and implications to the broader population of older travelers. Likewise, the implication made to other market segments, such as older consumers of other products and services, and travelers of other age categories, should be considered purely speculative in nature.

Further research is needed to determine to what extent older consumers are really different from travelers of other market segments. Research is also needed to determine if perceptions of importance of hotel/motel products and services vary with respect to different market segments within the older population. Specific information pertaining to the different market segments would enable lodging managers to provide better services for all guests/customers. Hence, specific hotel properties or concepts may find that they are best able to cater to specific older consumer market segments.

REFERENCES

Ananth, M., DeMicco, F. J., Moreo, P. J., & Howey, R. M. (1992). Marketplace lodging needs of older travelers. *The Cornell Hotel and Restaurant Administration Quarterly, 33*(3), 12-24.

Anderson, B. B. & Langmeyer, L. (1982). The under-50 and over-50 travelers: A profile of similarities and differences. *Journal of Travel Research, 20*(4), 20-24.

America's aging consumers. (1993). *Discount Merchandiser, 33*(9), 16-18.

Babbie, E. R. (1990). *Survey research methods,* 2nd edition. Belmont, CA: Wadsworth Publishing Company, Inc.

Babbie, E. R. (1989). *The practice of social research, fifth edition.* Belmont, CA: Wadsworth Publishing Company, Inc.

Berry, L. L. (1988). Delivering excellent service in retailing. *Retailing Issues Letter, 1*(4), 19.

Berry, L. L., & Parasuraman, A. (1991). *Marketing services: Competing through quality.* New York, NY: The Free Press.

Calver, S., Vierich, W., & Phillips, J. (1993). Leisure in later life. *International Journal of Contemporary Hospitality Management, 5*(1), 4-9.

Carlino, B. (1994). Operators strike gold with seniors. *Nation's Restaurant News,* *28*(39), 53-56.

Conaway, F. (1991). Segmenting will unleash mature market potential. *Public Relations Journal, 47*(5), 18-19.

Cooper, C. (1996). Room with a view–into the future. *Incentive, 170*(5), 15.

Dillman, D. A. (1978). *Mail and telephone surveys: The total design method.* New York, NY: John Wiley & Sons, Inc.

Doka, K. J. (1992). When gray is golden: Business in an aging America. *The Futurist, 26*(4), 16-21.

Dunkin, A., & Chandler, S. (1996, May 13). Business trips with tots in tow. *Business Week, 3475,* 160.

Engel, J. F., Blackwell, R. D., & Miniard, P. W. (1990). *Consumer behavior,* 6th edition. Hinsdale, IL: Dryden Press.

Fink, A., & Kosecoff, J. (1985). *How to conduct surveys: A step-by-step guide.* Beverly Hills, CA: Sage Publications, Inc.

Fisher, C. (1994, June 27). Kidding around making sense. *Advertising Age, 65*(27), 34,37.

Kerlinger, F. N. (1986). *Foundations of behavioral research,* 3rd edition. New York, NY: Holt, Rinehart and Winston.

Koss, L. (1992, May 11). Bonus programs survive. *Hotel & Motel Management, 207*(8), 1,31.

Koss, L. (1994). Hotels developing special packages to attract senior travelers. *Hotel & Motel Management, 209*(3), 37.

Lago, D., & Poffley, J. K. (1993). The aging population and the hospitality industry in 2010: Important trends and probable services. *Hospitality Research Journal, 17*(1), 29-47.

Legler, R. (1990). A close look at grandma and grandpa's bank accounts. *Bank Marketing, 22*(8), 58-59.

Mann, R. S. (1994). Tapping into the mature market. *Hotel and Resort Industry, 17*(5), 30-33.

McCleary, K. W., Weaver, P. A., & Lan, L. (1994). Gender-based difference in business travelers' lodging preferences. *Cornel Hotel & Restaurant Administration Quarterly, 35*(2), 51-58.

Moschis, G. P., Mathur, A., & Smith, R. B. (1993). Older consumers' orientations toward age-based marketing stimuli. *Journal of the Academy of Marketing Science, 31*(3), 195-205.

Owen, R. M. (1989). Winning the senior market. *Insurance Sales, 132*(7), 13-15.

Pollock, E. (1989). New ideas to woo older customers. *Bankers Monthly, 106*(12), 58-65.

Rager, L. (1991). The future grows older. *Nations Business, 79*(3), 48-49.

Rigby, J. (1990). Report on business travel: The smart traveler. *Canadian business, 63*(4), 73-84.

Rodeway seniors get choice room. (1993). *Lodging Hospitality, 49*(12), 11.

Rushmore, S. (1993). Beyond recycling: The ecotel. *Lodging Hospitality, 49*(9), 20.

Seniors: Who they are and how they spend. (1993). *Restaurant U.S.A, 13*(8), 37-43.

Spiller, L. D., & Hamilton, R. A. (1993). Senior citizen discount programs. *Journal of Consumer Marketing, 10*(1), 42-51.

Weiss, S. (1995). Market driven menus a coming of age. *Restaurants and Institutions, 105*(6), 62-86.

Williams, T. G. (1982). *Consumer behavior: Fundamentals & strategies.* St. Paul, MN: West Publishing Co.

Withiam, G. (1994). What seniors want. *Cornell Hotel and Restaurant Administration Quarterly, 35*(4), 14.

U.S. Bureau of Census (1992). *An Aging World II.* Washington, DC: U.S. Government Printing Office.

U.S. Bureau of Census (1991). *1991 current population survey.* Washington, DC: U.S. Government Printing Office.

U.S. Bureau of Census (1995). *Statistical Abstract of the United States: 1995.* Washington, DC: U.S. Government Printing Office.

Index

Note: Page numbers followed by f indicate figures; page numbers followed by t indicate tables.

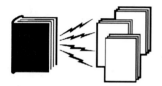

Haworth
DOCUMENT DELIVERY
SERVICE

This valuable service provides a single-article order form for any article from a Haworth journal.

- *Time Saving:* No running around from library to library to find a specific article.
- *Cost Effective:* All costs are kept down to a minimum.
- *Fast Delivery:* Choose from several options, including same-day FAX.
- *No Copyright Hassles:* You will be supplied by the original publisher.
- *Easy Payment:* Choose from several easy payment methods.

Open Accounts Welcome for . . .
- Library Interlibrary Loan Departments
- Library Network/Consortia Wishing to Provide Single-Article Services
- Indexing/Abstracting Services with Single Article Provision Services
- Document Provision Brokers and Freelance Information Service Providers

MAIL or *FAX* THIS ENTIRE ORDER FORM TO:

Haworth Document Delivery Service
The Haworth Press, Inc.
10 Alice Street
Binghamton, NY 13904-1580

or FAX: 1-800-895-0582
or CALL: 1-800-429-6784
9am-5pm EST

PLEASE SEND ME PHOTOCOPIES OF THE FOLLOWING SINGLE ARTICLES:
1) Journal Title: _____

    Vol/Issue/Year:_____Starting & Ending Pages:_____

Article Title:_____

2) Journal Title: _____

    Vol/Issue/Year:_____Starting & Ending Pages:_____

Article Title:_____

3) Journal Title: _____

    Vol/Issue/Year:_____Starting & Ending Pages:_____

Article Title:_____

4) Journal Title: _____

    Vol/Issue/Year:_____Starting & Ending Pages:_____

Article Title:_____

(See other side for Costs and Payment Information)

COSTS: Please figure your cost to order quality copies of an article.

1. Set-up charge per article: $8.00

              ($8.00 × number of separate articles) _____

2. Photocopying charge for each article:

              1-10 pages: $1.00 _____

              11-19 pages: $3.00 _____

              20-29 pages: $5.00 _____

              30+ pages: $2.00/10 pages _____

3. Flexicover (optional): $2.00/article _____

4. Postage & Handling: US: $1.00 for the first article/

              $.50 each additional article _____

              Federal Express: $25.00 _____

              Outside US: $2.00 for first article/

              $.50 each additional article _____

5. Same-day FAX service: $.50 per page _____

               GRAND TOTAL: _____

METHOD OF PAYMENT: (please check one)

❑ Check enclosed   ❑ Please ship and bill. PO # _____
           (sorry we can ship and bill to bookstores only! All others must pre-pay)

❑ Charge to my credit card: ❑ Visa;   ❑ MasterCard;   ❑ Discover;
            ❑ American Express;

Account Number:_____ Expiration date:_____

Signature: ✗ _____

Name: _____ Institution: _____

Address: _____

_____

City: _____ State:_____ Zip:_____

Phone Number: _____ FAX Number: _____

MAIL or *FAX* THIS ENTIRE ORDER FORM TO:

Haworth Document Delivery Service   **or FAX:** 1-800-895-0582
The Haworth Press, Inc.   **or CALL:** 1-800-429-6784
10 Alice Street   (9am-5pm EST)
Binghamton, NY 13904-1580